$ 39.00

LEBANON
Fire and Embers

LEBANON
FIRE AND EMBERS

A History of the Lebanese Civil War

Dilip Hiro

Weidenfeld and Nicolson
London

Weidenfeld & Nicolson Ltd
Orion House, 5 Upper St Martin's Lane
London WC2H 9EA

ISBN 0 297 82116 4

Printed in Great Britain by Butler & Tanner Ltd
Frome and London

Contents

Preface

Lebanon is unique in the Arab world in more ways than one. It is the only member of the Arab League with a Christian president. It gives official recognition to sixteen Christian, Islamic and other religious sects. As a proportion of its population, it has exported more emigrants than any other state in the Middle East, a sign of continued Levantine enterprise.

Despite the patchwork of religious sects within its boundaries – expanded by France at the expense of Syria during its mandate over the two territories after the First World War (1914–18) – and a history of bloody feuding between Christians and Muslims, the republic of Lebanon managed to build up an image of peace, harmony and dignity, well captured by its national symbol: a cedar.

But reality was different. This became embarrassingly apparent, to Lebanese and others, with the outbreak of a civil war in May 1958 between the pro-Western Christian community and the Muslim community inspired by Arab nationalism. It was brief, lasting only three months. In retrospect it proved to be a forerunner of a much longer and bloodier conflict which followed seventeen years later.

It is the purpose of this book to give an account of the 1975–90 civil war, one of the longest military conflicts of the century. The book begins with a historical background to the war, and the main narrative is divided into two parts: before the June 1982 Israeli invasion of Lebanon, and after.

Chapter 1 outlines the emergence of the Lebanese National Movement (LNM), composed of various nationalist and progressive Muslim-dominated parties, and aided by the Palestine Liberation Organization (PLO), as the dominant camp in the fighting, an outcome which was not to the liking of the Syrian president, Hafiz Assad. The next chapter fleshes out the military intervention by Syria which led to its emergence as the dominant foreign power in Lebanon.

The first Israeli invasion of Lebanon, which occurred in March 1978, forms the core of Chapter 3, which is followed in Chapter 4 by a description of the successful efforts of the Christian community to set up a mini-state of its own.

Israel's full-scale invasion of Lebanon in June 1982 and its aftermath occupy most of Chapter 5, which ends with the withdrawal of the Multi-National Force (MNF) of American, British, French and Italian troops in February 1984.

The next two chapters, dealing with the return of Syria and its dominance, show the limitations of Syrian power, just as Chapter 5 illustrates the limits of the Israeli-American axis to determine the future of Lebanon.

Chapter 8 deals with the crisis caused by the failure of the Lebanese parliament to elect a president in September 1988 and the rise of two competing governments, one of them headed by General Michel Aoun, a Maronite, who started a war of liberation against Syria. The intensified fighting led to active mediation by the Arab League and the convening of the Lebanese parliament in Taif, Saudi Arabia.

Chapter 9 describes how the accord reached in Taif by Lebanon's parliamentarians inadvertently became the trigger to ignite an internecine war among Christians, which weakened Aoun's camp. It paved the way for a swift military campaign by Syria against Aoun's forces, which came in mid-October 1990 against the background of President Assad joining the United States-led coalition against Iraq, the latter having invaded and occupied Kuwait two months earlier. This narrative takes up much of Chapter 10, the rest of which describes how the Lebanese government has been coping with the legacy of fifteen and a half years of armed conflict, and how it has formalized its relations with Syria as the big sister.

The concluding chapter summarizes the history of the civil war and two Israeli aggressions in an analytical framework.

Since there is no standard way of transliterating Arabic names and words, spelling them is always problematic. There is no uniformity even for such common words as Moslem/Muslim and Koran/Quran. When it comes to looking up an index, a particular difficulty arises where the same place or person is spelled with a different first letter, as in Geagea/Jaja and Gemayel/Jumayil. The problem is compounded in the case of Lebanon because of the French influence. Shouf is spelled as Chouf in French, and Shamoun as Chamoun. In each case I have chosen the spelling most widely used in the English-language print media, and stuck to it – except when the spelling of a book author or title is different from mine. I have also simply reproduced the published spelling in quoted matter. Whenever the Arabic name of a place is different from its English equivalent, I have given the Arabic name in brackets: Sidon (Saida), Tyre (Sur), etc.

Dilip Hiro
London, July 1992

Abbreviations and Acronymns

ADF: Arab Deterrent Force
Amal: *Afwaj al-Muqawama al Lubnaniya* (the Lebanese Resistance Detachments)
AUB: American University in Beirut
CIA: Central Intelligence Agency
DFLP: Democratic Front for the Liberation of Palestine
GCC: Gulf Co-operation Council
GDP: Gross domestic product
IDF: Israeli Defence Forces
IJLP: Islamic Jihad for the Liberation of Palestine
IJO: Islamic Jihad Organization
LF: Lebanese Forces
LFEC: Lebanese Forces Executive Committee
LNM: Lebanese National Movement
MNF: Multi-National Force
MP: Member of Parliament
NLP: National Liberal Party
NSF: National Salvation Front
OOTOOTE: Organization of the Oppressed of the Earth
OPEC: Organization of Petroleum Exporting Countries
PFLP: Popular Front for the Liberation of Palestine
PFLP–GC: Popular Front for the Liberation of Palestine: General Command
PLA: Palestine Liberation Army
PLO: Palestine Liberation Organization
PNSF: Palestine National Salvation Front
PSP: Progressive Socialist Party
RJO: Revolutionary Justice Organization
SAM: Surface-to-air missile
SLA: South Lebanon Army
SNF: Socialist National Front
SSNP: Syrian Social Nationalist Party

TOW: Tube-launched optically-tracked wire-guided
TWA: Trans World Airways
UAE: United Arab Emirates
UN: United Nations
Unifil: United Nations Interim Force in Lebanon
USA: United States of America
USSR: Union of Soviet Socialist Republics

LEBANON AND ITS NEIGHBOURS

CYPRUS

Latakia

0   km   100

Larnaca

SYRIA

Beirut

LEBANON

MEDITERRAEAN SEA

Damascus

Nahariya

GOLAN
HEIGHTS

JORDAN

Tel Aviv

WEST BANK

Amman

ISRAEL

Jerusalem

SAUDI ARABIA

GAZA
STRIP

--------- Ceasefire line until 1967

Land over 1500m

EGYPT

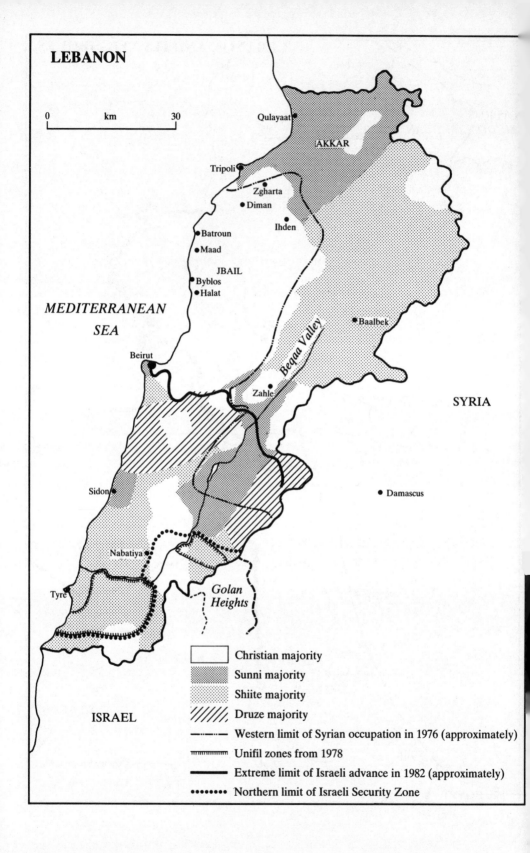

LEBANON

0   km   30

Qulayaat

AKKAR

Tripoli

Zgharta

Diman

Ihden

Batroun

Maad

JBAIL

Byblos

Halat

MEDITERRANEAN
SEA

Baalbek

Beqaa Valley

Beirut

Zahle

SYRIA

Sidon

Damascus

Nabatiya

Golan
Heights

Tyre

ISRAEL

☐ Christian majority

▨ Sunni majority

⠿ Shiite majority

▨ Druze majority

—·—·— Western limit of Syrian occupation in 1976 (approximately)

▥▥▥ Unifil zones from 1978

▬▬▬ Extreme limit of Israeli advance in 1982 (approximately)

••••••• Northern limit of Israeli Security Zone

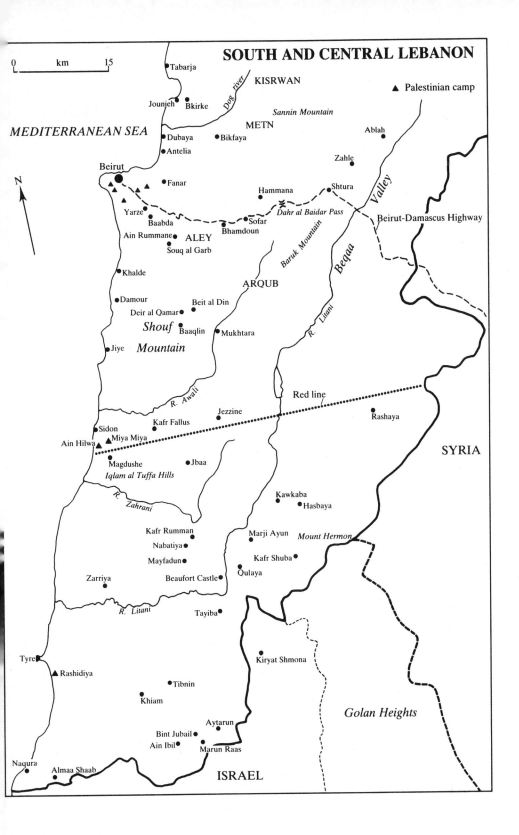

SOUTH AND CENTRAL LEBANON

0 km 15

▲ Palestinian camp

MEDITERRANEAN SEA

N

Tabarja

KISRWAN

Jounieh   Bkirke

Sannin Mountain

METN

Ablah

Dubaya   Bikfaya

Antelia

Zahle

Beirut

Fanar

Hammana   Shtura

Dog river

Yarze

Baabda   Sofar   *Dahr al Baidar Pass*   Beirut-Damascus Highway

Ain Rummane   ALEY   Bhamdoun

Souq al Garb

Baruk Mountain

Valley

Beqaa

Khalde

ARQUB

Damour   Beit al Din

Deir al Qamar

Shouf   Baaqlin   Mukhtara

R. Litani

Jiye   *Mountain*

R. Awali

Jezzine   Red line   Rashaya

Kafr Fallus

Sidon   Miya Miya

Ain Hilwa

Magdushe   Jbaa

Iqlam al Tuffa Hills

SYRIA

R. Zahrani

Kawkaba

Hasbaya

Kafr Rumman   Marji Ayun   *Mount Hermon*

Nabatiya

Mayfadun   Kafr Shuba

Zarriya   Qulaya

Beaufort Castle

R. Litani   Tayiba

Tyre

Kiryat Shmona

Rashidiya

Tibnin   *Golan Heights*

Khiam

Aytarun

Bint Jubail

Ain Ibil   Marun Raas

Naqura   Almaa Shaab

ISRAEL

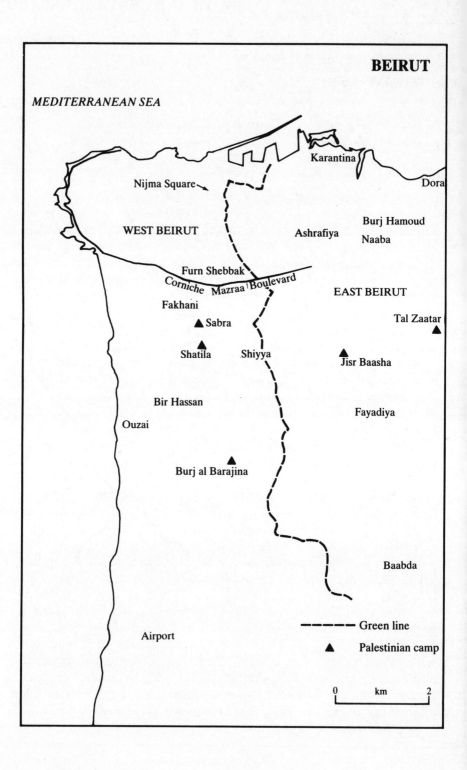

BEIRUT

MEDITERRANEAN SEA

Karantina

Dora

Nijma Square

WEST BEIRUT

Ashrafiya

Burj Hamoud

Naaba

Furn Shebbak

Corniche Mazraa Boulevard

EAST BEIRUT

Fakhani

▲ Sabra

Tal Zaatar ▲

▲

Shatila

Shiyya

▲ Jisr Baasha

Bir Hassan

Fayadiya

Ouzai

▲

Burj al Barajina

Baabda

Airport

------- Green line

▲ Palestinian camp

0   km   2

INTRODUCTION
The Background

The roots of Lebanon's brief civil war of 1958, as well as the much longer one from 1975 to 1990, lie in its history and geography. Over the centuries Lebanon's mountains became a magnet for the persecuted religious minorities of the region. But since these sects belonged to one of the two monotheistic religions at loggerheads with each other – Islam and Christianity – their mutual relationship was far from harmonious. Indeed it was often violently hostile, especially in the case of Maronite Christians and Druze Muslims.

Maronites were followers of Saint Maron, born in north-east Syria in the late fourth century. They became a formidable force under St John Maron, Patriarch of Antioch and All East (685–707). They were persecuted by the Byzantine emperors because they believed that Jesus Christ possessed not two natures but one – with two parts, one human, and the other divine. Imperial persecution forced them to migrate to the northern section of Mount Lebanon, called Metn. Following the success of the First Crusade (1095–9), resulting in the establishment of the Latin Kingdom of Jerusalem, and its subsequent extension to Sidon (Saida), Beirut, Byblos (Jbail) and Tripoli (Trablus), the Maronites of Mount Lebanon became part of the enlarged Christian realm.

By then the southern section of Mount Lebanon, called Shouf, had been settled by Druzes, a persecuted Muslim sect. They were followers of Hakim al Darazi, an eleventh-century Ismaili[1] missionary, who maintained that Hakim Bi-Amr Allah, the Fatimid caliph from 996 to 1021, was a 'Hidden Imam', and therefore divine. Known as Hakimiya, Druzes are secretive about their doctrine, which is an amalgam of Islamic, Christian, Judaic and Zoroastrian elements. Of the five obligations enjoined upon orthodox Muslims, Druzes do not feel bound by two: fasting during Ramadan and pilgrimage to Mecca. They were therefore persecuted by Muslim

rulers. In turn they tried to prove their loyalty to Islam by participating zealously in the battles against Christian forces. By the time
the local Muslim warriors had seized Acre, the last bastion of
Christianity, in 1291 after the Ninth Crusade (1271–2), the leading
members of the Druze clan of the Buhturs were acting as cavalry
officers and administrators of the Sunni Mamluke emperors
(1260–1517) in the Shouf region.

The advent of the Sunni Ottoman Turks as caliphs of the Islamic
empire in 1517 almost coincided with the transfer of power in the
Shouf from the Buhturs to the Maans, another eminent Druze clan.
Fakhr al Din Maan (1591–1633) extended his domain to the south
and north, including the Maronite areas, as well as eastwards – and
established the Emirate of Mount Lebanon, which is regarded by
many historians as the precursor of the modern state of Lebanon.
But he fell out with the Ottoman emperor, who ordered his execution
in 1635.

Meanwhile, Maronites had renounced their monotheistical doctrine and sought reconciliation with the Roman Catholic Church.
The establishment of a Maronite college in Rome by Pope Gregory
XII in 1584 was a major step towards unification. Maronites
improved their status further in 1648, when the Ottoman emperor
accepted France as their protector in his domain. Maronite links with
France flourished and the community thrived. Along with this came
a population explosion. Maronites began moving southwards to the
Shouf region, a migration facilitated by the fact that the Emirate of
Mount Lebanon included all of Mount Lebanon as well as the 10
km-wide Beqaa valley lying between Mount Lebanon and Mount
Anti-Lebanon. Whatever the causes of this demographic movement,
it sowed the seeds of an intractable confessional conflict, which has
since then erupted in ever-rising proportions, engulfing such other
sects as Shias, Greek Orthodox and Sunnis, who found themselves
ruled by Druze or Maronite governors as they expanded their
respective domains.

When the last Maan governor, Ahmad Maan (1667–97), died
without a son, his office passed on to the Shehabis. They reorganized
the emirate, now consisting of both Muslim and Christian settlements, in 1711. Three generations later a new twist was given to the
inter-communal tension when the Emir of Mount Lebanon, Yusuf
Shehabi (1770–88), abandoned Islam and joined the Maronite
Church, much invigorated by the formal links it had forged with the
Roman Catholic Church in 1736. Yusuf Shehabi's example was

followed by his son Bashir. He ruled as Bashir II until 1840 when, following his alliance with the Egyptian governor against the Ottomans, he was deposed by the Ottoman sultan. He left behind a Mount Lebanon which was socially divided between the north – where Maronites were the majority, with the minority Druzes tied as serfs to Maronite landlords – and the south, where the Maronite and Druze roles were reversed. The political ascendancy of Maronites at the expense of the traditional ruling Druze élite created instability. Bashir III – the young Shehabi governor who, like his predecessor, was a Maronite – proved incapable of controlling the Druze notables. The result was socio-political unrest which lasted a generation.

Vicious fighting broke out between Maronites and Druzes in 1845. The Ottoman court intervened and imposed a new administration, but to little avail. Inter-communal violence simmered on. In 1858 an uprising by the Druze serfs against their Maronite landlords in northern Mount Lebanon, the Metn, succeeded, and they gained their freedom. Two years later, as the Maronite peasants in the south prepared to attack their Druze feudal lords, the latter pre-empted them by masterminding a massacre of 11,000 Maronites in settlements such as Bhamdoun. Overall, the Druzes, though outnumbered, did well in the fighting. To save the Maronites from further persecution by the Druzes, France dispatched an expeditionary force to Lebanon. It succeeded in ending the conflict, and France emerged as a dependable protector of Maronites *in extremis*.

Yielding to pressures from France and other European powers, the Ottoman sultan transformed the Emirate of Mount Lebanon, excluding the major port cities of Tripoli, Beirut and Sidon, into an autonomous province in 1861, and placed it under a Christian governor. The imperial decree provided protection to Maronites and Druzes, and stipulated a council, elected on the basis of proportionality, to assist the governor. Since Maronites formed an overwhelming majority in the province, the Ottoman decree inadvertently turned the Druzes, the military victors, into political losers.

This arrangement lasted until 1915 when, in the course of the First World War (1914–18), the Ottomans ended autonomous administration and imposed direct rule on Mount Lebanon.

Following the break-up of the Ottoman empire in 1918, France obtained a mandate over Lebanon and Syria from the League of Nations. On 1 September 1920 it enlarged the Ottoman Emirate of Mount Lebanon by adding agrarian Muslim areas to its north, west and south (belonging to Ottoman Syria), and naming the new province Greater Lebanon. It did so to make the new entity economically viable while at the same time ensuring that Christians retained their majority. Its intention was to transform Greater Lebanon, about half the size of Wales, into an outpost of French influence to counter the hostile Arab nationalism emerging in the hinterland. France achieved this aim, but an enormous price was paid by Lebanon and its neighbours, as the subsequent history of the country has tragically shown. As Itamar Rabinovich, an Israeli specialist on Lebanon, notes: 'The net effect of the creation of Greater Lebanon was Syrian irredentism and the disruption of the demographic balance in the new state, resulting in discord between the traditional Christian ethos, which underlay its creation, and the heterogeneous composition of its population.'[2]

Having created a Christian-majority territory of Greater Lebanon, France treated it favourably. In 1926 it promulgated a republican constitution drafted by a commission of the Lebanese consultative council. It provided for a parliament empowered to elect the republic's president, who was authorized to appoint the prime minister and his cabinet.

The inter-war period was marked by animosity between the French-backed Maronites on one side and an alliance of Sunnis and Greek Orthodox Christians on the other. With their patriarch based in Damascus, Greek Orthodox Christians had a long history of harmonious relations with their Muslim rulers. They now allied with Sunnis in their opposition to the Maronite plans to create a Western-oriented state in an independent Lebanon, and sought the merger of their country with the adjoining Syria. In this conflict France played the role of a biased mediator.

When the presidential contest between a Muslim candidate and his Christian rival became too heated in 1932, Paris suspended the constitution and did not reinstate it until four years later, when the leftist Popular Front won elections in France and formed the government. In Lebanon Emile Edde, a Maronite, was elected president.

After the occupation of northern France in 1940 by Germany as a result of the Second World War (1939–45), and the subsequent establishment of a pro-German regime in Vichy in central France, control of the overseas French territories passed to the Vichy government. In mid-1941 the Vichy forces in Syria and Lebanon were attacked and defeated by the British, supported by the Free French troops under the command of General Charles de Gaulle, then operating from England. Prodded by the British, in March 1943 the Free French restored the Lebanese constitution, which had been suspended by the Vichy government. General Edward Spears, the British representative in Beirut, mediated between the feuding Muslims (led by Riad Solh) and Christians (led by Bishara Khuri) regarding division of the parliamentary seats. Using the 1932 census, which showed Christians to be 54 per cent of the population, Spears recommended the ratio of six Christian parliamentary seats to five Muslim.[3] This was accepted by leaders of both communities as part of the National Pact, an unwritten supplement to the constitution.

The National Pact encapsulated an overall compromise. The Muslim leaders accepted the existing boundaries of Lebanon, and gave up their demand for a union with Syria to recreate the Greater Syria of the past; their Christian counterparts agreed that Arabic should be the only official language of the republic, and that Lebanon should be free of any foreign (i.e. European) ties and should present an 'Arab face' to the world. The Pact stipulated that the republic's president should be a Maronite Christian, its prime minister a Sunni Muslim, its parliamentary speaker a Shia Muslim and his deputy a Greek Orthodox Christian. Of the 77 parliamentary seats, 42 were allocated to Christians – with Maronite Catholics receiving 23, Greek Orthodox 9, Greek Catholics 5, Armenian Catholics and Armenian Orthodox 4, Protestants and non-Muslim minorities (Jews and Bahais) one. The 35 Muslim seats were divided among 16 Sunnis, 14 Shias and 5 Druzes.[4] The first parliament with a 6:5 Christian–Muslim composition came into existence in August 1943. It elected Bishara Khuri, a Maronite, as president; and he called on Riad Solh, a Sunni, to form the government.

Thus, while the 1861 political arrangement under the Ottomans was predicated on a Maronite–Druze partnership, the new National Pact – given the status of an official decree by the French delegate-general in July 1943 – consecrated a Maronite–Sunni alliance.

Within a generation, modern Lebanon had crystallized as an entity built on the foundation of a confederation of sixteen proto-national communities – Armenian Catholic, Assyrian and Chaldenan Catholic, Greek Catholic, Maronite Catholic, Roman Catholic, Syrian Catholic, Armenian Orthodox, Greek Orthodox, Syrian Orthodox, Protestant, Bahai, Jew, Alawi, Druze, Shia and Sunni – each of which claimed the ultimate loyalty of its members. This system, which recognized the primacy of religious communities vested with political authority, came to be known as 'confessionalism'.

Since the political system rested on the base of confessionalism, it perpetuated the power and influence of traditional and religious figures. The allocation of parliamentary seats on a sectarian basis ensured the continued pre-eminence of communal leaders.[5] The in-built conservatism of the system inhibited the rise of modern politics based on broad socio-economic interests which transcend narrow sectarian and communal concerns. Parliament emerged as an institution mirroring the complex web of relationships between the traditional centres of power and patronage centred around clans, regions and sub-regions.

By blocking change and steady reform, the archiac, rigid con-fessionalist system forced popular discontent to build up to unbear-able proportions and explode, periodically, in widespread violence.

Independent Lebanon

The French finally left Lebanon in December 1946. The Lebanese parliament amended the constitution to make the president both the head of state and the chief executive, give legislative powers to a single chamber of deputies, and make the cabinet, appointed by the president, responsible to the chamber. The president, elected by a two-thirds majority of the deputies on the first count, and a simple majority on the subsequent ones, was to hold office for six years. Parliamentary elections were to be held every four years on the basis of adult suffrage, which until 1952 excluded women. Article 95 of the constitution sanctified confessionalism – that is, fixed communal representation – by stating that 'the [sectarian] communities will be equally [i.e. proportionately] represented in government employment and in the composition of the cabinet without jeopardizing the good of the state'.

In 1949 Bishara Khuri was re-elected president for six years. But, yielding to popular pressure, he resigned in September 1953 in the wake of charges of corruption, and gave way to Camille Chamoun (b. 1900, d.1987), the choice of the recently formed opposition Socialist National Front (SNF). The Front was led by Chamoun, Kamal Jumblatt (b. 1917, d. 1977), a radical Druze who headed the Progressive Socialist Party, and others concerned mainly with dom-estic reform in the government.

However, Chamoun showed more interest in external affairs than internal. Following the overthrow of Egypt's King Farouk by republican military officers on 23 July 1952, there was an upsurge in radical Arab nationalism propounded by the new Egyptian leader, Gamal Abdul Nasser (b. 1918, d. 1970). His success in nationalizing the Anglo-French-owned Suez Canal Company in July 1956 electrified the masses in the Arab world, including Lebanon. And the subsequent attack on Egypt by Britain, France and Israel in late October 1956 engendered a wave of anti-Western feeling in the region. In Lebanon this feeling was shared by Muslims and Greek Orthodox Christians, but not by most Maronite Catholics. Despite pressure from Muslim politicians, Chamoun refused to break relations with Britain and France. Following the May 1957 promise by President Dwight Eisenhower (1953–60) of United States economic and military aid to any Middle East country wishing protection against 'overt armed aggression from any nation controlled by international communism [meaning Nasser's Egypt, then friendly with Moscow]', Chamoun became one of the two Arab leaders to subscribe to the Eisenhower doctrine – the other being the prime minister of pro-Western Iraq, Nuri al Said. He thus emerged as an anti-Nasserist figure, and alienated himself from the pro-Nasser SNF.

The 1958 Civil War

Intent on getting the constitution amended to allow him a second term of office, Chamoun wished to rig the June 1957 parliamentary elections so as to assure himself a large majority in the chamber. In this he was aided, financially and otherwise, by the US Central Intelligence Agency (CIA) station in Beirut.[6] Chamoun succeeded to the extent that such popular leaders as Kamal Jumblatt lost their seats. This widened the gap between Chamoun and the predominantly Muslim Socialist National Front. The formation of the United Arab Republic consisting of Egypt and Syria in February 1958 boosted the morale of the SNF. Its mainly Muslim followers had come to resent the second-class status assigned to them by the administration of President Chamoun who, confident of unqualified American backing, was becoming increasingly intolerant of his opponents.

In this charged atmosphere the publisher of an opposition paper, Nasib Metni, a liberal-minded Christian who had just finished serving a gaol sentence for criticizing President Chamoun, was assassinated on 8 May. This led to anti-government rioting in Tripoli, which left thirty-five people dead. SNF supporters, now openly opposed to the President, paralysed the country in a three-day general strike, and their leaders urged Chamoun to resign or face civil strife. He declared a state of emergency.

On 12 May 1958 civil war erupted. The pro-Western followers of Chamoun confronted the nationalist-leftist forces headed by Jumblatt, with the 8,000-strong army, led by General Fuad Chehab, remaining neutral – on the ground that it might fracture along sectarian lines if ordered to fight. In Beirut barricades went up and fires flared. In the Shouf region Jumblatt set up a local administration around his base at Mukhtara. From there his 2,000-strong Druze militia mounted an offensive in mid-May to seize the summer presidential palace in Beit al Din, and faced the Chamounist forces consisting of the Lebanese gendarmerie and the Maronite militia, equipped *inter alia* with 500 submachine-guns supplied by Israel.[7] The fighting was so intense that General Chehab intervened to end it. An attempt by Jumblatt in late June to capture Beirut also induced intervention by the Lebanese army.

On 14 July 1958 the pro-Western monarch of Iraq, King Faisal II, was overthrown and executed by republican army officers. This deprived Chamoun of the only strong ally he had in the region. He now requested, and received, military assistance from Washington under the Eisenhower doctrine. Soon Lebanon witnessed the arrival of 10,000 US marines and airborne ground troops, backed up offshore by the 76-ship, 35,000-man US Sixth Fleet, equipped with nuclear weapons. This enraged the opposition Socialist National Front whose forces now controlled about a third of Lebanon. The civil war intensified briefly before coming to an end, with both sides accepting General Chehab as the sole presidential candidate, and the parliament electing him to that office on 31 July. The conflict took a toll between 1,400 and 4,000 Lebanese.[8]

Just as in 1860, so now the civil strife in Lebanon was brought to an end by foreign intervention.

By temporarily shattering the political-administrative system, however, the 1958 war opened up opportunities for accelerated socio-economic transformation and fuelled high popular expectations from the presidency of Chehab.

Fuad Chehab's Presidency: 1958–64

Aware of the bipartisan backing he had received, President Chehab pursued an external policy of blending his country's Christian identity with Arab nationalism. At home, supported by military officers and technocrats, he tried to modernize the Lebanese political-administrative machine – steeped in feudal values and sectarian cleavage – only to meet opposition from politicians, businessmen and senior civil servants, all intent on preserving their privileged positions built on interlocking networks of patronage. To bypass the political system he tried to strengthen the state apparatus. He used the government bureaucracy and military intelligence (known as the Deuxième Bureau, or Second Bureau) to divide and suppress the groups which were strong enough to withstand direct pressure from the Presidential Bureau. The result was a series of reforms – achieved without any change in the basic confessional nature of the Lebanese polity.

Nevertheless Chehab's road-building in rural areas had a profound impact on demographic movement. It accelerated migration to urban centres. A majority of the migrants were poor Shias, concentrated hitherto in the south and the Beqaa valley. They settled around the dozen or so camps of Palestinian refugees which had sprung up since the founding of Israel in May 1948. This was the beginning of an emergent alliance between Lebanese Muslims and the Palestinians: a phenomenon which later surprised and disappointed Maronites who, given to sectarian thinking, could not visualize Sunni Palestinians allying with Shia Lebanese.

Charles Helou's Presidency: 1964–70

In the summer of 1964 Chehab was succeeded by his nominee, Charles Helou. A weak leader, Helou lacked a political or military base of his own. In foreign affairs he continued the policy initiated by Chehab. At the summit of the Arab League – which Lebanon had helped establish in 1945 – held in October, he endorsed the proposal for a United Arab Command for the countries adjoining Israel: Egypt, Jordan, Syria and Lebanon.

However, events in the states contiguous with Lebanon had a divisive impact on Lebanese society. The suppression of the leftists and the Palestinians in Jordan by King Hussein ibn Talal in 1965, and the seizure of power by the radical wing of the ruling Arab Baath Socialist Party in Syria in 1966, accentuated the age-old fissures in Lebanon's socio-political structure.

On 5 June 1967, the Third Arab–Israeli War, popularly known as the Six Day War, pitted Israel against an alliance of Egypt, Syria and Jordan. The truce negotiated by the United States on 11 June left

Israel in occupation of Egypt's Sinai peninsula and the Palestinian Gaza Strip, Jordan's Palestinian West Bank (of the Jordan River) and Syria's Golan Heights. Since Lebanon did not participate in the fighting, it emerged from the conflict without any territorial loss.

But the upheaval caused tens of thousands of Palestinian refugees to pour out of the West Bank. A substantial proportion ended up in Lebanon. The Palestinians were by now organized under the umbrella of the Palestine Liberation Organization (PLO), a political-administrative body set up in 1964. Faced with an enlarged presence of Palestinians in Lebanon – some of whom resorted to mounting armed actions against Israel from the Lebanese territory – the right-wing Christians, belonging to the Phalange Party[9] of Pierre Gemayel (b. 1905, d. 1984) and the National Liberal Party of Camille Chamoun, sharpened their attacks against 'intruders' and 'foreigners', accusing them of subverting the Lebanese system. In contrast, the Lebanese Muslims by and large regarded providing refuge to displaced Palestinians, perceived as victims of Zionism, as a religious duty. They also considered helping the Palestinians an integral part of the 'Arab face' of Lebanon as stipulated by the 1943 National Pact.

In the May 1968 parliamentary elections Pierre Gemayel and Camille Chamoun combined with Raymond Edde, a moderate Christian leader of the National Bloc, to form the Triple Alliance. Their aim was to challenge the Christian candidates supporting the Chehabist policy of marrying Christian identity with Arab nationalism. Triple Alliance candidates argued that the activities of the Palestinian commandos in Lebanon were a serious threat to social stability and national security. They were apprehensive that, encouraged by the support of the armed Palestinians, the Lebanese Muslims would strive to strip the Christians of their traditional power. The Democratic Parliamentary Forum led by Rashid Karami (b. 1921, d. 1987), a son of the mufti (i.e. chief religious judge) of Tripoli, emerged as the chief rival of the Triple Alliance. By mounting a blatantly sectarian campaign, the Triple Alliance emerged slightly ahead of Karami's Democratic Parliamentary Forum.

The resulting impasse in parliament on the formation of the government was broken by the swearing-in of an emergency cabinet of two Maronites and two Sunnis, with Abdullah Yafi, a Sunni Chehabist, as prime minister.

On 28 December 1968, following a Palestinian attack on an Israeli plane at Athens airport, Israel retaliated. Its commandos landed on

Beirut airport and blew up thirteen civilian airliners. The radical
Lebanese parties called a general strike in Beirut to protest against
governmental incompetence. The event led to the resignation of
Prime Minister Yafi.

Among other things it demonstrated that the Palestinian resistance
was now an integral part of Lebanese politics. Since the secular,
progressive nature of Palestinian politics ran counter to the con-
fessionalist core of Lebanon's political life, the scene was set for the
destabilization of Lebanese society and state.

The new government formed by Rashid Karami in January 1969
excluded, as before, the three leaders of the Triple Alliance:
Gemayel, Chamoun and Edde. It reaffirmed its backing for the
Palestinian resistance. But this policy was ignored by the president
and the army commander, General Emile Boustani, both of them
Maronite. Consequently, there were bloody clashes between the
Lebanese army and the Palestinian commandos in the areas adjacent
to Israel (from where the Palestinians were hitting Israeli targets) and
Syria (which provided military aid to the radical Palestinians). This
led to such a severe protest by the pro-Palestinian elements in Beirut
in April that the authorities had to impose a state of emergency.
Prime Minister Karami resigned, stating that it had become impossible for his government to take sides on the Palestinian issue without
causing a severe division in the nation.

When the Lebanese army renewed its battles with the Palestinians
in late October, there were strong protests from Syria, Iraq, Libya,
Algeria and South Yemen. Responding to a mediation offer by
President Nasser of Egypt, President Helou sent General Boustani
to Cairo. Aware that the unity of the Lebanese army would be
threatened as clashes between the army and the Palestinian commandos became more bloody and frequent, and aroused strong
opposition from the Muslim community, Helou instructed Boustani
to be amenable to a compromise.

The resulting concord between Lebanon and the PLO, mediated
by Nasser, was signed on 3 November 1969 by Boustani and Yasser
Arafat, chairman of the PLO. It was decided to keep its text secret.
However, when a press leak in April 1970 revealed its contents, it
emerged that the PLO had been allowed to administer the Palestinian
refugee camps and establish armed units and posts inside them, and
also to hold transit routes and certain positions in south Lebanon
(which had emerged as a major Palestinian–Israeli battleground), in
return for the PLO's promise to respect Lebanese sovereignty.

Of the three Triple Alliance leaders, who opposed the Cairo Agreement, Pierre Gemayel and Camille Chamoun later changed their stance with the proviso that its terms should be strictly applied where the PLO's respect for 'full sovereignty of the Lebanese state over the whole of its territory' was concerned. At the same time they enlarged their party militias and upgraded their training.

For their part, both the Palestinian commandos and the Lebanese troops broke the terms of the Cairo Agreement as and when it suited them. Moreover, the Palestinians gradually began extending the cover of the Agreement to radical Lebanese parties. As a result these organizations, assisted by the Palestinians, started forming their own paramilitary forces.

The number of legal Lebanese parties increased dramatically when, in August 1970, Kamal Jumblatt, the interior minister, issued a ministerial order lifting the ban on political parties with links to extra-territorial organizations, which had been in force since 1949. This legalized not only the Communist Party but also the Arab Baath Socialist Party, the Arab Nationalist Movement and its off-shoots, various Nasserist organizations and the Syrian Social Nationalist Party, wedded to the concept of reconstituting Greater Syria. 'Jumblatt's order reflected the new political climate created by the 1967 [Arab–Israeli] war and its consequences', notes Tabitha Petran, a specialist on the Levant:

> The weakening of the central authority in the post-Chehab period . . . permitted a relatively open and stimulating political climate to develop. A shifting sectarian balance of power, effected by the appearance of the Palestine resistance movement, encouraged many new groups and individuals to take part in political life.[10]

In general, radical Lebanese parties viewed the National Pact as a façade behind which lurked the resolve of a bourgeois and mainly Christian élite to keep itself in power. They wanted to abrogate the principle of sectarian representation in public office and parliament, and introduce non-sectarian, popular representation. Only on such a just foundation could genuine national unity be achieved, they argued.

Suleiman Franjieh's Presidency: The First Half, 1970–73

In the September 1970 presidential election, the Chehabists nominated Elias Sarkis (b. 1924), the governor of the Central Bank since

1966, as their candidate. During Chehab's presidency he had run the Presidential Bureau. His rival was Suleiman Franjieh (b. 1910), a politician from Zgharta, a fiefdom of the Franjieh clan, which marked the northern boundary of the Maronite heartland that stretched unbroken to Jezzine at the southern tip of Mount Lebanon. However, as part of the hinterland of Tripoli, Zgharta was more tied to that Sunni-dominated city than to the Maronite core areas of Kisrwan and Metn to the south. Socially, the northern Maronites were more tribal than sectarian in their outlook. In the 1958 civil war the Franjiehs had battled alongside the insurgents against President Chamoun, with Suleiman Franjieh adopting a pro-Nasser stance. Two years later he was elected to parliament where he allied himself with Saeb Salam, a Sunni leader, and Kamil Assad, a Shia notable. He emerged as an anti-Chehabist parliamentarian.

In his presidential campaign, therefore, Franjieh received the backing of Chamoun and Gemayel who, as the backbone of the Maronite establishment, were anti-Chehabist. At the same time, because of his pro-Nasser leanings, Franjieh was acceptable to Muslim parliamentarians. In the presidential poll he defeated Sarkis, though only by a single vote. His victory signalled the end of the twelve-year Chehabist era, and a reversion to traditional political life.

On assuming office Franjieh called on Saeb Salam to form the new cabinet. His other principal ally, Kamil Assad, was elected speaker of the parliament. The Salam government purged the army and civil service of all Chehabist elements and disbanded the Chehabist military intelligence apparatus. This resulted *inter alia* in the loss of useful information on the Palestinian commandos.

The subject of the Palestinian guerrilla presence became urgent when, in the wake of bloody clashes between the PLO fighters and the army in Jordan in September 1970, many armed Palestinians arrived in Lebanon, followed by the transfer of the PLO headquarters from Amman to Beirut in late 1970. This led to an increase in anti-Israeli operations by the Lebanon-based Palestinians, which in turn raised Israel's retaliatory strikes against the Palestinian targets in Lebanon.

In one such action the Israeli commandos assassinated three Palestinian leaders in downtown Beirut in the early hours of 10 April 1973. The event stunned the populace. The gathering of 250,000 people (amounting to 10 per cent of the country's adult population) in the funeral procession was an indirect warning to the authorities to refrain from succumbing to the Israeli pressure and suppressing the Palestinian resistance. But President Franjieh seemed not to register it. Prime Minister Salam resigned in protest. Amin Hafiz, his successor, failed to form a satisfactory government and in early July gave way to Taqi al Din Solh.

Meanwhile, in May, there had been clashes between the Lebanese army and the PLO forces when the former had tried to besiege the Palestinian camps of Shatila and Burj al Barajina. For the first time, the militias of the Lebanese leftist and Nasserite parties fought alongside the Palestinians, thus setting a pattern for the larger conflict which was to erupt two years later. Partly because of the strong resistance offered by the Palestinians and their Lebanese allies, and partly because of Syria's sealing of the Lebanese border, resulting in the severance of Lebanon from its Arab hinterland, the Lebanese army lifted its blockade of the Palestinian camps. The immediate impact of this outcome was to weaken the position of Franjieh and strengthen the hands of President Hafiz Assad of Syria (1970–).

As for medium-term consequences, the return to the status quo solved nothing. The antagonistic camps regarded the recent clashes as curtain-raisers for something far bigger and bloodier, and for the next two years they prepared feverishly for the much-predicted conflict. The commanders of the militias of the Phalange Party, the National Liberal Party and the Franjieh clan started collecting large consignments of arms and ammunition, secured by their local and foreign allies, at Beirut port. On the other side, aided by Syria, Iraq and Libya, the Palestinians went on reinforcing their bases in Lebanon by shoring up their fighters and supplies.

The Palestinian political-military structure, built around the refugee camps, inspired and encouraged the radical, and largely underprivileged, Muslim groups of Lebanon, and crystallized their discontent with a system weighted in favour of the Maronite Christians, led by an oligarcy of businessmen and financiers. President Franjieh's gradual, but definite, adoption of an anti-Palestinian policy advocated by the right-wing Maronite politicians increased the existing anger and frustration among the pro-Palestinian, Arab nationalist Muslims as well as the middle-of-the-road Greek Orthodox Christians.

In the three decades since the adoption of the 1943 National Pact, demographic and other changes had favoured the Muslim side. The 1973 population estimates for Lebanese citizens put Muslims at 1,775,000 out of a total of 3,250,000 – or 54 per cent.[11] In other words, the proportions of Muslims and Christians in the national population had reversed over the thirty-year period. In Beirut the settlement of poor, mainly Shia rural migrants on the outskirts of the affluent Christian eastern part of the city accentuated sectarian antagonisms among people accustomed to more homogeneous surroundings. The large inflow of indigent Muslims into the urban centres, coupled with the mushrooming of radical Lebanese parties, subverted the power of the traditional Muslim leaders. This was well illustrated by the results of the 1972 parliamentary election. It introduced thirty-nine new faces in a chamber of ninety-nine. Yet there was no major change in the balance of power between the different groups.

This was the backdrop against which the prologue to the longest Lebanese civil war was to be enacted.

Prelude to the Civil War: June 1973–February 1975

The cabinet formed by Taqi al Din Solh on 8 July satisfied Damascus as it included some pro-Syrian Muslim politicians. Though Lebanon did not join Syria and Egypt in their hostilities with Israel in the October 1973 war, it made available to Syria not only its fuel supplies but also its radar station on Mount Baruk, south of the Beirut–Damascus highway.

On 6 October 1973 Egypt and Syria mounted a surprise attack on the Israeli units occupying the Egyptian Sinai and the Syrian Golan Heights, and made impressive gains in the first week. But the swiftly mobilized Israeli Defence Forces (IDF), bolstered by a continuous airlift of American weapons, forced the Syrians back, and cut a wedge through the Egyptian front to establish a bridgehead on the western bank of the Suez Canal. On 22 October the United Nations Security Council Resolution 338 called for an immediate ceasefire. Egypt and Israel accepted the resolution immediately, with Syria following two days later. The Israeli breach of the truce led to the second Security Council ceasefire resolution on 25 October, which finally ended the hostilities. The latest Arab–Israeli war had proved to be the bloodiest so far.

The fact that for the first time the Arabs had taken a military initiative against Israel, and held on to most of their early territorial gains, improved the morale of the Palestinians and their Lebanese supporters. The other, non-territorial consequence also proved beneficial to the Arabs.

During and after the October 1973 war, the petroleum-producing

Arab states used the 'oil weapon' against the Western states support-ing Israel. A two-prong stategy of selective oil embargo, and control over global production through the Organization of Oil Exporting Countries (OPEC), resulted in a quadrupling of the oil price during 1973–74.

Freshly aware of the power of the oil weapon, the Western nations, now keener on strengthening ties with the oil-rich Arab states than before, lost interest in the idea of preserving a Christian power base in Lebanon. This weakened the hand of the Christian, particularly Maronite, politicians there. They therefore turned increasingly to Israel for moral and material aid. Israel obliged, particularly when the most politicized sect among Christians, the Maronites, was turning daily more anti-Palestinian. In contrast to their Christian compatriots, the Lebanese Muslims were buoyed by the feeling of Arab and Muslim power sweeping through the region. Their leaders became less willing than before to accept Christian hegemony. This was particularly true of the new breed of leadership thrown up by the events of the previous decade.

These developments gave an impetus to Kamal Jumblatt, the Progressive Socialist Party leader, to expand and strengthen the Front of National and Progressive Parties and Forces (or Progressive Front, in short), an umbrella organization formed in 1972. Also the further weakening of the traditional Sunni and Shia notables assisted the Progressive Front, with Jumblatt gaining at the expense of such Sunni leaders as Saeb Salam and Hassan Khalid, the Grand Mufti of Lebanon.

As for the Shias, now the single largest sect, their politics had undergone a radical change. Nothing summed this up better than the slogan that the new Shia leader, Imam Musa Sadr (b. 1928, d. 1978), gave to a rally of 75,000 at Baalbek in March 1974; 'Arms are an ornament to men'. Criticizing the government for failing to protect the mainly Shia population from Israeli attacks in southern Lebanon, he announced the setting-up of training camps in the Beqaa valley for the Shias of the south.

Musa Sadr, born in the Iranian holy city of Qom, had arrived in Lebanon in 1957 as a representative of the Shia theological establish-ment of Qom. His task was to provide religious guidance to Lebanese Shias, the poorest and most exploited group, based principally in Beirut, south Lebanon and the Beqaa valley. Following his condem-nation of the Shah of Iran, Muhammad Reza Pahlavi, for suppressing a country-wide uprising led by Ayatollah Ruhollah Khomeini in

June 1963, Musa Sadr was deprived of his Iranian nationality. He then acquired Lebanese citizenship. In 1967 he formed the Higher Shia Communal Council and became a leading official spokesman of the Shias. In early 1974 the Council presented a series of social, administrative and economic demands to the government to ameliorate the living and working conditions of Shias.

This charter became the manifesto of the Movement of the Disinherited that Musa Sadr founded in February 1973. The Movement claimed to speak on behalf of the underprivileged of all sects. (Initially 20 per cent of its members were Christian; but later, as sectarian polarization intensified with the outbreak of a civil war, this percentage declined.) The Movement proved popular with Shias, dissatisfied as they were with their traditional, pro-establishment leaders. Through rallies, demonstrations and strikes, Musa Sadr made Shias aware of their strength.

The other factor which boosted Shia morale was the emergence of Hafiz Assad as the leader of Syria in November 1970. As an Alawi,[12] he belonged to the Shia school of Islam. After a quarter-century of political upheavals Syria achieved stability under Assad who, as a military strategist, was acutely conscious that Israel could use Lebanon to outflank Syrian defences. This happened at a time when Egypt lost its primacy in Arab affairs following the death of President Nasser in September 1970. These factors enabled Damascus to exert a degree of influence over Lebanon that it had not done since the dissolution of the Ottoman empire. Little wonder that the Lebanese politicians, who used to fly to Cairo in the 1960s to seek solutions to their internal and external problems, now took to visiting Damascus instead.

The inclusion of pro-Syrian Muslims in the Taqi al Din Solh government in July 1973 was another indication of Syria's rising star in Beirut. However, that did not improve the Solh administration's chance of implementing even the mild reform it promised in early 1974. Nor did it enable the government to strengthen the army to resist Israel's repeated violations of Lebanese sovereignty. In mid-April 1974 the IDF penetrated with impunity deep into Lebanon along an 80 km stretch of the Lebanese–Israeli frontier. At home, the internal security situation deteriorated as private militias grew larger and stronger. Government morale fell as individual Muslim ministers resigned. On 1 October Israel declared its intention to organize regular patrols and roadblocks on Lebanese soil to prevent infiltration across the border. In mid-December it went one step further by bombing the Palestinian refugee camps of Sabra and Shatila in Beirut.[13] Unable to take any retaliatory action against Israel, the Lebanese government resigned.

Rashid Solh, a cousin of the departed premier, formed a heterogeneous cabinet of eighteen ministers in January 1975. Lacking cohesion and power, the government failed to stop a slide into social anarchy, with extortions, kidnappings and murders becoming commonplace, and strikes and demonstrations plaguing the nation.

In late February a strike by fishermen in Sidon against a newly established company owned by Camille Chamoun, with plans to engage in trawler-fishing, became the catalyst which raised the simmering friction between the rightist Maronites and the leftist Lebanese Muslims to an incendiary level. Six weeks later came a violent confrontation between the right-wing Maronites and the radical Palestinian commandos.

These two events are commonly regarded as heralding the passing of Lebanon from a state of tottering peace to civil war. The first was part economic, part sectarian – pitting profit-hungry Christian entrepreneurs against poor Muslims intent on preserving their traditional means of livelihood. The second event stemmed from the traditional Maronite claim of being the prime guardians of Lebanese nationalism, which they saw as threatened by the ever-increasing presence of armed Palestinians.

Triggers for the civil war

On 26 February 1975 the predominantly Muslim fishermen of Sidon demonstrated against the government decision to give fishing rights to a freshly established company, headed by Camille Chamoun and engaged in producing protein supplements. One of the demonstrators' leaders, Maruf Saad, the local mayor, was shot dead by unknown assailants. His killing polarized the populace, dramatically pitting the forces at the opposite ends of the sectarian–political spectrum against one another.

The rioting that erupted in Sidon following the mayor's murder became so severe that the government deployed troops to restore order. This only exacerbated the problem. On 1 March the conflict between the soldiers and the protestors escalated into gun battles between the troops and the commandos from the nearby Palestinian camp of Miya Miya, resulting in sixteen deaths. Despite repeated appeals, Camille Chamoun refused to give up his fishing rights. The Muslim side saw the deployment of soldiers against civilian protestors as a dangerous precedent. The Christian side viewed the event as part of a plot to tarnish the image of the Lebanese government and its army. To show their backing for the continued use of troops in Sidon, the Phalange and National Liberal parties mounted a demonstration in Beirut on 5 March.

The root problem was that, given the Maronite dominance in the army's command structure, most Muslims regarded the army as a tool of the Maronite president, and therefore unfit to act as an impartial arbiter of internal conflicts. The popular backing given to the army by the Maronite parties only confirmed the feeling prevalent among Muslims, who rationalized the use of weapons by their co-religionists against the army in Sidon. Sharing the popular view of the army among Muslims, sixteen of their leaders, including six former prime ministers, demanded the reconstitution of the army command council in order to give parity to Muslims and Christians. Camille Chamoun and Pierre Gemayel opposed this. As a compromise, Prime Minister Solh placed the matter before a parliamentary committee on defence.

Some weeks later came another violent episode, which finally plunged Lebanon into civil war. On Sunday 13 April, Pierre Gemayel was attending the consecration of a Maronite church in Ain Rummane, a Christian suburb of East Beirut. A car pulled up outside the church, and a burst of fire from the car killed four people, including a bodyguard of Gemayel. The shocked and enraged militiamen of the Phalange Party assumed that the culprits were Palestinian commandos. That morning Palestinians were celebrating a successful guerrilla action inside Israel with a parade at Shatila camp in West Beirut. In the early afternoon a busload of Palestinians and their Lebanese Muslim allies, on their way back to the Palestinian camp of Tal Zaatar (in East Beirut) from Shatilla, passed the church in Ain Rummane, loudly singing Palestinian nationalist songs. The Phalangist militiamen ambushed the bus, killing twenty-seven Palestinians and Lebanese, and injuring nineteen.

The news of the Ain Rummane massacre spread like wildfire; and almost instantly, fighting between the opposing camps erupted all over the country.

An important external factor which determined the timing of the outbreak of the civil conflict had to do with the efforts of the US secretary of state, Henry Kissinger, to bring about an overall Arab–Israeli settlement in the wake of the October 1973 war. His 'shuttle diplomacy' in the Middle East, which led to the signing of troop withdrawal agreements between Israel and Egypt, and Israel and Syria, by the spring of 1974, ran out of steam early the following year. The assassination on 25 March 1975 of King Faisal ibn Abdul Aziz of Saudi Arabia, a pro-American monarch and a stabilizing factor in the region, by Faisal ibn Musaid, a junior prince of radical views, made Kissinger nervous. To divert the Arab states' attention away from the American failure to further the Arab–Israeli peace process, and to engage them in proxy, internecine conflict by supporting the opposing camps in Lebanon – a traditional arena for warring between competing ideologies and interests in the Middle East – Kissinger seemed to have decided to push Lebanon into a civil war. The agency to be used for the purpose was the CIA, which had long-standing connections with the Maronite political establishment, as illustrated by the CIA's funding of the 1957 Lebanese parliamentary elections through President Chamoun. In more recent times the CIA had acquired a powerful 'asset' in Bashir Gemayel (b. 1947, d. 1982), an overly ambitious son of Pierre and the leader of the Phalange Party. According to Winslow Peck, a former employee of the US National Security Agency, the American administration used its CIA station in Athens to activate the Phalange and 'kindle the fire'.[14]

The civil war, which continued until mid-October 1990, passed through nine phases: April 1975 to May 1976; June 1976 to February 1978; March 1978 to October 1978; November 1978 to May 1982; June 1982 to February 1984; March 1984 to January 1986; February 1986 to September 1988; October 1988 to September 1989; October 1989 to October 1990.

The single most important domestic factor which plunged the country into civil war was the perception shared by the Maronite leadership that the presence of the Palestinian commandos in Lebanon was a serious threat to Lebanese sovereignty. In the late 1950s President Chamoun had taken such a view of the rise of Nasserism in Lebanon. Just as in 1958 so now the Maronite religio-political establishment succeeded in mobilizing the community around the banner of Lebanese nationalism, thus precipitating civil strife. But there were major differences too between 1958 and 1975. Unlike in 1958, when the Maronite patriarch and the Maronite commander of the army provided a viable moderate leadership in the Christian camp, in 1975 there was no such alternative available to Christians; and the degree of military organization and armament among the Lebanese as well as the Palestinians was unparalleled.

History shows that whenever the Christian politicians in power, led by the republic's Maronite president, have implemented foreign policies which deviate sharply from those of the mainstream Arab world, and/or have pursued domestic policies which alienate the leadership of urban Muslims, they have destroyed the delicate equilibrium of the Lebanese political system and induced a severe crisis. The converse is true as well: that is, whenever the dominant Christian politicians have aligned their foreign policies with those of the Arab hinterland and co-opted the urban Muslim leadership in the running of the state, they have provided stability to the republic. In this respect the presidencies of Bishara Khuri (1943–53), Fuad Chehab (1958–64) and Charles Helou (1964–70) are illustrative.

In 1975 there were three major participants in the civil war: the conservative Lebanese Front, a confederation of Christian parties; the reformist Lebanese National Movement, a confederation of mainly Muslim parties; and the Palestinian resistance. In addition there were others on the fringes of the conflict: the traditional Muslim and Christian leaders and their followers, and the pro-Damascus Nationalist Front.

The Lebanese Front emerged in early September 1976 both as a political organ headed by Camille Chamoun, and as the Unified Military Command of the Christian militias, led by Bashir Gemayel. It evolved out of two Maronite summits – the first held in January 1976 (at the presidential palace of Suleiman Franjieh) under Chamoun, then interior minister, and the second in Kafur three months later. The constituents of the Lebanese Front stressed their distinctness from the Arab world by emphasizing that Maronite history, which centred around the Church and Mount Lebanon, stood apart from the mainstream Muslim Arabs and even non-Maronite Christians.

Politically and militarily, the most important of its constituents was the Phalange Party. Inspired by the Nazi Youth Movement's rallies, which he had witnessed during his visit to the Berlin Olympics in the summer of 1936, Pierre Gemayel founded the Phalange Party in November of that year. Its following came chiefly from among the Christian youths of the Metn region and Christian students of Beirut. It played an active role in the forging of the National Pact of 1943, which formalized Christian domination of the state machinery.

Following Lebanon's full independence in 1946, the party tried to widen its appeal. In this it was helped by the discovery in 1949 of a plot by the Syrian Social Nationalist Party to merge Lebanon with Syria, and the nationalist reaction that it aroused among Christians, who were determined to maintain Lebanon as an independent entity.

The party's pro-Western stance, coupled with its opposition to Nasser and Arab nationalism, led it to back President Camille Chamoun in the 1958 civil war. Its initial support for President Chehab began to wane as he tried to strengthen the powers of the state at the expense of the financial and commercial oligarchs who had led the Phalange since its inception. The reforming effort initiated by Chehab slowed considerably during the presidency of Charles Helou. Helped by the continuing prosperity of Lebanon – stemming mainly from its being a banking and tourist centre for the wealthy oil sheikhs of the Arabian Peninsula – the party swelled its ranks with recruits from the Christian petty bourgeoisie.

By aligning with the parties of Camille Chamoun and Raymond Edde in the 1968 parliamentary elections, the Phalange increased its share from four seats to nine among the thirty allotted to Maronites. However, with the economic boom petering out towards the early 1970s, disillusion set in among its members. The leaders directed this feeling against the Palestinians, whose presence in Lebanon had been bolstered by the June 1967 Arab–Israeli War and the Jordanian strife of 1970–1. As an extreme example of Arab nationalism, the Palestinians were a perfect target for hatred by the members of the Phalange Party, which, on the eve of the civil war, was 20,000 strong and had a militia under the command of Bashir Gemayel.

The National Liberal Party (NLP) revolved chiefly around the personality of Camille Chamoun, who had established it soon after the 1958 civil war. The main pillars of its ideology were Lebanese (as against Arab) nationalism and economic liberalism based on private enterprise. Unlike the older and better organized Phalange, the NLP was able to attract non-Maronite Christians. This had an important bearing on its strength in parliament. In the 1972 general election it secured thirteen parliamentary seats, the highest won by any party. It had contested that poll, and the one before, in alliance with the Phalange.

Both parties began building up their own militias in the late 1960s, with the NLP calling its fighters, led by Nihad Shalhat, Tigers. At first these militias aided the Lebanese army in attacking the Palestinian commandos. Later, in 1973, they took to assaulting the Palestinian partisans on their own. By the summer of the following year, the two Maronite militias were expanded to the point where jointly they were a third as large as the 18,000-strong Lebanese army.

A third Maronite armed force was called the Zghartan Liberation Army. Its Giants Brigade was commanded by Tony Franjieh, a son of Suleiman. It was formed in 1969 by the Franjiehs as a result of their conflict with the Palestinian commandos in the Tripoli area. But compared to the Phalangist and NLP militias it was small, its total strength fluctuating around 1,000 fighters; and it did not join the Unified Military Command of the Christian militias under Bashir Gemayel in September 1976.

Additionally, there were other smaller, but more militant, Maronite paramilitary forces: the Guardians of the Cedars and the secretive Al Tanzim (i.e. The Organization) belonging to the Maronite League and headed by Fuad Shamali. These came into existence soon after the civil war erupted in April 1975. Led by Etienne Saqr, the Guardians were ultra-nationalist and fiercely anti-Palestinian. They derived their ideology from the writings of Saad Aql, an intellectual and a poet, who believed that Lebanese identity was rooted in its distant Phoenician past and had little to do with Islam or Arabism. Aql went on to develop a version of the Latin alphabet which he claimed was more suitable to the 'Lebanese' language. His ideas appealed to Maronite intellectuals who, during the inter-war period, were intent on giving shape to a Lebanese identity distinct from Syria and the Muslim-dominated Arab hinterland. With the tide of Arab nationalism rising after the Second World War, Aql's particularist thesis lost ground. Later, the arrival of a large number of Palestinians in Lebanon revived Aql's ideology among Maronites, and the Guardians of the Cedars became its most enthusiastic supporters. Alone among the various Maronite groups, the Guardians were open about their links with Israel.

Then there was the Maronite Church establishment. The moderate Patriarch Boutros Khuraish was overshadowed by Sherbal Qassis, the head of the Association of Lebanese Monastic Orders, who sat on various Maronite forums as the representative of the Maronite Church. A militant nationalist, he was opposed to the idea incorporated in the 1943 National Pact that Lebanon should project an Arab face. Equally strongly, he resented the presence of the Palestinians in Lebanon, and wanted it drastically reduced. The Maronite monastic orders assisted the Maronite militias in two ways. As owners of vast plots of agricultural lands, they backed them financially. And they allowed the militias to use their monasteries as storage places for arms, ammunition and food.

The moderate opinion among the Maronites was represented by Elias Sarkis, a Chehabist, and Raymond Edde, son of former president Emile Edde (1936–41). An academic, and a parliamentary deputy since 1965, Raymond Edde led the National Bloc. He was opposed to both Camille Chamoun's tribal/feudal view of politics and General Fuad Chehab's use of military intelligence and other organs of the state to modernize Lebanese politics.

As the civil strife intensified, the Lebanese army, commanded by Major Fuad Malik, a Maronite, began to show cracks, with the mainly Christian officer corps openly fraternizing with the Lebanese Front.

Pitted against the Maronite forces was a reformist alliance called the Lebanese National Movement (LNM), which was backed by the Palestinians. Consisting of about a dozen Muslim-dominated Lebanese parties, some of which emerged during the civil war, the LNM was led by Kamal Jumblatt.

His staunch commitment to pan-Arabism neutralized any handicap Kamal Jumblatt had in the predominantly Muslim camp due to his Druze origins. Though his organization, the Progressive Socialist Party (PSP), formed in 1949, was predominantly Druze, it had some Sunni, Shia and Christian members. His feudal background enabled him to exercise strong influence over Druzes, whereas his leftist Arab nationalist views made him popular among urban, mainstream Muslims. He was a consistent opponent of confessionalism. To provide a common framework to the Lebanese groups of leftist persuasion and the Palestinian parties, he established the National and Progressive Front in 1969. His legalization of such transnational parties as the Communists and the Baathists in the summer of 1970 enlarged the size of the Front, to be called the Front of National and Progressive Parties and Forces in 1972, and later the Lebanese National Movement.

The Communist Party of Lebanon (CPL) grew out of the Communist Party of Syria and Lebanon formed in 1925. In more recent times it had participated in the 1958 civil war as part of the Socialist National Front dominated by pan-Arabists. The discrediting of Nasserism in the wake of the Arab defeat in the June 1967 war created fresh opportunities for the growth of the party in Lebanon. The ban on it was lifted formally three years later. Under the leadership of Niqula Shawi the party set up its own militia called the

People's Guards. By restoring to popular forms of agitation and propaganda, the CPL widened its base among the students, workers and peasants. Its successful call for a general strike in early 1974 gave a boost to its newly established National Union of Workers and Employees. On the eve of the civil war in April 1975, the CPL along with the PSP and the Communist Action Organization (led by Muhsin Ibrahim) formed the hard core of the Front of National and Progressive Parties and Forces. Unlike other parties the Communists combined military action with political education and propaganda. By the end of 1975 the party had acquired 15,000 members, half of them Shia and one-third Greek Orthodox.[15]

As a regional body, the Arab Baath Socialist Party had a long history dating back to 1940, when Michel Aflaq and Zaki Arsouzi, both history teachers in Damascus, formed groups of nationalist students to agitate for independence from the French. Three years later they decided to merge their groups and called the new body the Arab Baath Party. At its first pan-Arab congress in Damascus in April 1947, delegates from Syria, Iraq, Lebanon, Transjordan (later Jordan) and Morocco adopted a constitution and a programme. The party's basic principles were described as: the unity and freedom of the Arab nation within its homeland; and a belief in the 'special mission of the Arab nation', the mission being to end colonialism and promote humanitarianism. To accomplish it the party had to be 'nationalist, populist, socialist and revolutionary'. Later the pan-Arab organization changed its name to the Arab Baath Socialist Party. Due to the ban on transnational organizations imposed in the wake of the 1949 attempted coup by the Syrian Social Nationalist Party, the Baath Party acquired a semi-clandestine existence. In the mid-1960s, with the division of the pan-Arab organization into pro-Syrian and pro-Iraqi wings, the Lebanese party too split, with the pro-Iraqi faction led by Abdul Majid Rafii retaining the name, and the pro-Syrian wing led by Asim Qansu calling itself the Organization of the Baath Party.

Another regional organization, functioning in Lebanon and Syria, was the Syrian Social Nationalist Party (SSNP). It was formed in 1932 by Antun Saade, a Greek Orthodox journalist, with the aim of creating Greater Syria to accommodate all the people belonging to the Syrian nation, which Saade described as the ethnic fusion of Canaanites, Akkadians, Chaldeans, Assyrians, Arameans, Hittites and Metannis. He argued that 'a single healthy national loyalty' would ensure 'the revival of the [Syrian] nation'. He combined ultra-

INTRODUCTION

nationalism with secular ideas – including separation of church and state, and removal of barriers between various sects and religions – and a state-directed programme for modernizing society. He advocated absolute obedience to the Sole Leader. The French banned the party in 1935, but it managed to function clandestinely. The outbreak of the Second World War found Antun Saade in Latin America on a visit to forge links with the Syrian emigrants there. On his return to Lebanon in 1947, he re-established his control over the party, which derived the majority of its support from the non-Maronite section of the Christian community. Given his strong stand on adopting an all-embracing Syrian nationalism, he soon clashed with the Lebanese government. He went underground, but was allowed to resurface after he had affirmed his acceptance of Lebanon as a sovereign state.

The SSNP emerged as a bitter rival of the Phalange Party, wedded to the ideas of militant Lebanese nationalism and the centrality of the church in society. Following a bloody confrontation between the SSNP and the Phalange in June 1949, the government banned the party for plotting to overthrow the regime, and arrested 2,000 of its members.[16] Saade fled to Damascus, but was extradited to Beirut, where he was tried and executed. This weakened the party but, supported mainly by secular-minded non-Maronite Christians, it continued to function semi-clandestinely until the lifting of the ban on transnational parties in 1970. Led by Inaam Raad, it remained bitterly hostile to the Phalange Party.

The other organization which emerged as militantly anti-Phalange was the Independent Nasserites, formed in secret in the early 1970s by Ibrahim Qulaylat. A progressive social body which drew its following from the Sunni community, it backed the Palestinians and opposed partition of Lebanon. Its militia, the Murabitoun (literally, the Faithful of the Sermon), fought the Phalangists in Beirut.

In the course of the war, Nasserite organizations such as the Popular Nasserist Organization, led by Mustafa Saad, sprang up in Tripoli and Sidon, which were traditional Sunni centres. They participated actively in the armed conflict. In contrast, the traditional political and religious leaders of the Sunni community stayed out of the fray. However, they voiced opposition to the partition of Lebanon and the involvement of the Lebanese army in the civil strife.

As for the Shias, by July 1975 it became public that their radical leader, Imam Musa Sadr, had set up a militia adjunct to the Movement of the Disinherited. Called the *Afwaj al-Muqawama al Lubnaniya* (Lebanese Resistance Detachments), it was popularly known by its acronym Amal, which also means 'hope'.[17] While vehemently opposed to the traditional Shia leadership, Musa Sadr maintained friendly relations with the Sunni establishment with whom he shared the demand for political parity between Muslims and Christians. His Movement of the Disinherited was part of the pro-Syrian Nationalist Front, which included the SSNP.

Threatened by the loss of popular following to the charismatic Musa Sadr, such traditional Shia leaders as Kamil Assad and Adil Osseiran tried to conciliate the warring factions of Lebanon.

So far as the Palestinian resistance was concerned, consisting of half a dozen major parties, its moderate constituents – the Fatah (led by Yasser Arafat) and the Democratic Front for the Liberation of Palestine (headed by Nayif Hawatima) – refrained from fighting until January 1976. They were anxious not to invite intervention by the Lebanese army, or an external power, in the civil upheaval. The pro-Syrian Saiqa Organization (led by Zuhair Muhsin) followed the line pursued by Damascus. In contrast, such radical Palestinian organizations as the Marxist Popular Front for the Liberation of Palestine (headed by George Habash), the pro-Iraqi Arab Liberation Front (led by Abdul Wahhab Kayyali) and the Populist Struggle Front (headed by Bahjat Abu Gharbiya) allied with the Lebanese National Movement as soon as the war erupted.

PART I

PART I

1

Ascendancy of the reformist alliance

April 1975 — May 1976

The news of the Ain Rummane massacre on 13 April 1975 set Lebanon alight. For the next three days the Palestinian commandos, backed by the armed members of the Lebanese National Movement, fought the Phalangist militiamen, supported by the National Liberal Party's Tigers, on the streets of Beirut, Tripoli and Sidon. While the Palestinians and their Lebanese allies attacked the business premises and factories of the Maronites, the latter turned their guns and rockets against the Palestinian camps. Small fire intermingled with salvos of rockets and mortars. As in any civil war, there were no fixed battle lines and no well-organized armies. Often the partisans took up position behind hastily erected barricades in the streets. The government found itself powerless to stop the fighting until on 16 April the Arab League's general secretary brought about a ceasefire.

Protesting against a call by the Lebanese National Movement to isolate the Phalangists in Lebanon and elsewhere in the Arab world, three Phalange ministers resigned on 7 May. Their lead was followed by the NLP ministers, a move which left the government crippled. After the first bout of serious fighting the Palestinians refrained from active participation. They struck back only when they were hit by the Maronite militias.

Continuation of the conflict wiped out the political centre. The moderates, whether Christian or Muslim, abandoned their positions and joined the warring coalitions led respectively by Kamal Jumblatt and Camille Chamoun, who had headed the opposing camps in the 1958 civil war. The Maronites, it seemed, were intent on goading the Palestinians into a wide-ranging confrontation with a view to defeating them as a prelude to expelling them from Lebanon. Among others, Jumblatt saw through their strategy and intensified the fighting between the LNM and the Maronite militias. Prime Minister

31

Solh agreed with Jumblatt's assessment of the situation, but finding himself unable to frustrate the Maronite plans, he resigned on 15 May.

A fortnight later, President Franjieh called on Rashid Karami to form the next government. As the political crisis deepened, violence spread from Beirut southwards. Intense battles erupted in mid-June. Karami's efforts succeeded only when the Syrian foreign minister, Abdul Halim Khaddam, intervened. The new cabinet, containing a member from each of the six major Muslim and Christian sects, was sworn in on 30 June. Prime Minister Karami, who also held the defence portfolio, managed to secure the co-operation of the PLO and the Phalangists to stop fighting. The truce held until mid-summer.

Kamal Jumblatt reiterated the major demands of the Lebanese National Movement: ending the confessional system; amending the constitution to redefine the prerogatives of the various branches of the executive; changing the electoral law; reorganizing the army; and modifying the citizenship law to enfranchise such minorities as the Kurds living in Beirut. The LNM considered political reform as a prelude to socio-economic reform. It wished to abolish the existing political imbalance between the president on one side and the prime minister and parliament on the other. It also wished to broaden the scope for political participation by introducing proportional representation in parliament of the political parties formed on a non-sectarian basis.

The Christian leaders, particularly the Maronites, were opposed to these demands. Aware of the demographic dominance of the Muslims, they wished to cling to the provision of a powerful Maronite president. Replacing the present system with proportional representation for parties formed on non-sectarian grounds was bound to hurt the traditional leaders, both Christian and Muslim; and the Phalangists and the NLP were vehemently opposed to the idea.

The ceasefire of 16 April ended on 24 August. On that day hostilities between Christians and Shias erupted in Zahle, the administrative and commercial centre of southern Beqaa. More specifically, there was confrontation between the Phalangist militia and Amal, the Shia militia, whose existence and training camps near Baalbek, the administrative centre of northern Beqaa, had been acknowledged by Imam Musa Sadr some weeks earlier.

On 29 August fighting broke out in Tripoli between the units of the Zgharta Liberation Army (commanded by Tony Franjieh, son of the president) on one side and the Palestinian commandos and the Lebanese Sunni militia on the other. Prime Minister Karami tried to stop the Tripoli battle by interposing the Lebanese army. But when the troops killed thirteen Sunni militiamen, the army lost Muslim backing. Jumblatt called a general strike on 15 September in protest against the army action. Feeling harassed, Karami sought the help of the Syrian president, Assad, to control the situation. Assad responded by allowing 600 troops of the Damascus-based Palestine Liberation Army (PLA) to head for Tripoli to restore law and order there.

Although Jumblatt called off the strike on 14 September to cool tempers, his gesture failed to stop renewed clashes, which erupted in the hitherto neutral commercial district of Beirut. The Maronite militias, now in contact with Israel for military and intelligence assistance (as was to be revealed in 1976), were bent on reviving and escalating hostilities with a view to compelling Prime Minister Karami to use the army, under predominantly Maronite command, to curb the discontent. The LNM was opposed to the intervention by soldiers. It wanted an immediate reorganization of the army so that Muslim officers could share in the command at the highest level.

Intensified fighting brought the Syrian foreign minister, Khaddam, to the Lebanese presidential palace on 19 September. With his assistance a twenty-member Committee for National Dialogue was formed, and a ceasefire date of 25 September agreed. While Jumblatt wanted the new committee to discuss the LNM's demands immediately, the Maronite leaders insisted that no negotiations could be held so long as fighting continued.

The truce held only for about a month. Fierce fighting developed on 22 October in downtown Beirut and other fronts in Lebanon. Sporadic intervention by the army proved inadequate to contain the hostilities. To assist the Lebanese prime minister in his peacekeeping efforts, President Assad despatched a brigade of the Syrian-officered PLA from Damascus. However, Karami failed to secure the co-operation either of his president, Franjieh, or his interior minister, Chamoun. His efforts to convene the parliament were also in vain. His reconciliation with Franjieh in early November, at the intercession of the Syrians, failed to bolster his fast-sagging power and prestige.

In contrast, the Phalangists, working in collaboration with the American and Israeli intelligence agencies, felt aggressively confident. They decided to move out of their strongholds in East Beirut into the Muslim and mixed neighbourhoods of West Beirut, and made the hotel district their primary target. But they met stiff resistance from the Lebanese National Movement, and retreated.

In the course of bitter fighting, bloody retribution became commonplace, leading to periodic massacres. Following the murder of five Phalangists in the Christian-dominated town of Fanar on 6 December 1975, the Maronite militia abducted hundreds of Muslims in East Beirut at random, and brutally massacred between 53 and 200 of them. This reactivated all battlefronts in Lebanon. The Sunni Murabitoun militia attacked Christians at random in downtown Beirut. They and their allies expelled the Maronites from the hotel district. Battles raged up and down the country for eight days. It was only under the combined pressure of the PLO and Syria that the warring factions accepted a ceasefire on 15 December.

Both sides then decided to eliminate hostile pockets within their enclaves. In East Beirut and its suburbs the Maronites were vulnerable at three major points: (a) the exit to the coastal Beirut–Tripoli highway connecting the capital to the Christian hinterland to the north; (b) along the Beirut–Tripoli road near the Dog river; and (c) the exit to the Christian stronghold in the lower Metn region southeast of East Beirut. Since the Muslim slums of Karantia and Maslakh in the capital's port area were located along (a), the Palestinian camp of Dubaya along (b), and the Palestinian camps of Tal Zaatar and Jisr Baasha along (c), these were to become the targets of the Phalangists and NLP Tigers.

Between 4 and 14 January 1976 the Maronite militias blockaded the Palestinian camps at Tal Zaatar and Dubaya. Later they destroyed the Muslim slums of Karantia and Maslakh. The resulting slaughter of some 1,500 Palestinians and Lebanese Muslims in these slums by the Maronite militias led the moderate elements in the PLO – the Fatah and the Democratic Front for the Liberation of Palestine – to end their semi-isolationist policy and side actively with the Lebanese National Movement.

Aided by the LNM, the Palestinian units besieged the Christian-dominated coastal towns of Damour and Jiye south of Beirut. They introduced heavy artillery into the battles, and the Lebanese air force bombed the Palestinian positions around Damour. The Muslim militias from Sidon advanced north to strengthen the siege of Jiye. On 17 January, while Karantia and Maslakh fell to the Maronites, giving them unhindered access to the Christian hinterland to the north, the Muslim and Palestinian units captured Damour and Jiye. Most of the Christian residents had fled these towns before their fall.

Of those who stayed behind, some 300 to 400 were massacred by the attacking forces.

By now the whole country was aflame. In the northernmost region of Akkar, the Sunni tribesmen raided Christian villages. In the Tripoli–Zgharata area, fighting broke out between the Maronite Zgharatan Liberation Army and the Sunni militiamen and their Palestinian allies. In the Beqaa valley, battles raged in Zahle as well as in the area around Baalbek, where the Shia and Palestinian partisans attacked Christian settlements. Syria despatched a brigade of the Damascus-based PLA to aid the Lebanese–Palestinian alliance in its siege of Zahle.

The fierce, widespread fighting caused a virtual collapse of such vital state institutions as the army and the internal security force. Anarchy ensued. Public buildings became vulnerable to mob attacks and arson. The government offices in Baalbek, Tripoli, Sidon and elsewhere were ransacked and/or burnt. Many prisons were raided and their inmates released. The displaced residents of the slums and refugee camps resorted to occupying empty flats and houses in West Beirut.

The break-up of the Lebanese army brought in its wake the resignation of Prime Minister Karami on 18 January. Unable to cope, President Franjieh turned to Damascus. President Assad despatched Syria's foreign minister, chief of staff and air force commander to Beirut – a move endorsed by America, France and many Arab states. The Syrian team assisted in the forming of a Tripartite High Military Committee consisting of Lebanese, Palestinian and Syrian members. Its task was to monitor the thirty-third ceasefire, which went into effect on 21 January 1976, and maintain security.

Coinciding with the truce came the formation of the Unified Military Command of the Maronite militias of the Phalange, NLP, Guardians of the Cedars and Al Tanzim – now collectively called the Lebanese Forces – under the leadership of Bashir Gemayel. This was a great gain for the USA: the CIA had recruited him in the early 1970s when he had worked for an American law firm in Washington after finishing his studies in political science and law in Lebanon.[1] The founding of the Lebanese Forces strengthened the hands of those in the Christian camp who advocated partitioning Lebanon with a view to recreating a smaller, more compact Christian state encompassing Mount Lebanon, the northern littoral and eastern Beirut, with access to Beirut port. This scenario was unacceptable to the Lebanese Muslims, Palestinians and Syrians. To them the birth of a compact Christian Lebanon amounted to the creation of a second homeland for a religious minority in the Arab Middle East, Israel being the first. This was an outcome they were determined to abort at all costs.

By January 1976 the Maronite warlords had systematized the financing and procurement of arms. The funds came from Lebanese Christian businessmen at home and abroad, Maronite monastic foundations and such pro-American Arab states as Egypt and Saudi Arabia. Initially, the Maronites bought arms from Bulgaria, Czechoslovakia and East Germany, and later, clandestinely, from Belgium, France, Italy and West Germany. As for the Muslim militias, their principal source of weapons was Syria, which supplied them with arms made in the Soviet Union or eastern Europe.

Syria had by now emerged as an important player in the warfare in Lebanon. President Assad was determined to frustrate any plans to partition that country. He argued that the formation of a Christian state would demonstrate that Arab nationalism had ceased to act as a cement to hold together all Arabs, whatever their religious beliefs, that Islam was an intolerant faith, and that the PLO's objective of establishing a secular, democratic state in all of Palestine containing Muslims, Jews and Christians would seem a sham. At the same time, Assad was equally opposed to a clear-cut victory of the reformist Lebanese camp and its Palestinian allies. Such an outcome would, he believed, open floodgates of radicalism in Lebanon, a development bound to disturb the delicate balance of forces in the region, upsetting not only the pro-American Israel but also the pro-Soviet Syria. He did not relish the idea of finding himself sandwiched between radical Iraq, ruled by the rival wing of the Arab Baath Socialist Party, and radical Lebanon. Furthermore, in the name of protecting Lebanon's Christians, Israel was bound to intervene to quash the consolidation of power by the radical Lebanese and their Palestinian allies. If this happened, what would Syria do? If it tried to stop Israel, it would suffer defeat; and if it abstained, Lebanon would be lost to the Zionist enemy, with dire consequences for Syria and other Arab states. Either way Syria would lose.

The stance of Damascus could be understood in another, positive context. The increase in the size of its military supplied with sophisticated Soviet arms in the wake of the October 1973 war — combined with its growing influence over Jordan, the Palestinians and Lebanon — gave new confidence to Assad. He was able to build fruitful links with the oil-rich Arab Gulf states without compromising his traditionally strong ties with Moscow. Faced with a civil conflict in Lebanon, he resolved to extinguish it, thus not only ending a potentially disastrous war but also demonstrating Syrian dominance in the region. He was helped in this by Washington which, having burnt its fingers in the Vietnam War (1963–75), was reluctant to intervene directly, limiting itself to covert action mainly through the CIA.

January 1976 was a crucial month in another sense. It witnessed the formal break-up of the Lebanese army in the face of a continuing political-military crisis, with the Muslim segment claiming the loyalty of the majority of the ranks and lower-level officers, and formally calling itself the Lebanese Arab Army. Led by Lieutenant Ahmad Khatib, it took charge of twenty-five garrisons and camps in the Muslim-dominated areas.

The Lebanese Arab Army broke the latest ceasefire. Allying itself with the LNM forces, it embarked on an offensive strategy, expelling the Maronite units from downtown Beirut, bombarding the presidential palace at Baabda and forcing President Franjieh to flee to his home base of Ihden, and confining the Maronites to their enclave with the port of Jounieh, 20 km north of Beirut, as its undeclared capital.

Having tipped the balance against the Maronites, the Syrian president now wanted to moderate the progress of their Lebanese adversaries with a view to bringing the war to an end. He reckoned that the longer the fighting continued, the greater were the opportunities for Israel to fish in troubled waters to the detriment of Syrian and Arab interests.

A high-powered Syrian delegation persuaded President Franjieh to introduce long-overdue political reform. On 14 February 1976 he issued a Constitutional Reform Document. While leaving undisturbed the sectarian division of topmost jobs according to the 1943 National Pact, it specified Muslim-Christian parity in parliament, which was to take over the right to appoint the prime minister from the Maronite president. It promised electoral and socio-economic reforms.

The Lebanese National Movement regarded the Franjieh document as inadequate, while the PLO viewed Syria's rising power in Lebanon as threatening to the autonomy it enjoyed there. So the war continued to rage. On 11 March Brigadier-General Aziz Ahdab, the Sunni commander of the Beirut area, demanded Franjieh's resignation. The LNM leaders inside parliament and outside endorsed this call. The civil war intensified.

As days and weeks passed, the LNM–PLO alliance emerged victorious at the expense of the Maronite militias. By early April it controlled two-thirds of Lebanon, encompassing nearly all the areas that France had added to the Mount Lebanon region in 1920 to create the present state. This upset Assad who tried to roll back the situation, albeit subtly at first.

Assad displayed his displeasure by sending the Syrian-controlled Palestinian Liberation Army units 5 km inside Lebanon. He tried to wean the PLO away from the LNM in mid-April, but failed. He then boosted the presence of the PLA units inside Lebanon. This pleased America. 'President [Gerald] Ford has dropped his total opposition to outside military intervention in Lebanon, and approves Syrian actions there', said an official spokesman in Washington.[2] America's overt backing for his moves in Lebanon embarrassed Assad, but it did not deflect him from implementing the carrot-and-stick strategy he had devised towards the LNM–PLO alliance. To placate the LNM he went along, in principle, with its call for the immediate resignation of Franjieh (whose term was to expire in September), but settled for giving the demand a constitutional garb. He pressured the Lebanese parliament to amend the constitution to allow the presidential poll to be held within six months of the end of the incumbent's term instead of the existing two months.

As in the past, faced with the prospect of a humiliating defeat, the Maronites tried anxiously to find a foreign protector. America, still reeling from the effects of a military débâcle in Vietnam, was not prepared to consider helping them openly; nor was France or any other major nation of western Europe, made freshly aware of its dependence on Arab oil. Israel was an option, but turning to it would have alienated Assad irrevocably, an outcome that the Maronite leaders thought it prudent to avoid. In desperation, they turned to President Franjieh, whose cordial relations with Damascus dated back to the late 1950s. They supported his Constitutional Reform Document and, through him, set up a communications channel with Assad. The exercise proved fruitful.

The Maronite politicians succeeded in getting Assad to order his PLA units to switch sides and aid the (Maronite) Lebanese Front – for a price. The Maronite and other Christian deputies agreed to follow Assad's guideline when the parliament assembled on 8 May to elect the next president. They voted for Assad's choice, Elias Sarkis, who happened to be the only candidate. So too did Prime Minister Karami and other traditional Muslim leaders, thus ensuring the necessary two-thirds majority for Sarkis on the first count. However, the election of Sarkis went down badly not only in Egypt (now allied firmly with Washington), but also in radical Iraq and Libya.

Initially, Kamal Jumblatt, the LNM leader, viewed the Syrian–Maronite alliance positively, as a welcome opportunity to wean the Maronites away from France in particular and the West in general, and turn them eastwards towards Syria. He also urged negotiations to resolve the year-long crisis in the Lebanese army. But he was soon to be disappointed. As hostilities escalated, and President Franjieh refused to step down before the end of his term on 22 September, the chances of talks between the warring sides receded.

Assad's thinly disguised intervention to shore up the Maronite Lebanese Front failed to reverse its declining fortunes. This worried the Syrian leader. He was not prepared to co-exist with a radical Lebanon which, by giving revolutionary Palestinians unprecedented freedom of action, was likely to provoke Israel and alarm Western capitals. That a radical political-administrative entity was gradually taking shape in Lebanon became obvious to Assad when the Lebanese National Movement's steering committee began functioning as a cabinet led by Muhsin Ibrahim, the head of the Communist Action Organization; and when Jumblatt repeatedly ignored his appeals to cease fire, as did Yasser Arafat.

By mid-May 1976 Assad seemed to have decided to intervene directly in the Lebanese conflict by committing Syrian troops. But aware that such an action was liable to be misunderstood by Israel, he sought and secured American mediation. He assured Washington that his goal was to end the Lebanese civil conflict, and that the strength and the geographical distribution of his forces would not pose any threat to Israeli security.[3] The result was a 'red line' agreement – an unwritten, unsigned understanding – mediated by the USA. It ruled out the stationing of Syrian surface-to-air missiles (SAMs) in Lebanon, and imposed limits on the deployment of Syrian air, naval and land forces, including a ceiling of one brigade south of the Beirut–Damascus highway. Israel set out its conditions in a letter from its foreign minister, Yigal Allon, to the US secretary of state, Henry Kissinger, who passed it on to Damascus.[4] Aware of the impending attack on the progressive Lebanese and Palestinian forces by Assad, its long-term ally, the Soviet Union tried to dissuade the Syrian leader. Finding himself pulled in opposite directions by the two superpowers, Assad procrastinated.

Then, inadvertently, France ended the Syrian president's dilemma.

On 22 May the French president, Valéry Giscard d'Estaing, offered to send French troops to Lebanon if this were acceptable to all parties. Though only Pierre Gemayel, the Phalange leader, responded positively, Giscard d'Estaing's overture highlighted the prospect of a western European intervention in the Lebanese crisis – a development which Assad viewed as dangerously narrowing Syria's room for manoeuvre in Lebanon. He therefore decided to act.

On the night of 31 May–1 June, Assad despatched several brigades of Syrian armoured troops into Lebanon against the LNM–PLO alliance. This marked the first chapter of the civil war's post-Syrian phase, which lasted until the swearing-in of Elias Sarkis as president on 22 September 1976.

2

Syrian intervention and hegemony

June 1976 — February 1978

When attacked by the advancing Syrian troops from 1 June 1976 onwards, the Lebanese–Palestinian alliance, operating under a joint command, offered stiff resistance. Intense fighting developed in and around Beirut, Tripoli and Sidon; in the Palestinian stronghold between the Litani and Awali rivers; and in the foothills of Mount Hermon. While their armour enabled the Syrians to overpower the Lebanese–Palestinian resistance along the Damascus–Beirut highway and break the blockade of such Christian places as Zahle, elsewhere their unfamiliarity with the terrain proved a serious disadvantage.

Over the next few weeks, however, the Syrian position improved as the rejuvenated Maronite units began attacking hostile Muslim enclaves within the Christian territory, and the Syrians succeeded in severely disrupting the land and sea supply lines of their new adversaries. Symptomatic of the changed situation was the Maronite offensive on 23 June against the predominantly Palestinian camps of Tal Zaatar, containing 30,000 refugees, and the smaller Jisr Baasha in Beirut.[1]

On that day the prime ministers of Syria, Egypt, Saudi Arabi and Kuwait met in Riyadh to endorse the peace plan adopted a fortnight earlier by the Arab League foreign ministers in Cairo. It visualized an Arab Security Force of 6,000 to 10,000 troops eventually to replace the Syrian troops (some of whom were to be incorporated in the new force), and to supervise the ceasefire. The intervention of the Arab League, implying Arabization of the Lebanese civil war, was welcomed by the LMN–PLO Joint Command, who were bitterly opposed to the Syrian military intervention.

While the LMN–PLO alliance urged Moscow to pressure Damascus to withdraw its troops from Lebanon, the pro-Soviet Arab states of Iraq, Libya and Algeria publicly condemned Syria for its active co-operation with America and Israel in suppressing the LMN–PLO alliance. Their attacks came against a background of increasing evidence of substantial Israeli aid to the Maronite militias in money and military equipment and expertise.[2] To placate the Soviet Union, whose prime minister, Alexei Kosygin, was in Damascus when Assad moved his troops into Lebanon, President Assad sent his foreign minister to Moscow on 3 July to explain and justify the official policy. While puzzled and angry at the latest Syrian stance in Lebanon, the Kremlin was unwilling to alienate Damascus, its long-standing friend in the region, especially after its loss of Cairo as an ally four years earlier.

Meanwhile active fighting continued, with the Syrians and their Maronite allies gaining the upper hand. But the political-diplomatic price that Assad paid abroad was high, not to mention the quiet rumblings within the ruling Baath Party at home. Given the efficient intelligence services at his disposal, he was aware of this. Seizing the occasion of the inauguration of the newly elected provincial councils on 20 July, he delivered a long speech devoted almost exclusively to justifying the policy he had adopted in Lebanon.

Two days later Libya's mediation efforts bore fruit and led to a Syrian–Palestinian accord. It specified an immediate truce, and regularized the Palestinian presence in Lebanon according to the November 1969 Cairo Agreement and the 14 February 1976 Constitutional Reform Document. Having secured a ceasefire, the Lebanese National Movement leadership appointed the Central Political Council, and then (on 6 August) the Higher Organization for Civil Administration, to provide public services in West Beirut and elsewhere under the control of the LNM–PLO Joint Command. By so doing it merely followed in the footsteps of the Maronite Lebanese Front, which had established similar institutions.

The Libyan-brokered truce made no difference to the Maronite blockade of Tal Zaatar. It fell on 12 August 1976 after a siege of fifty-two days. Some 3,000 Palestinian civilians were killed, most of them after the camp had fallen. The capture and destruction of Tal Zaatar enabled Bashir Gemayel to consolidate his position as the head of the Unified Military Command of the Lebanese Front militias.

On the other side, the Tal Zaatar setback softened the LNM's friction with the Lebanese Arab Army, led by Lt Ahmad Khatib, which seemed to be leaning towards the traditional leaders of the Muslim community. Indeed, the LNM set up a committee to co-ordinate its actions with those of the Lebanese Arab Army. Having thus strengthened itself, the LNM refused to evacuate the areas it had seized earlier, in conjunction with the PLO, in the Metn and the Druze-dominated Aley region. It felt buoyed by Moscow's public call to Syria on 26 August to pull back its troops from Lebanon. Little wonder that the efforts of the Arab League envoy on 17 and 19 September to secure the LNM's withdrawal from the Metn and Aley areas failed.

Elias Sarkis inherited this situation when he assumed the presidency on 23 September. As expected, in his inaugural speech he thanked Damascus for its actions and underlined the need for the Syrian military presence in securing the well-being of Lebanon.

Having failed to secure the LNM–PLO withdrawal from the Metn and Aley regions through negotiation, Assad ordered a military offensive on 29 September. In early October some 13,000 Syrian troops, reinforced by armoured units, marched into Lebanon to expel the LNM–PLO alliance from the occupied Christian areas. Since the LNM–PLO Joint Command decided to resist the attackers, fierce combat ensued. The Syrians, being more powerful, won.

With the supremacy of the radical LNM–PLO having been virtually destroyed by Syria, King Khalid ibn Abdul Aziz, the pro-Western monarch of Saudi Arabia and the most important external player after Assad, considered further bloodshed counterproductive. This suited Assad, who came under renewed domestic pressure to moderate his campaign against the LNM–PLO alliance. Moreover, since Assad did not wish to end up depending on either of the warring sides in Lebanon (which would have happened if he had decimated one of them), he thought it was best to mediate between two enfeebled Lebanese camps. He therefore responded positively to Saudi Arabia's call for an emergency meeting in Riyadh of the belligerent parties – Lebanon, Syria and the PLO – as well as Egypt and Kuwait, both pro-Western. Their leaders unanimously adopted a peace plan, calling for an immediate truce and the deployment of a peacekeeping force sponsored by the Arab League. This suited Syria because its units had by then gained the upper hand on the battleground.

The decision of the Riyadh conference was endorsed by the Arab summit in Cairo on 25–26 October 1976. It sanctioned the formation of the Arab Deterrent Force (ADF) for an initial period of six months. Its 30,000 troops were to be drawn from Syria (25,000), Saudi Arabia (2,000), Sudan (1,000), South Yemen (1,000), Libya (600) and the United Arab Emirates (500).

Financed by the oil-rich Gulf members of the Arab League, the ADF was to function under Lebanese president Sarkis to maintain law and order. It was authorized to disarm all militias of their heavy weapons, and to see that the various fighting forces reverted to the positions they had held before 13 April 1975. Relations between the Palestinians and the Lebanese authorities were to be regulated by the 1969 Cairo Agreement. The Arab League appointed a four-member committee of Syria, Saudi Arabia, Egypt and Kuwait to work in conjunction with the Lebanese president.

Since Syria provided the bulk of the peacekeeping troops in Lebanon, Assad was quite pleased with the outcome. And since the Palestinians had their 1969 Cairo Agreement reconfirmed, they went along with the latest peace plan. But this was precisely what upset the ultra-rightist elements within the Maronite Lebanese Front. The Front's later, formal acceptance of the Arab League plan was at best reluctant.

However, the Lebanese Front's stance failed to impede the deployment of the Arab Deterrent Force over most of the country, including Beirut, by mid-November 1976. This signalled the virtual end of the nineteen-month civil war, which had resulted in 10,000 deaths.[3]

Along with the human and material losses went the fracturing of the country, with Syria administering large sectors of northern and eastern Lebanon; the Maronites ensconced in a Christian enclave north of Beirut, with its capital in Jounieh; the Franjieh clan controlling its traditional area sandwiched between the Syrian troops and the Lebanese Front militias; and the radical Lebanese and their Palestinian allies setting up a proto-state south and south-east of Beirut, and competing with Saad Haddad, a former Lebanese army major now commanding a pro-Israeli militia, for the control of south Lebanon. Nonetheless the truce created an environment for national reconciliation.

Aftermath of the November 1976 ceasefire

Signs of national and regional *rapprochement* could be perceived in the public acceptance by Kamal Jumblatt of Sarkis as the republic's president and Colonel Ahmad Hajj as the Lebanese commander of the Arab Deterrent Force, and in the Syrian prime minister's publicly expressed backing for the Palestinian resistance.

Reflecting the mood of reconciliation in the country, Salim Hoss, appointed prime minister by President Sarkis on 9 December, selected an eight-member cabinet composed almost wholly of technocrats. The parliament crowned its vote of confidence in the new government with an authorization to it to rule by decree for six months with a further extension of five months. However, there was a dark cloud in an otherwise clear sky: the south, where a mini-civil war erupted as Camille Chamoun and a section of the Phalange Party, encouraged by Israel, tried to deter the return of the Palestinians to the region.

Syria remained involved in the Lebanese conflict. This was reflected *inter alia* in the composition of the Arab Deterrent Force in January 1977. Of the 30,000-plus ADF soldiers and officers, 27,000 were Syrian, the rest being from Sudan, Saudi Arabia, South Yemen and the United Arab Emirates, Libya having quickly withdrawn its small contingent.

Following his visit to Damascus in early February, President Sarkis joined President Assad in issuing a communiqué which confirmed the importance of co-ordination between the two countries in 'everything related to their interests', and instructed presidential assistants to 'formulate a joint working plan inspired by the need for co-ordination between the two countries'. Soon Sarkis replaced the heads of the army and military intelligence, known to be pro-Lebanese Front, with pro-Syrian nominees. In the process he earned the ire of Camille Chamoun, the leader of the Lebanese Front. Arguing that the ADF functioned in lieu of the (much battered) Lebanese army, Sarkis declared that it was entitled to take up positions throughout Lebanon, including the areas being administered by the Lebanese Front. This was hotly disputed by Chamoun, who regarded the ADF as another name for the Syrian troops which, he insisted, were not entitled to enter the territories controlled by the Lebanese Front, especially East Beirut.

Given that the reconstruction of the Lebanese army was slow – with only the 3,000-strong Beqaa Command revived and deployed in the Beqaa and north Lebanon – Sarkis requested the Arab League to extend the mandate of the ADF for six months, until November 1977. The ADF was also assigned the job of implementing the 1969 Cairo Agreement between the PLO and the Lebanese authorities.

The 1969 Agreement was anathema to the Maronite leaders. Following a conference at a Maronite monastry, the Lebanese Front issued a communiqué on 23 January 1977; it aimed to 'liberate all the occupied Lebanese territory and to try to distribute the Palestinians residing in Lebanon among the member-states of the Arab League'.

The efforts of the Phalangists and the National Liberals to build up jointly the infrastructure of a modern state in the Christian enclave continued. Besides commissioning an airport and a harbour they instituted postal services, a food distribution system, courts, police and armed forces. They determinedly kept the Arab Deterrent Force out of the region they controlled. In the political negotiations that followed the truce, they insisted on a 'decentralized unity' of Lebanon, which their opponents saw as another term for partition.

Among those whom the Maronite camp considered its adversaries, Kamal Jumblatt was foremost. But he was as much opposed to the Syrian hegemony over Lebanon as were the Maronite leaders. Indeed, he became a serious impediment to Assad's realization of his three-point plan to consolidate and perpetuate Syria's influence in Lebanon: (a) by legitimizing the presence of Syrian troops inside Lebanon by occupying its eastern and northern parts, (b) by assisting the pro-Damascus President Sarkis to extend the domain of his administration into the Maronite-controlled region, and (c) by spawning pro-Syrian political elements in Lebanon. As a Lebanese patriot intent on maintaining a multi-party political system in his country (in contrast to the authoritarian set-up in Syria), Jumblatt resented the arrival of Assad in Lebanon as the sole power-broker. Indeed, he went on to attack Assad's rule in Syria itself in the mistaken belief that such a step would bolster the morale of the anti-Assad forces then believed to be planning a coup against the Syrian president. All this turned Jumblatt into Assad's number one enemy.

On 16 March 1977 Kamal Jumblatt and his two bodyguards were on their way from his castle in Mukhtara to Baaqlin, the largest Druze village in the Shouf region, when their car was intercepted by two gunmen. They blew off the top of Jumblatt's head before escaping. The shocked and enraged Druze followers of Jumblatt went on a rampage, attacking their historic enemies – Maronite Christians – in the Shouf, and murdering 170 of them. This was all the more deplorable because very few doubted the hand of Damascus in Jumblatt's assassination. Whatever the truth behind Jumblatt's violent death, it severely weakened the Lebanese National Movement and all those wishing to challenge the Syrian hegemony in Lebanon.

Walid Jumblatt, 29-year-old son of Kamal, succeeded his father as the leader of the Progressive Socialist Party as well as the Lebanese National Movement. Suppressing his suspicion of Syrian involvement in the assassination of his father, Walid Jumblatt visited Damascus in

April and again in July 1977. The communiqué issued by the LNM after his second visit to the Syrian capital was moderate. Instead of repeating the LNM demand for an end to confessionalism, the latest document merely urged consolidation of Lebanon's Arabism and restoration of its political and administrative unity, including the reconstitution of its 'patriotic and balanced army'.

To thwart any Palestinian plans to challenge the hegemony of Damascus in Lebanon, the Syrian-dominated Arab Deterrent Force posted its units at strategic positions outside the Palestinian camps. This had the additional advantage of reassuring the Maronite politicians, who kept demanding the expulsion of the bulk of the Palestinian refugees from Lebanon. Encouraged by the Syrian move, the Phalange leader Pierre Gemayel was able to make palatable the idea of Syria's domination of Lebanon to Chamoun, who had by now concluded that Assad was quite capable of unleashing his overwhelming military might against the Lebanese Christians, who could no longer count on assistance from any Western power.

On top of this, Damascus had by now fostered its own political camp in Lebanon. It consisted of not only the pro-Syrian Baath Party but also the religious leaders of the Muslim sects, and Rashid Karami, the head of a coalition called the Islamic Alignment.

By now it had become commonplace for senior officials in Syria and Lebanon to visit each other's capital for consultation and co-ordination of policies. For instance, in April 1977 a Syrian military delegation arrived in Beirut to discuss reorganization of the Lebanese army. In the same month President Sarkis replaced Colonel Ahmad Hajj, the Lebanese commander of the Arab Deterrent Force, with Sami Khatib, a former Lebanese army officer in exile in Syria since 1973.

On the eve of the second anniversary of the civil war on 13 April 1977, the state-run Radio Damascus could confidently declare: 'Syria acts with those loyal to Lebanon, and will not hesitate to take measures in order to decide the situation [there] and ensure the progress of peace and security [in Lebanon].' However, there was a Lebanese territory which was out of bounds for Syria: the southern region of Lebanon contiguous with Israel.

South Lebanon

The strip along the Israeli–Lebanese border had for a long time been a stronghold of militant Palestinians intent on attacking targets within the Jewish state. Among the various steps taken by the Israeli authorities to solve this problem was a programme of erecting frontier security barriers, which was implemented in 1974.

Following the disintegration of the Lebanese army in January 1976, its Muslim segment, called the Lebanese Arab Army, took up the positions of its predecessor along the Israeli frontier, with the overthrown Christian officers setting up their militias in the three Christian areas along the border: the tiny western enclave centred around the sole Christian village of Almaa Shaab; the central enclave of Ain Ibil-Rumaish sector; and the eastern enclave of the Marji Ayun-Qulaya sector. To aid these areas financially and politically, the Israeli government introduced a 'good fence' policy, which allowed the Lebanese Christians to work inside Israel. By so doing the Israeli authorities expected to recruit collaborators among Lebanese workers to collect information about the activities of the Palestinian commandos in the area.

With the fall of Tal Zaatar camp in Beirut in August 1976, followed by the migration of many Palestinian commandos to the south – particularly to the central enclave of Bint Jubail-Aytarun, and the eastern enclave of Khiam-Tayiba – tension between the Palestinian and Christian enclaves along the international border escalated. Since the 'red line' agreement between Syria and Israel precluded the deployment of Syrian troops in the south, the Damascus regime actively aided the Palestinian guerrillas in the region. And the Israeli government eagerly backed the Christian militias now being commanded by Saad Haddad. By the time the ceasefire imposed by the Arab League took effect in Lebanon in November 1976, Haddad's force had been turned into an early warning system for Israel.

In late March 1977 the Christian militias tried to link up their eastern and central enclaves; and this led to armed clashes with the Palestinian commandos, who were opposed to the idea of a continuous pro-Israeli buffer zone along the international border. The early Christian advance in the battle gave way to setbacks as the Palestinians struck back vigorously and retook their lost positions. The fighting was so vicious that about a third of the 600,000 residents of the area fled.

Unwilling to see the Palestinian commandos prevail totally in the south, and resort to reckless operations against Israel, the Syrian president encouraged his Lebanese counterpart to mediate between the warring parties. The resulting ceasefire, which came into effect in mid-April – and which elicited repeated commitments from the PLO and the Beirut government to honour the 1969 Cairo Agreement – held for three months.

The installation of the right-wing Likud-led government, headed by Menachem Begin, in Israel in May 1977 stiffened the attitude of the Maronite camp. As it was, once the mortal threat to Maronites posed by the 17,000 fighters under the LNM–PLO Joint Command[4] had subsided, the Lebanese Front leaders had no further use for Syria's continued role in their country. Little wonder then that they turned increasingly to Israel, their principal arms supplier, in the knowledge that its newly installed, hawkish administration would support them actively.

Indeed, in mid-July Danny Chamoun, the NLP Tigers' commander, announced that his men had carried out joint operations with the Israelis against the Palestinian positions in the south. This campaign was still unresolved when, in late July, a Syrian representative chaired a meeting of the military leaders of Lebanon, Syria, the PLO and the Arab Deterrent Force in Shtura to implement the 1969 Cairo Agreement. It decided that the Palestinians must withdraw to 15 km from the Israeli–Lebanese frontier, and allow the Lebanese army to move into the border strip; that the Palestinian commandos must be confined to the eastern Arqub sector of the frontier; and that the overall task of defending the southern littoral was to be assigned to the ADF. As for the control of the Palestinian camps and disarming of the commandos, the meeting specified a three-phase programme. The first two phases concerned controlling the Palestinian camps and disarming the fighters of heavy weapons, to be accomplished by the end of August. The Lebanese army was then to take over the positions vacated by the Palestinian units.[5] The political significance of the Shtura conference was that for the first time Syria became party to an agreement between the PLO and the Beirut government, a position previously enjoyed by Nasser's Egypt.

As for Israel and the Maronite militias, the Shtura resolution was a severe setback since it freshly legitimized a Palestinian presence in Lebanon. There was almost daily exchange of small fire and mortars between the Maronite militiamen and the Palestinian guerrillas, who also periodically attacked Israeli targets. The Israeli Defence Forces wanted to remove the 5,000 Palestinian commandos and their infrastructure deployed in south Lebanon, an objective it could accomplish either by intervening directly or by assisting in creating a Christian buffer in the area. It was opposed to the deployment of the Lebanese army in the south as this would have ended its policy of cultivating local Christians by letting them into northern Israel through its 'good neighbour fences'. Pursuing its strategy of limiting Palestinian military activity by bolstering the Christian militias, Israel participated in the Christian–Palestinian fighting in the latter half of September 1977, and enabled the Christians to capture Khiam. The Palestinians retaliated by hitting Israel with rockets. As the violence escalated, America mediated. The result was a series of understandings reached between Israel, Lebanon, Syria, the Palestinians and Saad Haddad, and a truce on 25 September.

In early November, however, the ceasefire broke down. Israel raised the stakes by hitting the Palestinian targets from the air in response to Palestinian rocket attacks on Israeli targets, which in turn were retaliation for shelling by the Israeli Defence Forces. However, the attention of Israel and its neighbours was soon diverted by the Egyptian president Anwar Sadat's visit to Jerusalem on 19 November in search of Arab–Israeli peace.

The shock and revulsion caused among Arabs by Sadat's precipitate action brought all other Arab leaders together. Links between Syria and the PLO strengthened sharply, and in south Lebanon the Palestinian commandos started harassing Christian villages from the Beaufort Castle near Qulaya. Given the pro-Israeli proclivities of the Maronite camp, relations between Syria and the Lebanese Front turned frosty. By the end of 1977 the Front's constituents had built up their respective militias – collectively known as the Lebanese Forces – to the point where they had 12,000 men under arms, more than twice the strength of the depleted Lebanese army. In late December the Phalange newspaper *Le Réveille* (The Call) demanded the resignation of President Sarkis for having placed the Lebanese army 'under the Syrian occupation', and was consequently suspended for three days. The growing confidence of the Maronite camp came to the fore when the Christian enclave north of Beirut, popularly known as Marounistan (The Land of Maronites), mounted a series of anti-Syrian demonstrations and strikes. This resulted in armed skirmishes between the Lebanese Forces and the Syrian-dominated ADF.

In 1977 there was growing awareness in Damascus that the alliance it had forged with the Maronites in the spring of 1976 was untenable politically, militarily and ideologically. Maronite leaders and their militias would never accept the Syrian hegemony over Lebanon that President Assad had in mind. Therefore he devised a two-prong strategy of reinforcing the pro-Damascus elements in Lebanon and weakening the power bases of the anti-Damascus forces both overtly and covertly.

In early 1978, faced with the prospect of failing to get the Arab League renewal of the mandate for the ADF, 90 per cent of whose 30,000 troops were Syrian,[6] Assad pressured President Sarkis to sign a defence treaty. Sarkis dithered while the Lebanese army units based at Beirut's Fayadiya garrison under the command of Colonel Antoine Barakat, close to Camille Chamoun, attacked ADF troops in early February 1978. Determined to teach its new adversary a humiliating lesson, the ADF called its units from Beqaa and shelled not only the Fayadiya garrison but also the (Chamounist) National Liberal Party headquarters and the Christian district of Ashrafiya in East Beirut. In the face of such pressure, the Lebanese army and its Maronite allies quickly accepted the offer of a ceasefire, which went into effect on 11 February. Assad pressured President Sarkis to retire Colonel Barakat and try the Lebanese army officer responsible for attacking the ADF before a joint Lebanese–Syrian military court.

By all accounts, therefore, Syria seemed to be consolidating its dominant position in Lebanon, much to the chagrin of the Maronite leaders and their foreign backer, Israel.

Damascus now tried to extend its influence to the Lebanese–Israeli border, albeit indirectly. For the first time the commandos of the pro-Syrian Saiqa Organization, a Palestinian party, became active in south Lebanon. They joined other Palestinian groups in their campaign on 3 March to capture Marun Raas in the central Christian enclave, and expel the Christian militiamen from there. They succeeded. This upset Israel, which saw this loss as the beginning of a process leading to the disappearance of the central Christian enclave of Bint Jubail-Rumaish, something it was determined to thwart.

Eight days later a party of (Damour-based) Palestinians reached northern Israel clandestinely by boat, and attacked a bus along the Haifa–Tel Aviv road, killing thirty-five passengers. Given the severity of the Palestinian action taken on a highway in central Israel, the Israeli government decided to solve, or at least alleviate, the south Lebanese problem by eliminating the presence of about 5,000 Palestinian guerrillas and their infrastructure in the area. This set the scene for an Israeli invasion of Lebanon.

3

The first Israeli invasion and aftermath

March — October 1978

On 14 March 1978 Israel invaded Lebanon. The campaign, code-named Operation Litani, was mounted with the aim of creating a 10 km-wide buffer zone along the 100 km-long border. The Israeli Defence Forces poured in 20,000 to 25,000 troops, and used US-made F-1 fighter planes and cluster bombs. Finding the Palestinians on the run, the IDF went beyond its original objective of acquiring a narrow border strip. It decided to seize much of south Lebanon – that is, the area below the Litani river, containing one-fifth of the national territory and a quarter of the Lebanese population – except the coastal city of Tyre (Sur). The retreating Palestinians had to be content with firing occasional rockets at targets in northern Israel. By 19 March the IDF had achieved its objective: it had occupied half of south Lebanon, or 10 per cent of the total Lebanese territory. It destroyed eighty-two villages and caused the deaths of 1,000 people and the displacement of 160,000, before agreeing to the United Nations Security Council's ceasefire call on 20 March.[1]

The Israeli action received strong condemnation in the Arab world, and cast a shadow over the Egyptian–Israeli peace talks then at a delicate stage. Washington was unhappy at the turn of events. When, at the Security Council, Lebanon prepared to introduce a resolution for an immediate Israeli withdrawal, the USA decided to take the diplomatic initiative. Out of this arose Security Council Resolution 425, which was passed on 19 March. Calling on Israel to cease fire and withdraw 'forthwith', it authorized the formation of the United Nations Interim Force in Lebanon (Unifil) to confirm the Israeli evacuation and assist the Lebanese government to assume effective control in the area. On 21 March Israel announced a ceasefire. Within two days the UN troops from France, Iran, Norway and Sweden began arriving to work under the command of General Emmanuel Erskine, a Ghanaian.

Damascus viewed Operation Litani as a device designed to entice it into a war with Israel at the latter's choosing. Determined not to fall into the Israeli trap, Syria said that it would choose its time and place for an armed conflict with the Jewish state. But that did not inhibit it from providing anti-aircraft fire cover to the Palestinians, and offering safe passage through its land and airspace to those who wished to join the Palestinian fighters. Among those who picked up the offer of safe passage were 600 'volunteers' from Iraq. This happened at a time when relations between Syria and Iraq had turned cordial, with their presidents engaged in talks to unify the two neighbouring countries.

After the truce Damascus actively co-operated with Unifil in order to facilitate Israeli evacuation. It was the same with the PLO, which felt that co-operation with the UN in general and Unifil in particular would add to its international standing. It was equally aware that its non-co-operation with the UN would provide the IDF with a rationale to extend their stay in south Lebanon.

During their occupation the Israelis built roads in south Lebanon for quick access the next time they decided to attack. They also accelerated their programme of making the local inhabitants economically dependent on Israel. They succeeded in making a majority of the labour force of Marji Ayun, a major Christian settlement in the eastern sector, work in Israel. The size of the Israeli-backed militia, consisting of the members of the Phalange, NLP and Guardians of the Cedars, rose by another 450; and its commander, Saad Haddad, named his force the South Lebanon Army (SLA).

On 11 April the IDF evacuated the easternmost sector and let in Unifil. Three days later they withdrew from an area adjoining the Litani river in the central sector.

Outside the southern region, the Maronites, having lost their fear of decimation, came to view Syria's pro-Muslim tilt with rising disdain, and began challenging the Syrian-dominated Arab Deterrent Force. As a result, between 9 and 14 April, there were exchanges of fire between the Christian district of Ain Rummane and the Muslim district of Shiyya across the Green Line in Beirut. The ADF intervened by shelling Ain Rummane heavily, and justified its artillery salvos as necessary to reimpose a truce. Christian leaders were unconvinced, and protested vehemently to President Sarkis. To pacify them he consented to replacing the Syrian units of the ADF with the Saudi and Sudanese contingents along the Green Line in Beirut.

On 23 April, a thirteen-member parliamentary commitee recom-mended to the full house a six-point national reconciliation plan, which included implementation of UN Security Council Resolution 425 requiring complete Israeli evacuation of South Lebanon, the halting of all Palestinian and non-Palestinian armed actions, and the reconstitution of the Lebanese army on a 'sound and correct national basis'. Four days later parliament (whose membership had been raised from seventy-seven to ninety-nine in 1960) adopted the recommendations by seventy-five votes to none, with twenty mem-bers, including Rashid Karami and Tony Franjieh, son of Suleiman Franjieh and head of the Zghartan Liberation Army, abstaining, well aware that the peace plan did not include any mechanism for its implementation.

Having concluded that his administration would gain legitimacy at home only if it showed some degree of independence from Syria, President Sarkis started to drift away from Damascus. He followed up his rejection of Syria's proposal of a defence pact with support for the Maronite Lebanese Front on the Palestinian issue. Israel's invasion of south Lebanon, and the subsequent posting of Unifil there, had made the 1969 Cairo Agreement redundant, the Lebanese Front reasoned, adding that a new accord needed to be concluded between the PLO and the Lebanese government. This was the argument Sarkis presented during his talks with Assad in Latakia, Syria, on 31 May–1 June 1978. It was rejected by the Syrian president who, agreeing with the PLO, wanted the Cairo Agreement to stand. He demanded the removal of some right-wing Christian military officers, and advised Sarkis to prepare the Litani Brigade to take over from the departing Israelis in the south.

However, when the IDF carried out its major withdrawal on 13 June – evacuating a border zone 4–12 km wide and 80 km long, from the Mediterranean to Kafr Shuba, with a population of 40,000 Christians (mostly Maronite) and 60,000 Muslims (mostly Shia) – it handed over its positions to Haddad's Christian militia. By then it had massively re-equipped and resupplied this force of 2,000 to 3,000 men with tanks and heavy guns, and decided to arm, train and finance it. The IDF did not allow the Syrian-dominated ADF to cross the Litani, nor did it permit the Beirut government to deploy its 1,500-strong Litani Brigade alongside Unifil in the south. Some weeks later Haddad declared the area 'independent', and refused to let the regular Lebanese army into the territory. Thus, Israel achieved its objective of securing the border, albeit through a proxy.

Overall, Operation Litani was an Israeli success. It eliminated the Palestinian presence and infrastructure from the immediate border region. It legitimized and strengthened Israel's relations with the Christians in south Lebanon. It enabled the Jewish state to pursue its interests through its Lebanese proxies, who were to be increasingly seen by Unifil as obstructionist agents of Israel. The only disadvantage to the IDF, stemming from its invasion, was that the Unifil presence compelled it now either to launch air strikes at its Palestinian targets or to use the extreme eastern flank to reach them overland. On the other hand, the presence of 4,000 Unifil troops became an additional obstacle to the Palestinians wishing to reach Israeli targets.

Following the IDF occupation of south Lebanon, ties between Israel and Maronites became stronger and less inhibited. There was a long history of Maronite sympathy for Israel and the Zionist movement. 'Since 1948 . . . the hardcore Maronites identified with Israel as an enclave society that, like itself, was surrounded by the Muslim world', notes Sandra Mackey, an American specialist on Lebanon.

> While the [Lebanese] Christians' Arab side expressed sympathy for the Palestinians, their Western side demanded that Israel be considered among the Christians' scant instruments of survival. Throughout the Arab–Israeli Wars of 1948, 1956 and 1967, the Christians refused to fight Israel over the Palestinians. Yet they sought to awaken the West to the Palestinians' plight.[2]

The growing Maronite–Israeli alliance reached a high point in May 1978, when Pierre Gemayel and Camille Chamoun visited Israel secretly, and reportedly signed arms deals there. The presence of Israeli military advisers in the Christian mini-state increased to the extent that there were 1,500 such personnel in East Beirut alone.[3] Funds for weapons came from the contributions made by the Lebanese Christian diaspora, particularly in North America, and the revenue collected by the Lebanese Forces (LF) at home. Estimates of the yearly LF income from taxes on petrol, restaurant and nightclub bills, illicit gambling casinos and real estate transactions, and customs duties, ranged from $100 million to $300 million. Bashir Gemayel, the young chairman of the LF Command Council, became increasingly ambitious and intolerant of rivals within the Maronite community. An attack by Phalangist gunmen on Raymond Edde, the leader of moderate Maronites, left him wounded and drove him into exile in Paris. Bashir Gemayel's next victim was to be Tony Franjieh.

The growing militancy of the Lebanese Front, as manifested in the events of Fayadiya garrison in February and of Ain Rummane two months later – coupled with its increasingly public ties with Israel – alienated Suleiman Franjieh, who had never shared the anti-Palestinian bias of Pierre Gemayel and Camille Chamoun. In parliament his son, Tony, was a member of the group of independent Maronite deputies formed in February 1978 to show that the Lebanese Front did not represent all Maronite Catholics, much less all Christians. He abstained on the crucial national reconciliation resolution put to the vote in late April. So did Rashid Karami, a traditional Muslim rival of the Franjiehs in north Lebanon. This paved the way for reconciliation of Rashid Karami with Suleiman Franjieh (who had by now stopped attending the Lebanese Front meetings), a goal which had been high on the agenda of Assad.

With Bashir Gemayel determined to monopolize power in the Maronite community, the struggle between the Phalangists and the Franjieh clan for unrivalled influence in the Christian part of north Lebanon intensified. The Franjieh clan resisted the intrusion of Phalangists in its traditional fiefdom, with the Franjiehs' Marada (i.e. Giants) Brigade assassinating hostile Phalangist figures. In early June Joud Bayeh, a Phalange leader in the area, was murdered. 'No one can prevent the Phalangist expansion in the north', Bashir Gemayel declared on 7 June. 'It is time to put an end to feudalism there.' Later, following the massacre of the Franjieh family at the summer palace of Suleiman Franjieh at Ihden, 20 km from Zghorta, Bashir Gemayel was to claim that it was in search of the murderers of Joud Bayeh, thought to be in the Ihden palace, that some Phalangists, led by 26-year-old Samir Geagea, had headed for the place. In fact, the attack on the Ihden palace was carried out by about a hundred Phalangists on 13 June 1978 at 4 a.m. Within fifteen minutes they murdered thirty-four people, including Tony Franjieh, aged 36, his wife, Vera, aged 32, and their 30-month-old daughter. The chief reason for Tony Franjieh's assassination was that Bashir Gemayel considered him a serious rival for the presidency of Lebanon. The Ihden massacre turned Suleiman Franjieh vehemently against the Lebanese Front and the Gemayels. His clan retaliated by murdering thirty Phalangists in the Baalbek area towards the end of June. The violent confrontation between the Franjieh clan and the Lebanese Front underscored Assad's argument that the Front's vociferous propaganda of a Muslim war of extermination against Christians was a lie.

In the meantime, on 21 June, declaring that seeking the assistance of the ADF was 'not always possible or ideal', President Sarkis announced a security plan, devised by his defence and foreign minister, Fuad Boutros. It divided the country into three zones – with one allocated exclusively to the Lebanese army, another jointly to the Lebanese army and the ADF, and the remaining to Lebanon's internal security forces and the ADF. After implementing the plan in the Metn area in late June, President Sarkis extended it to Beirut in early July.

This went down badly with President Assad, who had not been consulted by his Lebanese counterpart. He strongly disapproved of the exclusion of the 30,000-man ADF from a certain region of Lebanon, and its being relegated to an auxiliary position to the Lebanese army (which was only about 7,500 strong then) and internal security forces elsewhere. He found an ally in Prime Minister Hoss, who disagreed with Sarkis and Boutros on the deployment of certain army units in Beirut and the south.

Meanwhile, in late June, the LF fired on the Syrian-dominated ADF units to provoke them. Assad retaliated by ordering heavy shelling of East Beirut. It went on for five days and elicited a response from the Israeli prime minister, Begin. He declared that it was the 'duty' of his country to 'defend the rights of Lebanese and save them from a holocaust'. But his threat changed little. Syria's bloody action undermined the position of Sarkis in the Christian community, which blamed him for the unusually vicious shelling. He offered his resignation on 5 July, and then directed to Damascus his conditions for withdrawing the resignation: real authority over the ADF; disarming of all non-official armed forces; implementing the agreement with the Palestinians; and a free hand to secure national reconciliation. Assad was indifferent to the Lebanese leader's resignation since Sarkis had lost his usefulness to Damascus. 'The ADF has the right to defend the system of [Lebanese] security in any way that Syria sees fit in order to strengthen [its] legitimacy in Lebanon', declared Assad on 18 July.[4] Confident of the support of Prime Minister Hoss, who was close to him, Assad despatched one of his confidants to Suleiman Franjieh to sound him out on taking over the presidency from Sarkis.

This alarmed the Lebanese Front leaders. They reacted in two complementary ways. Pierre Gemayel and Camille Chamoun undertook a two-day trip to Israel, an event made public by a Beirut newspaper on 11 July. Their purpose was to finalize plans for an 'independent' Christian administration in south Lebanon should Sarkis's resignation become effective. Concurrently, apprehensive that Assad would replace Sarkis with Franjieh as president, they pressured Sarkis to withdraw his resignation. So too did Riyadh and Washington. Yielding to these pressures, Sarkis retracted his step.

In late July–early August, Assad prevailed upon Sarkis to send a 700-strong battalion of the Lebanese army under Lt-Colonel Adib Saad from Beqaa to the southern town of Tibnin, controlled by Unifil, which supported the idea. But instead of approaching Tibnin over the bridge in the central zone south of the Litani, Saad's troops approached it via the eastern town of Marji Ayun, a stronghold of Haddad. When they arrived at the nearby village of Kawkaba, they were attacked by the militia of Haddad, who alleged that they were members of a pro-Syrian Lebanese unit trained in eastern Lebanon. When, having beaten off the attack, the army unit failed to counter-attack Haddad's militia, it came under fire from the neighbouring Palestinians; and it disintegrated in mid-August.

The lesson of this episode was clear. The hegemony of Syria applied only to the area north of the Litani. In the Lebanese territory south of the Litani, Israel was the dominant foreign power, exercising its authority through its proxy, the Haddad-led militia.

However, the failure of the pro-Damascus side to reclaim the south had no adverse impact on Assad's continuing efforts to consolidate his control of Lebanon beyond the borders of the Christian mini-state. He pursued a twin-track policy of (a) bolstering those Lebanese who backed his policies in Lebanon and (b) undermining those who opposed them. In parliament he had secured the support of three groups: the Maronite MPs led by Tony Franjieh; the National Parliamentary Bloc of Shia deputies (formed on 23 March 1978 in the face of the Israeli occupation of south Lebanon) headed by Speaker Kamil Assad; and the Islamic Alignment of Sunni MPs led by Rashid Karami. Outside parliament, the Syrians aided Suleiman Franjieh to inflict his revenge on the Phalangists for murdering his son along with his family. Within two months of the atrocity in Ihden, the total number of reprisal murders of Phalangists and their families reached 342.[5] During his three-day visit to Damascus in mid-August, Suleiman Franjieh conferred with Assad at length.

This set the scene for a meeting between Suleiman Franjieh, Rashid Karami and Walid Jumblatt. It took place on 31 August 1978 at Franjieh's summer palace in Ihden. The three leaders issued a statement backing Syria's policy in Lebanon as well as the presence and activities of the ADF in their country.[6]

The Syrian-dominated ADF had become active since early August, when it started to sweep the country in stages with a view mainly to curbing the power of the Maronite militias. The latter, commanding the loyalties of 12,000 to 15,000 fighters, were now aggregately larger than the 9,000-strong Lebanese army commanded by a predominantly Christian officer corps. The Maronite military muscle appeared all the more threatening to Assad, who worried over the increasingly close ties between the Maronite leadership and Israel, the latest manifestation of which was Bashir Gemayel's first clandestine visit to Israel on 30 July 1978, after having earlier been briefed by Mossad, the Israeli intelligence agency, aboard a gunboat off Cyprus.[7] Assad considered any Israeli role or presence in Lebanon as a mortal threat to Syria's security, and was ready to do anything to eliminate it. 'Lebanon is our security belt', explained a Syrian official later. 'The whole picture will change if the Christians make a complete link with the enemies of the Arab nation. On this there can never be any bargaining.'[8]

The Syrian-dominated ADF encircled the LF units in the Christian enclave from the north, tightening its grip over Batroun from the east as well as from the Beqaa valley, northern Lebanon and the mountain range overlooking the Kisrwan and Byblos districts. By September 1978 the ADF had cleared a third of the Maronite heartland of the LF militiamen.

However, in late September, when the ADF tried to establish control over Ashrafiya, a strategic Beirut suburb which links East Beirut with the Christian hinterland to the north, the LF units put up stiff resistance. The ADF shelled East Beirut and other Christian strongholds intensely, causing heavy casualties and extensive damage, and in the process suffering substantial losses itself. About 800 people were killed and 3,000 wounded. Hundreds of apartments were destroyed, making some 200,000 people homeless, with the bulk of them fleeing to the mountainous hinterland.[9] Syria imposed land and naval blockades, but this did not deter Israel. It managed to breach the sea blockade and deliver 300 tons of food, arms and ammunition twice a week to the Christian-controlled port of Jounieh.[10]

At Washington's initiative, the UN Security Council met on 6–7 October. It called for a ceasefire and urged 'all Lebanese groups' to try to 'reach a national reconciliation based on the unity of Lebanon and her territories, independence and national security'. The US president, James Carter, aired the idea of an international conference on south Lebanon, which fell on deaf ears. However, following a trip to Damascus by President Sarkis to meet President Assad, there was a ceasefire which endured longer than most.

Sarkis then flew to other Arab capitals, including Riyadh, in pursuance of his plan to limit Syrian power in Lebanon. But he failed. At the end of a three-day conference at the Lebanese town of Beit al Din, the foreign ministers of the Arab states providing troops and/or cash for the ADF – Syria, Saudi Arabia, Sudan, United Arab Emirates, Kuwait and Qatar – adopted resolutions on 17 October 1978 which were basically in line with the stance of Damascus. The conference condemned 'illegal military manifestations and radio stations' – an allusion to the Lebanese Front's activities – and demanded an end to them. A three-member committee of Syria, Saudi Arabia and Kuwait was set up under the chairmanship of President Sarkis 'to undertake whatever tasks the [Lebanese] president assigns to it within the framework of the principles mentioned above'.

The government of Prime Minister Hoss endorsed the Beit al Din resolutions and formed a cabinet committee to supervise their implementation. On 26 October 1978 – two years after the ADF's formation – its mandate was extended for another six months.

In sum, within six months of the Israeli evacuation of south Lebanon, the Syrian hegemony in Lebanon was once again in place, a situation which progressively encouraged the Maronites to consolidate their mini-state.

4

Consolidation of the Christian mini-state

November 1978 — May 1982

It was generally agreed that the Syrian armed services had by now emerged as a crucial element in the complex Lebanese equation. As members of a conventional military organization, equal in size to the Lebanese army and the Maronite militias combined, the Syrian troops in Lebanon were a formidable force. They were capable of altering the balance of power in the country, and had actually done so. No matter what their detractors said, on the whole they had emerged as a stabilizing factor. And this came to be recognized by all concerned parties, either publicly or privately.

Aware that none of the Lebanese factions dared to see a total Syrian military pull-back from Lebanon – a scenario pregnant with renewed civil war, which none of them wished to see rekindled – Assad took to using the threat of withdrawing his troops as a lever to make Sarkis or other Lebanese leaders follow his counsel. He did so for the first time in mid-December 1978 in the case of Fuad Boutros, minister of defence and foreign affairs. He succeeded in getting Boutros divested of the defence ministry. The commander of the army, General Victor Khuri, was promoted to defence minister. These changes occurred against the background of two parliamentary committees debating a defence law.

The Lebanese army, now about 18,000 strong, was divided on religious lines. Its Christian segment, commanded by pro-Lebanese Front officers, was deployed around Mount Lebanon; and its Muslim segment, commanded by pro-Syrian officers, was centred around Ablah in Beqaa. A similar divide had arisen within the regime, with President Sarkis now leaning towards the Lebanese Front, and Prime Minister Hoss towards Syria. While sharing Assad's displeasure with Sarkis for his pro-Lebanese Front tilt, Hoss attempted to reconcile the two presidents. He travelled to Damascus in January 1979 for this purpose, but failed to make much headway.

The two parliamentary committees debating a defence bill reached agreement in mid-March 1979. The new law, adopted unanimously on 20 March, shifted the joint control of the military from the hands of the president and the military commander, both Maronite, to the president and the cabinet. It established a Military Council, headed by the defence minister and consisting of senior Maronite, Greek Orthodox, Greek Catholic, Sunni, Shia and Druze leaders, to deal with the military aspect of the defence policy. This policy was to be formulated by the cabinet and implemented by the newly appointed Higher Defence Council, composed of president, premier and defence, foreign, interior and finance ministers. It stipulated conscription from 1 July 1979 – a measure which, thanks to the predominance of Maronites in the high command, was to be postponed.

One of the military decisions of the cabinet in mid-April was to despatch 500 troops and officers, mostly Muslim, to the south via the coastal road and Sidon. The battalion was posted near Tibnin in the central sector of Unifil, headquartered at the port of Naqura. Soon the Lebanese battalion came under two-prong attack by the militia led by Haddad, who announced the establishment of the Free State of Lebanon in the border strip, 4–12 km wide and 80 km long, with a mixed Muslim–Christian population of 100,000. While the Lebanese Front expressed 'an understanding' of Haddad's actions, the Beirut government and Muslim factions condemned them.

The Muslim camp felt reassured when the Arab League extended the mandate of the Arab Deterrent Force by three months, from 27 April to 27 July 1979. With the departure of the Sudanese troops (in February), followed by the Saudis (in March, due to tension along the Saudi–North Yemeni border) and the United Arab Emirates (in mid-April), the ADF became a purely Syrian force. After conferring with Syrian officials in Damascus in April, the Lebanese and Palestinian leaders agreed to form a Syrian–Palestinian–Lebanese National Movement committee to co-ordinate their military and political moves.

In contrast, the distance between Syria and the Maronite Lebanese Front grew, primarily because the Front's co-operation with Israel increased, and secondarily because its commitment to maintaining Lebanon as a single, unified state was at best doubtful. As for the Maronite leaders free of contacts with Israel, Assad was willing to have normal relations with them. President Sarkis was one such. So Assad let Prime Minister Hoss continue his mediation efforts.

62

Following his visit to Damascus in April, the two presidents met in the Syrian capital on 14–15 May 1979. No joint communiqué ensued. But it was learnt reliably that Assad agreed with Sarkis that concluding a defence treaty between their countries would have to wait until after a government of politicians was formed to replace the present cabinet of technocrats, and that the function of the (Syrian-manned) ADF as a security force should be progressively taken up by the Lebanese army. In return, Sarkis promised to co-ordinate his major policies with Damascus.

The next day Hoss resigned in order to facilitate the formation of a government of politicians representing a broad parliamentary coalition. While the Lebanese National Movement wanted to exclude those who maintained ties with Israel, Chamoun wanted the new cabinet to be capable of coping with 'the foreign military presence in Lebanon'. The LNM demanded that the Lebanese Front should be disarmed according to the Beit al Din resolutions of October 1978, whereas the Lebanese Front stressed that the issue of the Palestinian presence be tackled first, and that the task of maintaining public order should be transferred immediately from the ADF to the Lebanese army. Little wonder that it took Hoss two months to assemble a political government. Yet the twelve-member cabinet formed on 16 July had only three politicians of high standing: Hoss, Charles Helou (a former Maronite president) and Fuad Boutros (a Greek Orthodox leader). Of the remaining ministers, seven were parliamentary deputies. The new government satisfied the LNM which, in the wake of the March 1979 Egyptian–Israel peace treaty, adopted a policy in July of forming 'a wide political axis that will confront those who co-operate with Israel and will act towards uniting the national ranks' and co-operate with 'other [anti-Zionist] forces' – namely, Suleiman Faranjieh, Saeb Salam and Rashid Karami.

In early August the cabinet, noting that the Beit al Din resolutions had won parliamentary approval earlier, proclaimed its intention to restore security and sovereignty in south Lebanon, and formally adopted the policy of 'maintaining the close brotherly ties which characterize our relations with fraternal Syria on the basis of mutual respect and common interest'.[1] This was the gist of the programme it presented to the chamber of deputies. On 8 August the chamber approved the government by fifty-four votes to nine, with thirty-two abstentions. It also extended its own term by two more years.

This happened against the background of change in the Maronite camp's military composition. When faced with renewed Syrian shelling of East Beirut in February 1979, the leaders of the factions forming the Lebanese Front decided to merge their respective militias. But this did not stop the Phalange and the NLP competing for recruits in East Beirut – an ongoing rivalry which provided a fertile ground for the Syrian intelligence agents within these parties to cultivate open conflict between them. In mid-May there were bloody clashes between the Phalange and the NLP. Pierre Gemayel and Camille Chamoun acted swiftly to control the situation. Then, to abort any future recurrence, they decided to unify their party hierarchies – a tricky decision to implement in view of the inflated egos and ambitions of the first-line leaders of the two parties. Unsurprisingly, in mid–June another round of fierce fighting between their ranks erupted. When the efforts of Gemayel and Chamoun failed to bring about a ceasefire, they appealed to Sarkis to send Lebanese army troops to East Beirut. He did. About 1,000 soldiers entered East Beirut on 18 June, and pacified the area.[2]

None of this made much difference to Bashir Gemayel's overall plan to monopolize power on the Christian side. Having cleared the Christian enclave of the Palestinians and Shias, he tried to establish control over the Armenian Orthodox districts of Burj Hamoud and Naaba in north-east Beirut. Claiming to eradicate illegal gambling dens there, the Phalangist militia attacked these districts in September 1979 because the (Armenian) Tashnak Party, despite its right-wing politics and closeness to the Phalange, had insisted on maintaining 'positive neutrality' in the civil war. The Armenian militia succeeded in repulsing the Phalangist attack; and this battle led to forty deaths.[3]

During the summer the problem of south Lebanon intensified. This had to do with the new strategy adopted by General Raphael Eitan, appointed the IDF chief of staff in April 1978. Discarding the traditional pattern of responding to the Palestinian attacks, he initiated a continuous campaign against the Palestinian targets on the ground, in the air and from the sea. By so doing he intended to put the Palestinians totally on the defensive, and rob them of any opportunity to mount armed attacks on Israel. His campaign consisted largely of aerial raids on the bases of the Palestinians who, in the wake of the Israeli invasion of Lebanon, had concentrated on rebuilding their military strength north of the Litani.

So now the Lebanese territory up to Sidon came under repeated Israeli air attacks, causing much Palestinian exodus from the south. This alarmed Syria. Disregarding one of its 'red line' agreements with Israel, it began sending its warplanes into the Lebanese area being bombarded by Israel. On 27 June 1979 there was an encounter between attacking Israeli planes and Syrian interceptors which flew in combat formation. This forced the IDF to scale down its air campaign sharply. But not for long. It escalated its air activity gradually until Syria again tried to intercept Israeli warplanes in September. Following this incident, the IDF curtailed its air campaign in south Lebanon drastically. But it was not until mid-November that the Israeli bombing virtually ceased. By then it had resulted in the deaths of 1,000 people and the displacement of 260,000, and had caused damage worth L£1,400 million, or $408 million.[4]

Faced with a deepening south Lebanese crisis, President Sarkis tried to convene a mini-Arab summit in mid-September to address the problem. His attempt failed. In early October the US president, James Carter, endorsed the idea of an international conference on south Lebanon to consider *inter alia* disbanding the Haddad militia and moving the Palestinians to the territory between the Litani and Zahrani rivers. France expressed its support; but nothing came of it. Attention then turned to the forthcoming Arab summit in Tunis from 20 to 22 November 1979. It adopted a seven-point resolution on south Lebanon. Noting that the Palestinians had abstained from staging military operations through south Lebanon, the resolution called for applying 'pressures' on 'the Israeli enemy to have it cease attacks on south Lebanon and withdraw from there'. The resolution asserted 'the right of the armed Palestinian presence in the area [to be] included in the international forces' sphere of operations, the right being based on the Lebanese government's agreement with the PLO [in 1969]'. It also backed the Lebanese administration's efforts to deploy its army in the south. Equally importantly, the summit decided to give Lebanon a grant of $2,000 million over a five-year period, with $400 million to be paid in 1980. Though generous in absolute terms, the aid did not even match the total estimated war damages of $2,500 million during the first two years of the conflict, with the private sector accounting for 82.5 per cent of the total.[5]

President Sarkis expressed satisfaction with the Arab summit resolution. But the Lebanese Front stated that it was not bound by it, and vowed to 'continue the war of liberation against any alien occupier of the homeland territory by various means'. The Lebanese cabinet took a middle position, expressing reservations about the resolution sanctioning an armed Palestinian presence in the Unifil area of operations in the south. As for deploying its army in the south, it made several attempts in December and January, but these failed, partly because Damascus did not back the action fully.

In late December the ruling Baath Party congress in Damascus resolved that the Syrian troops in Lebanon should be posted more evenly between the Christian and Muslim areas. On the eve of the Arab League's extension of the ADF mandate on 23 January 1980 for another six months, Syria evacuated the Muslim coastal area from Khalde southwards to the Zahrani river – moving half of the troops to western Beqaa and the other half to Syria – ceding their positions to the Lebanese Arab Army and the Damascus-controlled PLA units. However, when in early February the Syrians announced the next stage of their withdrawal plan – from Beirut – all parties, including the Lebanese government and the Maronite Lebanese Front, urged them to maintain their forces in the capital in order to forestall a revival of the civil war.

As a foretaste of the bloodbath to come, fighting broke out in mid-February between the Phalangist militia and the Marda fighters (of Suleiman Franjieh) in the north, and between the Palestinian guerrillas and Amal. The latter, following the 'disappearance' of Imam Musa Sadr in August 1978 during his visit to Libya, had come under the leadership of Shaikh Muhammad Mahdi Shams al Din and Hussein Husseini, who had forged strong links with Iran after a successful Islamic revolution there in February 1979.

Undeterred by these clashes, between 5 and 7 March 1980 Syria thinned out its troops in the north, Beirut and the adjoining mountain areas, and handed over its positions to the pro-Damascus Lebanese and Palestinian forces. The latest reduction brought the Syrian military strength down from 30,000 to 22,000, about equal to the Lebanese army's. However, at 500 personnel, the Lebanese air force was tiny ; and so was its 250-strong navy. Of the nearly 23,000 armed personnel (excluding the 5,000 men who belonged to the Lebanese internal security force), only 6,000 soldiers were professional and apolitical, the remaining being politically biased. They were equipped mainly with weapons supplied by Washington following the exchange of visits by the American and military delegations after the Israeli invasion, and paid for by US credits. On the other hand, Lebanon's annual military budget of $300 million (L£1,000 million) compared favourably with $160 million a year that the Arab League spent on maintaining its Arab Deterrent Force.[6]

On the political side, President Sarkis made a move on 5 March 1980 that was meant to be the first step towards national reconciliation. He announced fourteen principles that underlay the Lebanese entity. Drawn up to represent the minimum acceptable to both warring sides, these included: strengthening state authority, and especially the army, which should be non-sectarian; continuation of Lebanon's parliamentary system and market economy; friendly ties with other Arab countries, with special relations between Lebanon and Syria taking into account 'historical bonds, mutual interests, common struggle and kinship between the two peoples'; supporting the Palestinian cause and implementing the existing agreements with the PLO, while opposing any scheme which might result in the permanent settlement of Palestinians in Lebanon; and rejecting all forms of collaboration and co-operation with the Israeli enemy, and reversing the Israeli occupation of south Lebanon. The Sarkis principles were endorsed by the cabinet.

Neither the Sarkis statement nor its endorsement made much impact on Lebanon's politics. The differences between the Lebanese Front and the Lebanese National Movement remained as acute as before. The Front insisted on resolving the Palestinian and Syrian problems first, aware that this would weaken the Muslims' position. In contrast, the LNM wanted immediate moves to reform the system while its Syrian and Palestinian allies were still able to lend it support. Similar divisions existed within the administration, with Sarkis viewing national reconciliation as a prelude to reducing Syria's influence in Lebanon, and Hoss regarding it as a prelude to the implementation of a security plan in co-operation with the Syrian ADF and the institutionalization of Lebanon's special relationship with Syria. However, both leaders were in favour of securing national reconciliation, and so too was Assad.

The Syrian leader was relentlessly pursuing his long-term policy of weakening his opponents, and fomenting internecine violence among Maronites was at the centre of it. Minor skirmishes between the Phalangists and the National Liberal Party in November 1979 proved to be a prelude to more serious clashes two months later. A repetition of serious fighting in April and May 1980 in Kisrwan and Byblos districts led to ten deaths and public recriminations, with the Phalangists accusing the NLP leader Camille Chamoun of contacts with the PLO, and the latter accusing his rivals of cosying up to Syria. To resolve the conflict, Pierre Gemayel and Camille Chamoun agreed to discuss the merger of their parties. But nothing came of it. With a heavily armed force of 6,000 to 8,000 militiamen under their command, the Phalange leaders were unwilling to compromise.

In the event, the contest was settled through brute force. On 3–4 July and again on 7 July, under the active command of Bashir Gemayel, the Phalangist militiamen attacked the NLP Tigers in east and south-east Beirut, north of the capital, and in Kisrwan. The conflict centred on who was to control the illegal ports between Beirut and Jounieh, trading *inter alia* in hashish, and who collected the local levies on petrol, restaurant meals, gambling casinos, etc. The fighting on 7 July, which resulted in 150 deaths – including those of thirty civilians and forty-five Pakistani dockers at one of the five NLP-controlled ports – ended only when Danny Chamoun, the leader of the NLP Tigers, went into exile in Paris. These battles left a total of 350 dead and 500 wounded, and led to the fall of twelve offices and two garrisons of the NLP to the Phalangists.[7] Camille Chamoun and Pierre Gemayel met on 8 July, and announced political unification of the NLP and the Phalange. But, disregarding this decision, the NLP Tigers later handed over their remaining military positions to the Lebanese army, and not to the Phalange.

As for the government, having failed to move towards national reconciliation, Prime Minister Hoss submitted his resignation on 7 June. But it was not until 10 July that President Sarkis accepted it. On 16 July he called on Taki al Din Solh to form the next cabinet. Solh's attempt failed, and he stepped down on 9 August.

The political vacuum created by the absence of a government encouraged Bashir Gemayel's forces to expand their turf to the point of forcing the Lebanese army, commanded by Christian officers, to act against them. It did so, successfully, in East Beirut on 10 September.

After consulting Damascus, Sarkis called on Shafiq Wazzan, the Sunni head of the Supreme Islamic Council, on 22 October 1980 to form the next government. He did so three days later. Of the twenty-two ministers, divided equally between Christians and Muslims, ten were parliamentary deputies.

On 27 October the Phalangists attacked the remainder of the NLP Tigers in Zahle – a predominantly Christian city of 160,000, with the Greek Orthodox Church being the leading denomination – and in Beirut's suburbs of Ain Rummane and Furn Shebbak. The Lebanese army, which had controlled all Beirut suburbs since mid-June 1979, failed to prevent the Phalange–NLP clashes, and withdrew. This allowed the Phalangist militia to occupy Ain Rummane and Furn Shebbak. The army's behaviour dashed the hopes of the silent majority among Christians and Muslims, which looked forward to the day when the military would perform its constitutional role of restoring security and order. The Lebanese National Movement and Muslim leaders protested at the army's withdrawal. Responding to this, on 19 November the government took disciplinary action against the officers responsible for the débâcle, including the chief of staff, General Victor Khuri.

But the damage had been done. Accepting the unrivalled supremacy of the Phalangist militia – which had by now virtually transformed the Lebanese Front, commanding the loyalties of twenty-eight Christian MPs, into its political arm – Camille Chamoun and his followers decided to honour their latest unification agreement with the Phalange signed in early November. To bolster the authority of the Lebanese Front, the unified leadership declared conscription of all males, aged 16 to 45, in the areas under its control. Vowing to keep the Lebanese army out of these territories, it assigned internal security to the National Guard, which was to be composed of all Christian militias in the area.

On the political front, Bashir Gemayel and his father, Pierre, produced the Lebanese Front manifesto, entitled: 'The Lebanon We Want to Build'. Signed among others by Pierre Gemayel, Camille Chamoun, Bashir Gemayel, Edouard Hanayn (the Front's secretary-general) and Father Bolous Naaman, the document set out the Maronite position in broad terms. The signatories agreed to abandon the 1943 National Pact in favour of some sort of federation or confederation within the framework of a single unified Lebanon. Calling on the Arab world and the West to guarantee Lebanon's independence, they demanded an end to the Syrian occupation of Lebanon, and rejected the concept of permanent settlement of the Palestinians in their country. Bashir Gemayel's interpretation of the Lebanese Front manifesto was quite plain. Since Christians played a special role in Lebanon, he argued, they were entitled to a special position, irrespective of the size of their population. Only if the Christian aura and power structure were preserved would Lebanon remain unified. If not, then the Christians would go for a smaller Lebanon – consisting of East Beirut, the Metn region and the coastal areas north of Beirut – arising out of partition or cantonization.

The Lebanese Front document was released a week after the Wazzan government had secured a vote of confidence in mid-December on a programme of national reconciliation along the lines of Sarkis's 5 March statement and the establishment of special ties with Syria.[8] Heresy to both the Muslim side and many non-Maronite Christians, the document proved highly divisive.

The growing confidence of Bashir Gemayel emanated from the rising power of the Lebanese Front and its tightening links with Israel, which found it easier and more efficient to be dealing with one Maronite party. By the time he launched the Lebanese Front manifesto in late December 1980 Gemayel was ready for a showdown with Damascus. Earlier in the month, General Raphael Eitan had visited Jounieh and reportedly promised Israeli backing to the Lebanese Front in the event of its confrontation with Syria.[9] Both parties were aware that Syria's decision to back Iran in the Iran–Iraq War, which had erupted on 20 September, had isolated it in the Arab world, which was well illustrated by its boycott of the Arab summit in Amman on 23–5 November.

The Zahle crisis

Thus reinforced, the Lebanese Forces militia, commanded by Bashir Gemayel, tried to extend its influence to Zahle on the eastern slopes of Mount Lebanon, which bounded the Christian enclave in the north. Following the tactics they had used against the NLP Tigers, the LF wiped out the opposition in the city. Then, in December 1980, they ambushed a unit of the Syrian-manned Arab Deterrent Force, killing several of its members. In retaliation the ADF encircled the city and subjected it to artillery fire. Once the predictable ceasefire came into effect, the Lebanese internal security forces took charge of the security of Zahle, with the Syrian ADF returning to their checkpoints in the city.

Following these events, the Lebanese Forces, assisted by Israeli military advisers, fortified their military posts on the hills surrounding Zahle in early 1981, and started to build a military road north of the city to connect it with the Maronite enclave north-east of Beirut, ostensibly to bypass a possible future Syrian blockade. The overall purpose, however, was to transform Zahle into a strategic link between the Lebanese Forces in the north and the IDF-backed Haddad militia in the south-eastern strip along the Israeli border, and thus with Israel. Such an encirclement would have excluded the Syrian forces from most of central and southern Lebanon. But since Zahle is situated near the strategic Beirut–Damascus highway, Syria's lifeline to Lebanon, the Syrian ADF could not allow it to be developed into a 'dangerous enclave' in the predominantly Muslim

70

Beqaa valley along the Lebanese–Syrian border. This, as a possible Israeli invasion route, remained vital to Syria's defence.

Following the visit to Jounieh by General Eitan on 1 April – when he promised Bashir Gemayel that, if his Lebanese Forces were attacked by Syrian warplanes, Israel would use its air force against the Syrians[10] – the LF ambushed a Syrian unit near Zahle. This was a deliberate ploy by the LF hawks to draw Israel into the conflict. The Syrian ADF responded by attacking the LF positions in and around Zahle and dislodging the Maronite militia from the mountain posts. Assisted by the Palestinian and Lebanese National Movement units, the Syrian ADF besieged Zahle and subjected it to heavy artillery fire. The eight-day-long salvos resulted in 250 deaths and 500 injuries.

The intensity of the fighting split the Lebanese government, with eight out of the ten Christian ministers calling for a ceasefire and receiving the backing of President Sarkis. They were opposed by Prime Minister Wazzan and twelve ministers, two of them Christian. Abroad, appeals for a truce came from the United Nations, America and France. Israel's prime minister, Menachem Begin, warned against an attempt to massacre the Lebanese Christians, and threatened 'more than diplomatic action' from Israel if Syria continued to 'conquer' Lebanese. IDF forces carried out a series of land, sea and air strikes against many PLO bases and Lebanese army units, and some Unifil positions. However, at the United Nations, moves by the USA and France to censure Syria were frustrated by the Soviet Union.

In Lebanon, Wazzan's pro-Syrian position had the backing of the Lebanese National Movement and the PLO. Blaming Israel for instigating the crisis, they argued that, since Zahle was close to the strategic Damascus–Beirut highway, it needed to remain under Syrian control. While talks were in progress to defuse the crisis, Syrian ADF troops occupied the hills surrounding Zahle. Towards the end of April, as a detailed truce agreement was being worked out to open the Beirut–Baalbek highway passing through Zahle, the Syrians attacked the LF units occupying the summit of Mount Sanin, north-west of Zahle, which dominates both the Beqaa to the east and the Christian heartland to the west. After three days of heavy fighting, the Syrians captured the Sanin summit. On 28 April, just as Damascus was preparing to accept the ceasefire in the region, Israeli warplanes shot down two Syrian cargo helicopters in the Metn area, as a warning, according to Begin, that the Israeli government would act 'to prevent the annihilation of the Christian community in Lebanon'. The open intervention by Israel in the Lebanese conflict came after it had confirmed that its chief of staff, General Eitan, had visited Jounieh on 1 April. Its action reversed the cooling off in the region that had been in train over the previous week or so.

The next day, 29 April, Assad moved SAM-2s and SAM-6s (surface-to-air missiles) into the Beqaa valley. Prime Minister Wazzan described these missiles as defensive weapons intended to improve Lebanon's capacity to resist Israeli bombing raids. He was backed by the Lebanese National Movement and Amal, which called for a general mobilization. Begin decided to strike at the Syrian missiles on 30 April, an action that would have been welcomed by the LF. During this period contacts between Bashir Gemayel and his aides and the Israeli military and intelligence representatives intensified, with the Gemayel camp urging Israel to mount a military operation which would result in the expulsion of the Syrian and Palestinian forces from Lebanon, thus engendering an environment in which Gemayel would emerge as the only credible candidate for the presidential election due in the summer of 1982. However, poor weather conditions on 30 April frustrated Begin's plan, and helped to douse the rising tension. This provided time for America to pressure Begin to step back and avoid creating a crisis in US–USSR relations – and to appoint Philip Habib, an Arab-American academic, as a special envoy to help resolve the Zahle crisis.[11]

It also provided time for the Arabs to rally round Damascus in the face of Israel's military threats against the Syrian forces. The Arab foreign ministers' meeting in Tunis on 22 May promised Syria all required aid including combat troops to meet the Israeli threat. The Gulf states, led by Saudi Arabia, placed their resources at Syria's disposal and prepared to resume financial aid to it. Even Iraq, then engaged in armed conflict with Iran, promised to fight alongside Syria in any warfare with Israel. In short, the Zahle crisis enabled Syria to end its isolation in the Arab world which had resulted from its siding with Iran in the Iran–Iraq War.

To assist national reconciliation in Lebanon, the Arab foreign ministers' conference decided to revive the earlier Follow-Up Committee, consisting of the foreign ministers of Lebanon, Syria, Saudi Arabia and Kuwait as well as the Arab League general secretary, with the Lebanese president as the Committee chairman. During June, when the Israelis were engaged in their election campaign, the mediation of the Arab League Follow-Up Committee succeeded in getting the Maronite Lebanese Forces to leave Zahle, and the Syrian ADF to lift the siege. In late June a ceasefire went into effect.

Erratic progress towards national reconciliation

As for talks on national reconciliation, Syria and its Lebanese allies insisted that the Lebanese Forces must first cut all links with Israel. This was not forthcoming. 'If some consider that buying weapons amounts to the kind of relationship they talk about, we can bring matters under control', said Pierre Gemayel. 'But a weapons ban on us should go hand in hand with a weapons ban on others.'[12]

On 9 July 1981, the day the Israeli general election returned right-wing Likud to power, and various parties in Beirut were discussing national reconciliation and the LF's ties with Israel, the IDF resumed attacks on Palestinian targets in south Lebanon. The PLO retaliated with rocket fire aimed at Kriyat Shimona in northern Israel. After minor raids for the next few days, the IDF attacked twelve targets in Lebanon and shot down a Syrian warplane. On 15 July the PLO's rocket attacks on Nahariya left three Israelis dead and twenty-five injured. The nxt day the IDF launched air raids on the bridges and roads used by the PLO commandos, an unprecedented step. On 17 July, IDF war planes bombed West Beirut with the aim of destroying the command headquarters of two of the PLO's major constituents. However, of the ten buildings hit by Israeli bombs, only two were partially occupied by the PLO groups. The IDF raid on a densely populated area left 300 people dead and over 800 injured, most of them civilian and Lebanese.[13]

The Lebanese government appealed to the UN, and called on the Arab League for support. In mid-July the UN Security Council called for an immediate ceasefire. On 20 and 21 July the Israelis and the PLO exchanged heavy rocket and artillery fire. The next day IDF planes bombed civilian traffic in south Lebanon, killing forty people with direct hits. On 23 July the IDF bombed Sidon and Tyre. That night the Arab League's Joint Defence Council, meeting in Tunis, threatened to take 'global measures' against 'all countries' continuing to help Israel. The following day the PLO and the Lebanese National Movement forces foiled Israel's attempt to land its forces at Jiye, 20 km south of Beirut. US mediation by Philip Habib brought about a ceasefire between Israel and the PLO on 25 July. This was part of a three-way understanding between Israel, Syria and the PLO. It allowed Syria to deploy missiles in the Beqaa so long as they were not fired; Israel was permitted to continue its reconnaissance flights over Lebanon on the understanding that it would not target the Syrian missiles; and Israel and the PLO agreed to cease cross-border attacks, with the Syrian president guaranteeing the PLO's compliance.[14]

On 25 July the Arab League's Follow-Up Committee met to discuss Bashir Gemayel's promise to President Sarkis to start talks based on the latter's fourteen-point declaration of 5 March 1980. Later, in a private letter to Sarkis, Gemayel expressed his willingness to sever relations with Israel if this was in Lebanon's interest 'as perceived by the president'. Assad did not consider this good enough.[15]

During his visit in August 1981 to Washington, where he met William Clark, the US assistant secretary of state, Bashir Gemayel said that he sensed American readiness to solve the Lebanese crisis, and that he hoped that such a solution would include a Syrian withdrawal from Lebanon. This angered Damascus. In early September, on the eve of the meeting of the Arab League Follow-Up Committee, Syria demanded that the Lebanese Front sever all its links with Israel. Thus pressured, its leader, Camille Chamoun, repeated the Front's promise to do so. This signified a formal return of the Lebanese Front leadership to the Arab fold, and its preference for diplomatic mediation by Arabs to resolve the chronic Lebanese crisis rather than a military alliance with Israel. With this, the movement towards national reconciliation in Lebanon gathered pace in late 1981.

On the eve of the Arab summit in Fez, Morocco, at the end of November, Arafat promised Sarkis an end to Palestinian operations against Israel from south Lebanon. Sarkis was under pressure from the Lebanese Front to place the overall Lebanese problem before the summit. Opposing this, Syria proposed putting before the gathering only the south Lebanese problem because of the deep Israeli involvement in it. Syria prevailed, and the summit endorsed the Beirut government's attempts to invigorate its army and deploy it in the south.[16]

In late November, on the forty-fifth anniversary of the Phalange, Bashir Gemayel expressed his interest in presidency, when he declared that Lebanon needed a 'strong president' who could restore peace. Given his commitment to bringing about a Syrian withdrawal from Lebanon, Damascus was opposed to his candidacy. Relations between Syria and Gemayel soured further when in early 1982, at the time of heightened activity in Syria of the oppositionist Muslim Brotherhood, Damascus publicly accused Gemayel of assisting the Syrian Muslim Brotherhood and of maintaining contacts with Israel. The second accusation was confirmed by *Time* in early February 1982. It reported that Bashir Gemayel had secretly met the Israeli defence minister, Ariel Sharon, who had informed him of Israel's intention to invade Lebanon and move north as far as Beirut's international airport. This story, broadcast by Voice of Lebanon on 8 February 1982, deeply embarrassed the Gemayel camp. Its denial was unconvincing; and the Phalange newspaper, *Al Aamal* (The Labour), conceded that the revelation had damaged the cause of the party. In fact, during his visit to East Beirut in January, Ariel Sharon, a leading hawk who believed in *Pax Hebraica*, and who had been appointed defence minister by Prime Minister Begin five months earlier, had conferred with most of the Lebanese Front leaders to plan an Israeli invasion of Lebanon.[17]

By mid-February 1982 Israel had resumed arms and ammunition shipments to the Maronites, the delivery point being a cove at Tabarja. In mid-March the independent *Al Nahar* (The Day) reported 'well-informed speculation' that Bashir Gemayel was seriously contemplating a military operation to 'liberate' Lebanese territories from the Syrians, 'perhaps in conjunction with an Israeli invasion'.[18] Beginning in March, as Israel started evacuating the Sinai peninsula to implement its March 1979 peace treaty with Egypt, US intelligence pictures showed the deployment of Israeli troops near the Lebanese border. Concurrently, Israel stepped up its allegations of PLO violations of the ceasefire which had been in effect since 25 July 1981. Following the complete pull-back of the IDF from Sinai on 25 April, the pace of Israeli activity against Lebanon accelerated.

On the other side, the Lebanese National Movement leaders concluded in early 1982 that they had either to impose effective central authority on the areas they held – just as the Lebanese Front had been doing since mid-1980 on the territory it controlled – or to urge the Lebanese state to do so. They felt irked by the increasing challenge that they faced from Amal, the fast-rising organization of Shias, which gained most of its recruits in West Beirut from the 300,000 Shia emigrants from south Lebanon, who had abandoned their homes due to the IDF bombings triggered by the PLO's anti-Israeli actions. Due to their numerical superiority in Lebanon, and the emergence of an Islamic republic in predominantly Shia Iran under Khomeini, Lebanese Shias gained growing prominence from early 1980 onwards.

Following the resignation of Hussein Husseini as the general secretary of Amal in April 1980, Imam Musa Sadr's son, Sadr al Din Sadr, was elected secretary-general, and Nabih Berri chairman. Berri worked in conjunction with Shaikh Muhammad Mahdi Shams al Din, head of the Higher Shia Communal Council. They took to presenting Amal as a political movement which had its own militia of the same name, now 5,000 strong. While co-operating with the Lebanese National Movement, Amal had refused to join it, mainly because the LNM contained such atheistic parties as the Communist Party and the Communist Action Organization. In the wake of the IDF's intense bombing of Beirut on 17 July 1981, which led to hundreds of Lebanese casualties, Amal clashed with the Palestinian commandos, blaming them for the deaths and destruction. Next month it fought the militias of the Communists and other left-wing groups : these confrontations left thirty dead. To secure the ceasefire that followed, it was decided to form the Higher Security Co-ordination Committee, consisting of the ADF, the PLO, the LNM and Amal – a development which signified the formal recognition of Amal as a distinct entity, quite apart from the LNM.

As an important step towards formalizing its authority in the areas it controlled, on 27 March 1982 the LNM Central Council announced elections to the 300-strong popular council in West Beirut on 19 April. It then issued a comprehensive charter which, aimed at unifying all LNM constituents, called for the building of a national Lebanese–Palestinian–Syrian alliance.

However, soon some Muslim organizations inside and outside the LNM began arguing against the holding of elections, saying that such a step would provide the Lebanese Front with a precedent to hold similar elections in East Beirut as a step towards formalizing a *de facto* partition of Lebanon. This view got strong backing at the Amal conference held in early April under the dual leadership of Nabih Berri (b. 1938) and Shaikh Shams al Din. On 13 April fierce fighting between Amal and its secular, leftist adversaries erupted in the Nabatiya–Zahrani area in south Lebanon, and then spread to south Beirut. It ended only after the Higher Security Co-ordination Committee intervened. To stabilize the truce, the LNM leadership decided to postpone the 19 April 1982 local elections in West Beirut.[19]

In Israel, Ariel Sharon continued to press on with his plan to invade Lebanon. On 20 May he travelled to Washington and held private consultations with Alexander Haig, the US secretary of state, noted for his strong pro-Israeli bias. For the first time in its history, Israel was prepared to start a war in which its own existence was not threatened. It looked for an excuse to march into Lebanon. It came on the night of 3 June 1982 in the form of an assassination attempt on Shlomo Argov, the Israeli ambassador in London. It made little difference to the Israeli government that Nawal Rosan, the would-be assassin, was a member of a Palestinian group led by Abu Nidal, a notorious terrorist who had sentenced Yasser Arafat to death, and on whose head Yasser Arafat had placed a heavy price.

The invasion of Lebanon by Israel on the night of 5–6 June 1982 marked the end of the first part of the Lebanese civil war, which was now more than seven years old, and which had claimed 55,000 lives.[20]

Ironically, during this phase of the conflict, Lebanese living standards either remained stable or rose, with per capita income growing from $1,415 in 1974 to $2,011 in 1982, an increase of 42 per cent, and with the minimum wage rising 45 per cent, from $135 to $195. This was due to a number of factors.

First, Lebanon had considerable economic reserves. During the previous decade, per capita income had increased from $400 in 1965 to $1,415 in 1974, giving an annual growth rate of 6 per cent at fixed prices. The country had a foreign currency surplus of $4 billion. At the start of the war there were enough public and private economic and financial reserves to overcome the losses and dislocations of the first few years.

Second, the upsurge in the demand for labour in the Arabian peninsula in the wake of the oil price boom of 1973–4 saw the number of Lebanese migrant workers there grow from 50,000 in 1970 to 98,000 in 1975 (forming about one-eighth of the total Lebanese workforce) and to 210,000 in 1979–80 (constituting about a third of the national workforce). Their remittances jumped from $250 million in 1970, amounting to about one-sixth of the national income, to $2,254 million in 1980, accounting for about one-third of the national income. This allowed Lebanon to maintain a pre-war level of imports and consumption despite seven years of civil strife. It also funded growth in banking, construction, engineering, printing and publishing. Individual enterprises raised bank loans by mortgaging real estate, whose value rose sharply.

Third, there was a steady inflow of foreign political money to fund the numerous Lebanese and Palestinian militias and seventeen intelligence services. The total amounted to $300 million a year, forming 6 per cent of the gross domestic product (GDP) of $5,000 million.

Fourth, there was a substantial Palestinian economy. In 1981 it estimatedly generated 15 per cent of GDP, with the total PLO budget probably being larger than the Lebanese government's. The PLO with its own bureaucracy, army, institutions and activities ran 100 schools, eight hospitals and 108 diplomatic missions, and employed 15,000 fighters.

Finally, the civil war, which was accompanied by all sorts of extortion by the newly formed paramilitary groups, brought about redistribution of wealth in favour of the underprivileged and the lower middle class. Squatting, seizures, looting, forced taxation, extortion and other forms of forced transfers favoured: (a) the petty bourgeoisie and sections of the working classes at the expense of the traditional bourgeoisie; (b) suburban areas and the periphery of Lebanon at the expense of Beirut and central Lebanon; (c) the deprived sections of Muslim sects at the expense of better-off sections of Christian sects; and (d) private militias and sectarian factions at the expense of the state's administrative and financial institutions. Interestingly, the resulting social mobility caused an increase in the demand for housing, schooling, university places and durable consumer goods.[21]

At the same time the war inflicted much damage, direct and indirect, on the Lebanese economy. The direct annual cost was estimated to be $900 million. Of this, $300 million came from abroad as direct subsidies to various factions, and $400 million represented the PLO's expenditure on its forces as well as those of its military allies. So the burden borne by the Lebanese economy was only $200 million. The indirect cost was much higher though. It included the physical destruction of factories, hotels, houses and other facilities; a drop in Lebanese exports of industrial and agricultural products; an increase in costs of salaries, energy, transport and machinery replacements; the loss of trade to competing ports in Syria and Jordan; the partial deindustrialization of textile, footware and furniture industries; and a weakening of the commercial infrastructure, transport system, and personal and recreational services. This loss could not be compensated by the $2,000 million subsidy promised in 1979 by the oil-rich Gulf states to Lebanon over the next five years, particularly when the actual aid amounted to about a quarter of what had been promised.[22]

PART II

PART II

---------- *5* ----------

The second Israeli invasion and aftermath

June 1982 — February 1984

The June 1982 Israeli invasion of Lebanon, followed by occupation, was of such magnitude and speed that it left most Lebanese and Lebanon-based Palestinians dazed. More importantly, it rearranged the power equation in the republic in favour of Israel's allies, the Maronites.

While the advance of the Israeli Defence Forces from the international border to the outskirts of Beirut was swift, their efforts to expel the PLO from the Lebanese capital took many weeks to succeed. The subsequent period up to February 1984 – when the Western powers withdrew their peacekeeping forces stationed in Beirut in the wake of the Israeli withdrawal from the city – can be seen as constituting the aftermath of the Israeli invasion.

June to mid-September 1982

Once Sabbath ended on the evening of Saturday 5 June, the Israeli defence minister, Ariel Sharon, and his chief of staff, General Raphael Eitan, presented Operation 'Big Pines' to the cabinet, presided over by the prime minister, Menachem Begin. It was meant to last one or two days and lead to the capture of the Lebanese territory up to 40 km north of the border – with the IDF advancing in the direction of Sidon in the western sector, the Zahrani river in the central sector, and Hasbaya in the eastern sector, thus avoiding combat with the Syrian troops. The goal was to clear the area of the Palestinian commandos and make northern Israel safe from their artillery and rocket fire. If the USA did not object too much, then, argued Sharon and Eitan, they could implement the more ambitious Operation 'Peace in Galilee'. Its aims were to see the evacuation of all foreign forces from Lebanon, including those of the PLO, and the

81

establishment of a new Lebanese regime under Bashir Gemayel with a view to having it conclude a peace treaty with Israel.

In the event, Israel implemented its Peace in Galilee plan. Under Major-General Amir Drori of its Northern Command, it was to throw into the campaign some 76,000 troops, 1,250 tanks and 1,500 armoured personnel carriers (APCs), providing them with naval and air support. On the other side were 25,000 Syrian and Syrian-controlled PLA troops, equipped with 300 tanks and 300 APCs, under the command of Major-General Said Bairaqdar – plus about 15,000 PLO fighters belonging to eight separate commands and bearing an assortment of weapons, and their Lebanese allies.[1] The Lebanese army, obeying the order of its commander, was to stay out of the fray.

Early on the morning of Sunday 6 June, under heavy air cover in the central and western sectors, Israel invaded Lebanon. About 40,000 soldiers marched into Lebanon across the border – divided into eastern, central and western sectors – supplemented by amphibious landings near Sidon and Tyre. Ignoring Security Council Resolution 509 of 6 June, calling on Israel to withdraw immediately to its border with Lebanon, the largest contingent of the IDF advanced along the coastal highway to Tyre, 21 km north of the frontier, which fell the next day. Backed by more amphibious landings near Sidon, the IDF captured the city on 8 June. Leapfrogging along the coastal road, and reinforced by additional troops, the IDF easily overcame the resistance offered by the small units of Palestinian–Lebanese Joint Forces, who decided to implement an orderly withdrawal to the north, concentrating on inflicting casualties on the enemy, rather than defending territory. Israel's amphibious landings on the night of 8 June near Damour prepared the ground for the fall of the town on the following day. In the central sector, the IDF column moved through the territory under Unifil to seize Beaufort Castle with its line-of-sight view of Israel's Galilee region. It soon captured most of the PLO's southern heartland between the Litani and Zahrani rivers. In the eastern and central sectors, where the regular Syrian and PLA units under the Syrian command were fairly close to the border, the Palestinian–Lebanese Joint Forces resorted to the guerrilla tactics of retreat and harassment of the enemy.

By 8 June, while Israel's Prime Minister Begin was publicly calling on President Assad to order his troops not to attack Israeli soldiers, the IDF had acquired highly advantageous positions. Their column in the central sector had outflanked the Syrian forces in the southern

Beqaa valley, while their western column was pressing eastwards from Sidon into the Shouf mountains to envelop Syria's forward positions at Jezzine before heading north, and their eastern column under Major-General Avigdor Ben-Gal was concentrating on getting a foothold in southern Beqaa with a view to advancing to the strategic Beirut–Damascus highway. Indeed, late on 8 June, an IDF armoured unit reached a village 16 km south of the road, thus threatening to cut off the Syrian forces in Beirut and to encircle those in Beqaa. But it was held in check for two days by the Syrians, who strengthened their ground positions with armour against the background of intense Syrian–IDF aerial battles.

On the afternoon of 9 June, after Israeli electronic countermeasures had crippled the Syrian radar, IDF warplanes destroyed seventeen of the nineteen Syrian batteries of SAM-2s, SAM-3s and SAM-6s. The ensuing air battle, involving seventy Syrian and a hundred IDF supersonic jets, resulted in the loss of twenty-nine Syrian warplanes. By confusing the Syrian radar, the Israeli drones complemented the efficiency of the US-made Hawkeye aircraft, equipped with avionics capable of monitoring Syria's entire air defence system. Despite these losses, the next day President Assad, a former air force commander, deployed his air force on a large scale in order to slow down the Israeli advance. Damascus lost thirty-five more warplanes, but gained valuable time. On that day, 10 June, a Syrian armoured division, equipped with advanced Soviet T-72 tanks, engaged an IDF armoured brigade in the Rashaya area near the Lebanese–Syrian border, and forced back the enemy several kilometres while destroying thirty-three of its tanks.[2]

In the western sector, on the night of 9 June, the IDF tried to stage amphibious landings near Beirut as part of their plan to infiltrate the capital. But a vigorous defence of the beaches by the Palestinian–Lebanese Joint Forces frustrated the Israeli effort.

Following the Syrian air losses, President Assad dashed secretly to Moscow to urge the Soviet hierarchy to protect his country. This resulted in the Soviet leader, Leonid Brezhnev, contacting President Ronald Reagan on the Moscow–Washington hotline. With the rival superpower becoming openly agitated about the fate of its allies, Syria and the PLO, the US administration pressed its special envoy, Philip Habib, to intensify his peacemaking efforts.

As a result, a ceasefire between Israel and Syria came into effect at noon on 11 June, bringing the fighting in the eastern and central sectors to a halt. By then the IDF had seized a quarter of southern

Lebanon below the Awali river. The Syrian–IDF truce marked the end of an important and successful phase of the Israeli invasion. The IDF defeated the Syrians in Lebanon without the latter extending the conflict to the Israeli-occupied (Syrian) Golan Heights or getting the Soviet Union directly embroiled. And a ceasefire in the eastern and central sectors allowed the IDF to increase pressure on its adversaries in the western sector – until the next day, 12 June, when Habib brokered a truce between Israel and the PLO.

While the second ceasefire signalled the termination of the intense phase of the Israeli invasion, however, the fighting as such was far from over, as the subsequent events were to show.

Taking advantage of the truce, the IDF brought in reinforcements. On 13 June Ariel Sharon led Israeli armour into Baabda, a Beirut suburb measuring 10 square kilometres, which housed the Lebanese government. Once the IDF had expelled President Sarkis from his official palace in Baabda at night and linked up with Bashir Gemayel's Lebanese Forces, half a million Lebanese and Palestinians – including 14,000 Syrian and PLO troops – living in the 8 square kilometres of West Beirut found themselves under siege. Their encirclement was enforced by the combined military might of the Lebanese Forces and the IDF, which deployed 400 tanks and 100-plus heavy artillery pieces as well as offshore gunboats and an (unopposed) air force. It resorted to bringing in supplies through the Maronite port of Jounieh, and deployed tanks and artillery in East Beirut and the heavily populated hills overlooking West Beirut.

By Monday 14 June, Ariel Sharon had not only neutralized the Syrians in Lebanon but also produced an option for Israel to expel the PLO from Beirut – either through negotiations or by force. Choosing force, Sharon set out to eject the PLO from the capital in two stages. In the first stage, lasting from 13 June to 12 July, he tried to secure unconditional PLO surrender first by heavy artillery salvos (from 13 to 25 June), and then by staging air raids coupled with cutting off water and electricity supplies as well as fuel, fresh fruit, vegetables and bread (4 to 12 July).

Sharon intensified the bombing of West Beirut while his prime minister, Begin, was away in Washington from 20 June onwards. Begin's meeting with President Reagan and his defence secretary, Caspar Weinberger, was reportedly tense, with the Israeli leader facing sharp questioning on his country's military actions in Lebanon. But this had no impact on Sharon's aggressive stance. On 22 June, violating the eleven-day-old truce, his forces attacked the

Syrians along the Beirut–Damascus highway east of Baabda and removed them from the road for 15 km eastwards, up to Sofar, depriving them of any leverage over the battle for West Beirut, where one of the Syrian brigades was trapped. By the time the battle ended three days later, the Israelis had seized the Dahr al Baidar pass, east of Sofar, on the Beirut–Damascus highway.

The Israeli attack on the Syrians caused the collapse of the National Salvation Council of Lebanon – consisting of Shafiq Wazzan (Sunni), Bashir Gemayal (Maronite), Fuad Boutros (Greek Orthodox), Nasri Maluf (Greek Catholic), Nabih Berri (Shia) and Walid Jumblatt (Druze) – which had been formed by President Sarkis after his expulsion from the official palace. This signified a major shift in the balance of power in Lebanon against the Muslim and nationalist forces, a fact not acknowledged by them until after the end of the war.

On 24 and 25 June the IDF unleashed intensive artillery fire, naval gunfire and aerial bombardment against West Beirut: a development which caused reverberations in Washington. On 25 June the US secretary of state, Alexander Haig, resigned under pressure. His overindulgent attitude towards Israel – coming on top of his lack of team spirit and abrasive differences with leading presidential advisers – became unbearable to the White House. Haig's resignation ended the deal he had struck with Sharon in May to let Israel virtually take over its northern neighbour. However, it was another fortnight before Haig's successor, George Shultz, could assume full operating powers.

The Arab League foreign ministers' meeting in Tunis on 26–7 June declared that PLO activities from Lebanon should be ended and its armed military presence there removed, and that the Lebanese government should be helped to exercise its authority and sovereignty over all of Lebanon through its army and its paramilitary internal security forces. Though the meeting did not extend the Arab Deterrent Force's mandate, due to expire in late July, the Lebanese government did not formally request Damascus to pull out its troops. It did not wish to put the Syrian troops on a par with Israel's by demanding their withdrawal, or to upset the Muslim–nationalist camp, which reckoned that the withdrawal of the PLO and the Syrians would put them at the mercy of the Israeli–Maronite alliance.

On 27 June Israel demanded for the first time that all PLO forces leave, not just its leaders. This seemed unlikely. The morale of the Palestinians was high. They and the Lebanese inhabitants of West

Beirut had taken to hunkering down in candle-lit basements, glued to their transistor radios, listening to news from various stations run by the Lebanese government, the Christian militias and the Lebanese leftists, as well as the Israelis, Britons, Americans and French. Sharon did not intend to place his soldiers in the streets and alleys of West Beirut to wage guerrilla warfare, since the casualties would have been intolerably high for Israel. He pressed Bashir Gemayel to order his Lebanese Forces to expel the PLO from West Beirut. But Gemayel refused to do so. He feared that confrontation between his militiamen and thousands of heavily armed PLO commandos would result in unbearable human and material losses on his side: an outcome which would lower his popularity to such an extent as to damage severely his chances of becoming Lebanon's president. Moreover, he argued that if Israel wished to emerge as the regional superpower by imposing political change through a military campaign, it should be prepared to pay the price that the capture of West Beirut was bound to extract. Having declared the PLO's eviction from Beirut as its prime aim, Israel could not afford to back down: its failure to achieve its objective would now be interpreted by the world at large as a victory for the Palestinians.

On 3 July the IDF seized the Green Line, thus sealing off West Beirut from East Beirut. The next day they cut off all food, water and fuel into West Beirut, and subjected it to intense artillery bombardment. Four days later, responding to President Reagan's appeal, they restored water and electricity. On 9 July there was a strong military response from the PLO, which led to intense raids by the IDF for the next three days. Then came a ceasefire, which held until 21 July. The Israeli blockade had little impact on the PLO, which had stored ample supplies of food and ammunition.

On 21 July the PLO attacked the Israelis behind their lines. In response, Sharon escalated his campaign against West Beirut in two phases, primarily to highlight the IDF's awesome destructive power and secondarily to empty West Beirut as the American envoy, Habib, negotiated the terms for the PLO commandos' departure. The IDF started using aircraft to hit PLO positions in West Beirut, and combined this with naval and artillery attacks. Yet PLO morale remained high, with Yasser Arafat, surrounded by journalists, freely travelling around West Beirut. From 22 to 29 July, Israel staged more intense bombing of West Beirut and coupled it with bombardment of the entire Syrian front in the Beqaa, in response to Assad's alleged permission to the Palestinian guerrillas to harass the Israeli troops there. But the PLO in West Beirut refused to surrender, demonstrating that it was capable of withstanding savage pounding by the enemy. It had done so for a sufficiently long period to be able to retrieve its honour from the jaws of an imminent military defeat.

By now, the pattern of the conflict could be summarized thus: explosions of booby-trapped cars by remote control alternating with non-stop artillery, naval gunfire and aerial bombing, and periods of relative peace. The latest ceasefire went into effect on 30 July – as the proverbial lull before the storm.

Finally, from 1 August to 12 August, the IDF subjected West Beirut to more intense bombardment from air, land and sea. On 1 August it carried out fourteen hours of non-stop air, naval and artillery pounding of West Beirut. Two days later the PLO–Israel talks, being conducted through Habib, seemed to be stalling. On 4 August the IDF opened up heavy artillery fire all around West Beirut. It went far beyond the southern suburbs and the Palestinian refugee camps south of the Corniche Mazraa boulevard, which had so far been the military boundary of West Beirut. Now the Israelis fired heavy weaponry against those parts of West Beirut where the Palestinian population was about 1 per cent and no Palestinian commandos were posted. Perhaps Israel was attempting to expel the Muslim Lebanese inhabitants of West Beirut as well. Since the IDF siege nearly half of West Beirut's residents had departed, the remainder being either too poor or too rich (and therefore afraid of losing their well-appointed apartments to squatters) to leave. The Israeli ground troops tried to seize the PLO headquarters in the Fakhani district, but failed to advance due to strong resistance by the PLO, which showed a surprising degree of internal cohesion under adverse circumstances. In the process the IDF lost many of their comrades, and the attempt brought home the cost that Israel would have to bear if it engaged in house-to-house fighting.

On 6 August Lebanese sources announced that an agreement between the warring sides had been concluded along the lines proposed by Philip Habib. For the next two days there was no military action by the IDF while the Israeli government studied the plan. On 8 August, having obtained the consent of seven Arab countries to accept the PLO fighters from Lebanon, Habib announced that, as a member of the Multi-National Force (MNF), America would contribute 1,000 marines to help maintain order in West Beirut as well as escort and protect PLO commandos boarding vehicles, ships or aircraft on their way out of Lebanon.

On 9 and 10 August the Israelis bombarded the three PLO camps of Sabra, Shatila and Burj al Barajina. For the next two days, as the PLO leadership considered the Israeli demands for evacuation, the IDF staged intense bombings to overcome the stiff resistance it faced as it tried to advance along the Corniche Mazraa boulevard. It failed. The IDF's plan to sever the Palestinian camps from the northern part of West Beirut also failed.

On 12 August, later to be called Black Thursday, Ariel Sharon ordered saturation bombing on the scale of the Allied attacks on Dresden, Germany, in the Second World War. From dawn all areas south of Corniche Mazraa boulevard were subjected to non-stop air, artillary and naval bombardment for eleven and a half hours by the Israelis, who cut off water supplies and let the city burn. According to a report by an International Commission headed by Sean Mac-Bride, a Nobel peace prize winner, Israel used concussion bombs to bring down civilian buildings as well as phosphorus shells, high explosives and, in at least sixteen locations in West Beirut, US-made cluster bombs.[3] When the onslaught, which caused the deaths of at least 500 civilians, finally ceased, the IDF units rushed to man the roadblocks, making sure that no food or fuel entered West Beirut. Sharon's action sent shock waves not only through the Arab world and outside, but also through the Israeli government.

'The reaction to the [12 August] attack within the Israeli cabinet was anger', noted Richard A. Gabriel, an Israeli defence expert. 'Most of the cabinet, even Sharon's supporters, concluded that he had exceeded his authority by ordering the attack. Its intensity seemed almost gratuitous in its attempt to crush the remaining PLO forces of West Beirut.'[4]

Sharon's saturation bombing angered Washington. It pressured Prime Minister Begin, who intervened to lift the 63-day siege of West Beirut and order a ceasefire. Peace returned on 13 August. The next day the Syrians announced that they would withdraw from West Beirut when they were given the opportunity to do so. On 19 August Israel accepted the PLO's evacuation plan.

Summing up the long ordeal West Beirutis had suffered, Sandra Mackey, a resident American journalist, wrote:

For seventy days, the Israelis pounded Beirut with bombs and mortar rounds. Shelling came from the north, from the hills, and from the sea. Night after night, the skyline exploded in flashes of orange and yellow accented by ascending spirals of white smoke from exploding munitions. Israeli gunners, known for their precision, landed rounds on hospitals marked with red crosses and crescents as well as on the headquarters of the International Committee of the Red Cross. Hysterical people piled into basements they knew would become tombs if the building above were hit.[5]

Along with the general destruction of West Beirut went the specific Israeli aim to assassinate Yasser Arafat, which never quite succeeded, and which in its train caused hundreds of deaths. Israeli agents, equipped with portable radios, constantly supplied information about Arafat's whereabouts to the IDF command centre, which deployed war planes to hit the area. In the process eight buildings, including apartment blocks, were razed to the ground. Arafat took to operating from, and even sleeping in, his car, which was constantly on the move.

With the lifting of the siege, popular attention turned to the impending evacuation of the PLO fighters from West Beirut, and the presidential election. Significantly, on 25 July, in the midst of heavy IDF bombing of West Beirut, Bashir Gemayel, aged 34, announced his candidacy for high office. Demanding that the election be held on time, he said that only a strong president could lead Lebanon to its salvation. He was opposed not only by the Lebanese National Movement but also by the most senior Sunni religious leader, Hassan Khalid. But the opposition to Bashir Gemayel was not united or wide enough to be able to offer its own credible candidate. Therefore, advised by Syria, the anti-Gemayel camp decided to follow the line being taken by Rashid Karami, Suleiman Franjieh, Raymond Edde, Nabih Berri and Saeb Salam. Insisting that the poll be conducted only after the Israelis had departed, they had called for the boycott of the presidential election being held on 19 August.

As it was, the poll was postponed to 23 August because the venue, the parliament house, was judged to be unsafe. The new venue was Fayadiya army barracks near the presidential palace in Baabda. Thanks to the alliance struck between Bashir Gemayel and Kamil Assad, the Shia speaker who had won his office in October 1981 with the help of the Gemayel supporters, and a liberal use of threats (by the Lebanese Forces) and money (mainly by Saudi Arabia), the turnout was sixty-five deputies, forming more than two-thirds of the surviving total of ninety-two. Among Muslims, five out of nineteen Sunnis attended, as did twelve of the eighteen Shias, and all five

Druzes. Among Christians, six out of eleven Greek Orthodox attended, as did five of the six Greek Catholics, twenty-seven of the twenty-eight Maronites, and all five Armenians. On the first ballot Bashir Gemayel failed to secure the required two-thirds of the total membership. But on the second ballot he easily surpassed the simple majority of forty-seven to win a total of fifty-seven votes. His election was greeted with ecstatic enthusiasm in the Maronite camp and denounced by Jumblatt as the victory of 'the candidate of Israeli tanks'.

On 21 August the first units of the Multi-National Force (MNF) arrived, composed of American, British, French and Italian troops. The next day, Sunday, the first PLO contingent of 379 armed men departed. This was the start of a process which saw the evacuation by 1 September of 14,344 Palestinian combatants – 8,144 PLO commandos, 3,500 Syrian-controlled PLA troops and 2,700 Syrian soldiers of the 85th Brigade – with the Syrians and PLA units departing by truck for Syria, and the PLO fighters boarding ships bound for various Arab states. As the PLO fighters left they handed over their weapons to the MNF units. Their families stayed behind, guaranteed protection by the MNF troops deployed in West Beirut.

This signalled the formal end of the Israeli invasion, which left 17,000 to 19,000 mainly Muslim and Lebanese civilians dead, and 34,000 to 40,000 injured. The losses on the Israeli side were 350 killed and 2,100 wounded.[6]

On 1 September President Reagan offered a Middle East peace plan, drafted by his secretary of state, George Shultz. Reagan affirmed UN Security Council Resolution 242 as the 'cornerstone' of American peace diplomacy, and interpreted it to mean an Israeli withdrawal from all Arab lands occupied since the June 1967 war. He called on Israel not to build new settlements in the Occupied Territories or to enlarge the existing ones. He came out in favour of Palestinian self-government 'in association with Jordan', thus excluding an independent Palestinian state as well as Israeli annexation, sovereignty or permanent domination over the Occupied Territories. Referring to the 1978 Camp David Accords, which had mentioned the legitimate rights of the Palestinian people, the US president proposed widening the Camp David process to include Jordan and the Palestinians so that a self-governing Palestine authority could be elected to succeed Israeli rule. The Israeli prime minister, Menachem Begin, who had not been consulted, rejected the plan outright, and it died an instant death.

The timing of the Reagan initiative clearly demonstrated that it was taken to placate the Arabs in the wake of the PLO's expulsion from Beirut and a large-scale use of lethal US-supplied weapons by Israel in its invasion of Lebanon, culminating in a nine-week siege and the destruction of West Beirut. Washington also signalled to Israel that, following its success in expelling the Palestinians and the Syrians from Beirut, it should not embark on a creeping annexation of the West Bank and Gaza.

At its 6–9 September summit in Fez, Morocco, the Arab League outlined its terms for peace in the Middle East: an Israeli pull-back to the pre-1967 frontiers; the uprooting of Israeli settlements in the Occupied Territories; the translation of the Palestinian right to self-determination under PLO leadership into the establishment of an independent state on the West Bank and Gaza with its capital in East Jerusalem; and the right of Palestinian refugees to return home or receive compensation. By stating that the UN Security Council should guarantee peace for all the states in the region, the Arab summit implicitly recognized the right of Israel to exist in peace.

In Lebanon, however, public attention was focused on the forth-coming presidency of Bashir Gemayel. He had already begun for-mulating, and announcing, his policies on important issues. He called for the withdrawal of all foreign forces – Syrian, Israeli and Palestin-ian. By so doing he equated Syria, an Arab state which had been called on by the Arab League to contribute its troops to the Arab Deterrent Force, with the invading forces of Israel: a step which turned President Assad into his mortal enemy. In Damascus, Gemayel was seen as nothing more than an Israeli stooge.

During his clandestine meeting with Prime Minister Begin on 1 September, Gemayel came under pressure to sign a peace treaty with Israel. While pledging to co-operate with the Jewish state, he reportedly refused to say when he would conclude a peace accord with it. Both agreed, however, that an 'exchange of representatives' between the two countries did not have to await a formal treaty. At home President-elect Gemayel faced hostility from the Muslim community and the Lebanese National Movement. Saeb Salam, a Sunni leader close to Saudi Arabia, intervened to conciliate the two sides. A conference of eminent Muslim and LNM leaders on 6 September demanded an end to the Israeli occupation, and rejected the idea of a peace accord which Israel wished to impose on their country. They also called for the dissolution of all militias, Muslim and Christian.

Externally, Bashir Gemayel had better success with Western powers, particularly America which, having approved of his candidacy, wanted to strengthen his presidency. On 9 September, 1,200 US marines left West Beirut, handing over their positions to the Lebanese army.

Two days later Salam met Gemayel at the presidential palace in a congenial atmosphere. But before his mediation could improve relations between the president-elect and his opponents, Gemayel was killed.

On 14 September 1982 a bomb explosion at the Phalange Party headquarters in Ashrafiya, East Beirut, killed Bashir Gemayel and twenty-six others, and wounded thirty-seven more. Voice of Lebanon Radio announced later (on 2 October) that the Lebanese Forces had arrested Habib Tanios Shartuni, aged 26, for committing the outrage. He was later identified as a secret member of the pro-Damascus, anti-Phalangist Syrian Social Nationalist Party, which was committed to aiding Assad in thwarting Israeli ambitions in the region. (A branch of Syrian intelligence was rumoured to have assisted Shartuni in placing the bomb, though the link could not be proved.) Shartuni and his sister and grandparents occupied the top floor of the building which accommodated the Phalange Party's headquarters. He had used a sophisticated long-range electronic detonator for the explosives, which had been supplied to him by an SSNP military commander, who subsequently disappeared.[7] The assassination of Bashir Gemayel pushed his Maronite and Israeli supporters into hysterical rage, and led them to vow revenge.

Disregarding the terms of the agreement Israel had signed, Sharon ordered IDF troops into West Beirut on 15 September. Within twenty-four hours they had taken full control of the city. Privately, the Israelis put it about that the PLO had murdered Bashir Gemayel. Publicly, to rationalize his move, Sharon alleged that the PLO chairman, Arafat, had left 2,000 undercover commandos behind in Sabra and Shatila camps. That day at 6 p.m. the head of the IDF Northern Command, Major-General Amir Drori, authorized the élite force of Elie Hobeika, the intelligence chief of Bashir Gemayel, to search the camps for the alleged undercover PLO fighters.

IDF officers had been privately taunting such LF commanders as Elie Hobeika, Joseph Eddees and Michel Zouins for not getting involved in confronting the PLO earlier. Suffering the additional anguish of having failed to protect their young, charismatic leader, Bashir Gemayel, the LF commanders took to massacring the Palestinian refugees with an unprecedented vengeance. The carnage continued for thirty-eight hours, until 8 a.m. on 18 September, while the IDF sealed off the camps and fired flares to illuminate them and aid the Maronite murderers inside. About 2,000 men, women and children were butchered. The US mediator, Philip Habib, had made the Palestinian refugees vulnerable by evacuating the commandos, and the Pentagon had then withdrawn its marines to let the Lebanese army under Maronite officers enter West Beirut. 'Sharon was a killer, obsessed by hatred of Palestinians', Philip Habib later told Patrick Seale, a British specialist on the Middle East. 'I had given Arafat an undertaking that his people would not be harmed, but this was totally disregarded by Sharon whose word was worth nothing.'[8]

The entry of LF militiamen into West Beirut, with full Israeli collusion, went hand in hand with their entry into the Shouf mountains, where they battled with the Druze fighters, and the south, where they started harassing the Lebanese Muslim population as well as the Palestinians in refugee camps.

Having announced his candidacy for president on 17 September, Amin Gemayel (b. 1942), the elder brother of Bashir, condemned the Sabra and Shatila massacres, and appealed for national unity. The butchering of the innocent in these camps brought most of the Lebanese politicians together around Amin Gemayel. Unlike Bashir, Amin Gemayel did not have connections with the CIA or Israel's Mossad. Also, unlike Bashir, Amin Gemayel had been a parliamentary deputy since 1970 and had proved a level-headed politician. Given this, and the fact that as a member of the Gemayel family and a Phalangist he provided continuity, he received the backing of Syria. Interestingly, Walid Jumblatt and Raymond Edde – two of the three important leaders who opposed him – did so from self-exile, the exception being Suleiman Franjieh, whose hostility towards the Gemayel family remained undiminished.

Little wonder that all but twelve of the surviving ninety-two parliamentary deputies assembled at Fayadiya barracks on 21 September; and that Amin Gemayel, who entered the auditorium along with Saeb Salam, secured seventy-seven votes, with only one deputy opposing. Two days later he assumed the high office at the age of 39.

President Amin Gemayel received much support in the international community and, more significantly, from Syria. At home he proved more popular in West Beirut, now free of the fighters of the PLO and the Lebanese National Movement, than in East Beirut. There, the bulk of the Lebanese Forces, who had been commanded by his brother, Bashir, failed to transfer their loyalty to him. They refused to disarm when he ordered them to. Later, feeling vulnerable in the wake of the Israelis' departure from Beirut, they shipped their weapons to rural Maronite monastries for safe-keeping.

While the assassination of Bashir Gemayel had the overall effect of unifying the Lebanese nation, albeit temporarily, it had a converse impact on Israel and its politics. It depressed Prime Minister Begin, and the subsequent Sabra and Shatila massacres severely stained the image of his government at home and abroad. On 25 September Israel witnessed the largest protest demonstration in its history, with 400,000 marchers demanding an official inquiry into the Sabra and Shatila massacres and the recall of IDF troops from Lebanon.

More and effective pressure on Israel came from the nations contributing troops to the Multi-National Force: America, Britain, France and Italy. Following the departure of the PLO fighters, they had withdrawn their forces from West Beirut, thus inadvertently creating an environment in which massacres could occur. They realized that Palestinian civilians needed protection, and were prepared to offer it – but only after the Israeli troops had departed. Thus pressured, Sharon pulled out his soldiers, along with 520 tons of weapons and other military material, from West Beirut by 29 September.

This marked the end of a particularly bloody chapter in the history of strife-torn Lebanon.

From October 1982 to February 1984

The withdrawal of the Israeli troops from West Beirut following the Sabra and Shatila massacres prepared the ground for a full-scale entry of the Lebanese army into the city. And the departure of the Palestinian and LNM fighters from West Beirut enabled the moderate, traditional Muslim figures, inclined towards compromise with the Maronites, to reassert leadership of the community.

Against this background, President Amin Gemayel prepared to re-establish the authority of the Lebanese army over the capital in stages. First, he distinguished between those Palestinians who had arrived in Lebanon before or during 1948 – the year Israel was founded – and those who had come after 1948, describing the latter as 'illegal, anti-government elements'. It was estimated that about half of the 500,000 Palestinians in Lebanon belonged to the 'illegal' category. Then, on 1 October 1982, after (nominally) reuniting the two divided sectors of the capital, President Gemayel ordered the Lebanese army to search western and southern parts of the city for the 'illegal' Palestinians. This led to the arrest of hundreds of them as well as the confiscation of arms caches worth $138 million.[9]

President Gemayel called on Prime Minister Shafiq Wazzan to form a new cabinet. On 7 October Wazzan assembled a government of ten ministers: two Maronites, two Sunnis, two Greek Orthodox, two Shias, one Greek-Catholic and one Druze. Significantly, none of the ministers or important presidential advisers was from the pro-Bashir Gemayel section of the Phalange Party or the Lebanese Forces. A month later the parliament approved the government by fifty-eight votes to one, and provided it with emergency powers for six months to govern by decree. One of its first decisions was to put into effect conscription, which should have been enforced on 1 July 1981.

Thus strengthened, Amin Gemayel flew to Washington in mid-November 1982. President Reagan pledged economic aid for Lebanon's reconstruction and backing for its campaign to secure the withdrawal of all foreign troops. From America, Amin Gemayel went to France and Italy. Though he tried to underline Lebanon's Arab credentials by visiting Saudi Arabia, and by congratulating President Assad on 15 November on the twelfth anniversary of his assumption of power, the overall pro-Washington bias of his government, with a pro-US politician, Elie Salim, running the foreign ministry, could not be masked.

Amin Gemayel was under American pressure to negotiate directly with Israel with a view to concluding a peace treaty. At home, Fadi Afram, the new chairman of the LF Command Council, reiterated the right-wing Maronite argument that the common destiny shared by Lebanon's Christians and Israel's Jews, both being minorities in hostile surroundings, called for peace between Lebanon and Israel through direct talks. But Amin Gemayel was unconvinced. Sensitive to the Arab hostility towards Israel, he refused to enter into bilateral negotiations with Israel, preferring to engage in tripartite talks with America as the mediator. Such negotiations started on 28 December 1982 under American chairmanship and were conducted alternately in Khalde, a Lebanese port, and Kiryat Shimona, a border town in north Israel. While willing to enter into security arrangements along the common frontier, the Lebanese delegation insisted on total Israeli withdrawal from their country. For their part, the Israelis wanted a peace treaty, with their defence minister, Ariel Sharon, demanding that Israel retain bases in south Lebanon and that the Lebanese government put the security of the south into the hands of Saad Haddad, a renegade Lebanese officer. Amin Gemayel rejected these demands, arguing that the position of Saad Haddad was a domestic affair for Lebanon, and that he would resist an imposed decision which was damaging to the morale and dignity of the Lebanese army.

At home, President Gemayel moved to consolidate his hold over the capital. He offered a plan to create Greater Beirut, consisting of the capital and its suburbs, stretching from the Dog river in the north to Khalde in the south, a distance of 20 kilometres. On 31 January 1983 Phalange leaders endorsed his Greater Beirut plan. Armed with this, he confronted the LF, and compelled it to allow the Lebanese army into East Beirut and its suburbs. In mid-February he ordered the deployment of 5,000 troops in Greater Beirut. On 7 March the Lebanese army completed its control over East Beirut by moving into the busiest dock of the port, thus ending its illegal use for smuggling, which had deprived the government of customs revenue. This was an important economic and political achievement.

Elsewhere in Lebanon, however, the anti-Gemayel elements, intent on countering the rising American–Israeli influence, began to flex their muscles. Pro-Iranian Shias emerged as an important force in this camp. They drew their inspiration and training from the 2,000 Iranian revolutionary guards that President Assad had allowed into Baalbek, in northern Beqaa, during the Israeli invasion of Lebanon.[10] In July 1982, accusing the Amal leadership of collaboration with Israel, Hussein Musavi, a member of the organization's Command Council, left Amal to set up the Islamic Amal Movement, a militant Islamist party which co-operated with the Iranian revolutionary guards based in Baalbek.

The Islamic Amal grew stronger in the wake of the Lebanese army's search operations in southern Beirut, which involved the destruction of the 'illegally built' houses of Shia migrants and led to clashes between the troops and the Shias. To get even, followers of the Islamic Amal, aided by the Iranian revolutionary guards, attacked the Lebanese army's Shaikh Abdullah barracks near Baalbek on 22 November, the national independence day, and occupied them. They soon became the nucleus of anti-Israeli and anti-American activities in Lebanon, stepping up guerrilla attacks on the IDF troops in south Lebanon, and pushing the total IDF fatalities since its June 1982 invasion past the 500 mark by March 1983. On 18 April a truck loaded with explosives rammed the US embassy in West Beirut, destroying much of the building and killing sixty-three people, including seventeen Americans. Seven of these were CIA officers, including the station chief. Convinced that the Iranians were the real culprits, the CIA suspected Syrian complicity.[11]

By now, having re-equipped its armed forces with advanced Soviet arms, Damascus had regained its military strength and self-confidence. Its refurbished armoury included SAM-5s, which the Soviet Union had not supplied to any country outside the Warsaw Pact. While Israel protested against the deployment of these missiles by Syria, the latter complained of the former's aggressive intentions to the UN Security Council. But the regional temperature did not rise. 'We have no intention of going to war against Syria over the new missiles or for any other reason', said General Raphael Eitan, the IDF chief of staff.[12] Eitan's comparative dovishness stemmed from the fact that – following the publication of a critical report on the Sabra and Shatila massacres by an Israeli commission headed by Yitzhak Kahan, president of the supreme court – his ultra-hawkish defence minister, Ariel Sharon, had been forced to resign in February 1983 and had been replaced by Moshe Arens, a Likud leader of centrist tendencies.

Behind all this, US efforts to lead Lebanon towards signing a peace treaty with Israel continued unabated, with the US secretary of state, Shultz, and his roving envoy, Habib, deliberately ignoring Syria. Against the background of shuttle diplomacy by Shultz, President Gemayel set out his terms in a radio broadcast on 22 April. While normalization of relations with Israel was 'out of the question', he said, security arrangements with it were 'unavoidable'. But he ruled out any IDF presence in Lebanon. By 4 May, Shultz had on hand a draft peace treaty between Lebanon and Israel.

On 7 May Shultz travelled to Damascus to secure Assad's endorsement. This was not forthcoming. Assad argued that he was opposed to the accord because, by letting Israel alter Lebanon's Arab character and impose its hegemony in the region, the USA was rewarding it for its aggression against Lebanon. He offered to pull back his forces from Lebanon after Israel had done so unconditionally. He demanded a full implementation of the UN Security Council Resolution 508 of 5 June 1982 (calling for the cessation of hostilities declared by the Security Council Resolution 490 of 1981) and Resolution 509 of 6 June 1982, demanding unconditional Israeli withdrawal to the international boundaries of Lebanon, which America had voted for.

The draft treaty between Lebanon and Israel formally ended the state of war between the two countries, and enjoined upon Lebanon to ban any demonstration of hostility towards Israel (ranging from verbal propaganda to commando actions) and the passage through its land territory or airspace of any troops, arms or equipment to or from any country not having diplomatic ties with Israel. Moreover, the document required Lebanon to abolish, within a year, any regulations, laws or treaties that were in conflict with the Lebanese–Israeli accord. These included all the commitments that Lebanon had made as a founder-member of the Arab League since 1945. Though full normalization of diplomatic links had to await total Israeli evacuation of Lebanon, Israel gained the immediate right of setting up a 'liaison office' in Lebanon. The treaty imposed limits on the Lebanese government's control over its southern region. Israel's surrogate force in the south, the militia commanded by Saad Haddad, was given the right to function as an independent force patrolling the area up to the Zahrani river. In addition, the accord stipulated the establishment of eight Lebanese–Israeli supervisory teams charged with detecting and destroying any armed guerrillas in the area. Between the Zahrani and Awali rivers, the Lebanese government could station no more than a brigade equipped with limited weaponry. Overall, Lebanon was forbidden either to probe Israel with its military radars or to station high-altitude surface-to-air missiles on its soil. Unsurprisingly, the treaty was hailed in Israel, with an eminent Israeli leader declaring that with this, the Jewish state had achieved 'its major goal of neutralizing Lebanon and putting it in the American sphere of influence'.[13]

On 16 May Lebanon's parliament met to discuss the accord. Of the seventy deputies present, sixty-four voted for it and two against (with the rest abstaining), confident that the peace treaty would bring about total Israeli withdrawal from their country.[14]

The next day Israel signed the treaty. At the same time it addressed a secret letter to the USA, which tied phased Israeli withdrawal from Lebanon to a similar exercise by Syria and the remainder of the PLO forces. There was jubilation in Israel, with Lebanon becoming its second Arab neighbour to sign a bilateral peace treaty with it just three years after Egypt had done so.

In contrast, there was anger and frustration in Damascus. It decried the accord for curtailing the sovereignty of Lebanon and transforming the country into a virtual Israeli protectorate. Coming after the Israeli annexation of its Golan Heights in January 1982, Syria found the idea of south Lebanon being transformed into an Israeli zone of influence intolerable. This did not surprise Washington. 'We know Syria won't willingly accept the terms of this accord', said Philip Habib. 'It must now accept them unwillingly.'[15] In the event, the contrary happened. Habib and the rest of the US administration had clearly underestimated the cunning and perseverance of Assad and the strength of the opposition to the treaty among large segments of Lebanese Muslims and certain sections of the Christian community.

Following their conclave in Zgharta from 13–16 May, Suleiman Franjieh, Rashid Karami, Walid Jumblatt, George Hawi (of the Lebanese Communist Party), Inaam Raad (of the SSNP) and Asim Qansu (of the Lebanese Baath Party) denounced the Lebanese–Israeli treaty. There was open opposition to the accord from the Shias in south Beirut. They demonstrated on 17 May, and faced firing from the Lebanese internal security forces, commanded by a Sunni: it resulted in several deaths.

In contrast, Prime Minister Wazzan backed the treaty. On 29 May President Gemayel addressed a rally of 20,000 Sunnis, all of them followers of the traditional Sunni leaders, where he praised the new treaty.

On 4 June the Lebanese government informed the Arab League that the Arab Deterrent Force in Lebanon, now manned only by Syrians, had ceased to exist, thus creating an environment in which Israel's withdrawal could occur along with Syria's. And to put pressure on Israel, President Gemayel refrained from signing the Lebanese–Israeli treaty after it had been ratified by parliament.

But in the following weeks, as the growing opposition to the accord consolidated itself, with the security forces again clashing violently with the protesting Shias on 9 July, President Gemayel found himself sandwiched between the alliance of his local adversaries with Syria on the one hand, and Israel on the other. On 18 July he flew to Washington only to find that the USA had singled out Assad as the culprit, thus adding its weight unequivocally to the Israeli side.

Encouraged by Syria, an enlarged meeting of all those opposed to the treaty with Israel gathered in Tripoli, and formed the National Salvation Front (NSF) on 23 July 1983. It was the first time since the Israeli invasion of a year before, that the constituents of the Lebanese National Movement had met under a single banner and adopted a common programme. Describing President Gemayel's administration as an instrument of the 'Phalangist hegemony', the NSF charter pledged to overturn this hegemony, destroy the Lebanese–Israeli treaty, confront the Israeli occupiers, and reconstruct a 'new Lebanon'.[16]

Though not a member of the NSF, Amal, now led by Nabih Berri, was strongly opposed to the accord. A failed attempt by Maronite extremists to assassinate Berri on 9 August, resulting in the death of one of the attackers, reinforced Amal's stance on the treaty. The incident also highlighted the historic friction between the Maronites and Shias, with the Maronites allying with the Sunnis to rule Lebanon, thus marginalizing the Shias.

The rising domestic opposition undermined the position of President Gemayel. This encouraged Assad to harden his stance. Only if Israel and the Multi-National Force withdrew from Lebanon unconditionally, and the country was ruled by a government of national unity, would he consider pulling out Syrian troops from Lebanon, he said. He remained bitterly opposed to the Lebanese–Israeli pact, which he attributed to the USA. 'America masterminded this agreement', he told the *Los Angeles Times* on 14 August 1983. 'America has to abrogate it.'

As for Israel, having failed to obtain President Gemayel's ratification of the peace treaty, it decided to stop protecting his regime. Instead, it strengthened its ties with the Lebanese Forces. Moshe Arens, the Israeli defence minister, held meetings with LF leaders during his visit to East Beirut on 16 August. Thus emboldened, the LF Command Council opened ostentatious new barracks in East Beirut.

The Israeli decision did not lead to any softening in the stance of Amin Gemayel's domestic opponents. If anything, the leading figures of the opposition – Nabih Berri, Walid Jumblatt, Rashid Karami and Suleiman Franjieh – came to view him increasingly as a Phalangist president intent on protecting the interests of his party and family,[17] and totally disinterested in effecting the political reform which should have been introduced after the Israeli invasion, if not before. The overbearing tone and behaviour of the Maronite camp – well encapsulated by Pierre Gemayel's statement on 11 August, 'Let the war come, and let the strongest win'[18] – hardened attitudes on the other side, and paved the way for a revival of the civil war during the next few weeks.

In late August, following the visit of a Shia delegation to Damascus, Amal challenged the Amin Gemayel government. The president ordered 3,000 troops to re-establish control in West Beirut and its

Shia suburbs in the south. The fighting lasted from 28 August to 1 September, with forty soldiers and many more Amal militiamen losing their lives. Though the army re-established control of West Beirut, it failed to reach the Amal headquarters in the Burj al Barajina area. Overall, the five-day battle heralded the arrival of Shias into the mainstream of Lebanese politics.

The Shia uprising in West Beirut coincided with an upheaval in the Druze-inhabited Shouf mountains, which control access to Beirut and its suburbs from the hinterland. Following their arrival into the Shouf on the coat-tails of the Israelis in June 1982, the LF units tried to repatriate those Maronite residents of the area who had fled in the wake of the Druze offensive against them after Kamal Jumblatt's assassination in March 1977. The Druze militia, angered by the LF's overbearing behaviour towards the Druzes, resisted the move. While LF overconfidence stemmed from the presence of the IDF units in the area, the IDF itself adopted an ambivalent stance. Unlike Israeli Arabs, Israeli Druzes were represented in the IDF, and many were posted in Lebanon; and they disapproved of the LF's heavy-handedness towards their fellow Druzes. So, when fighting erupted between the LF and the Druze militia in November 1982, mainly in the Aley area,[19] the IDF stayed neutral. By the time it enforced a ceasefire on 6 February 1983, 130 people had been killed in the fighting, a majority of them Maronite.

Three months later tension rose sharply as Lebanon got ready to sign a peace accord with Israel, and President Gemayel prepared to send Lebanese army units, freshly armed and trained by the USA, [20] into the Shouf. The Druze militia shelled Beirut. In a meeting with President Gemayel on 11 May, the Druze leaders – Walid Jumblatt, Majid Arsalan and Shaikh Muhammad Abi Shaqra – warned that their militia would not allow the Lebanese army into the Shouf without a prior political agreement paving the way for a more representative administration. Such an accord was not on the president's agenda. Therefore the situation in the Shouf worsened, with Syria arming the Druzes and the Israelis arming the LF. The total toll of the battles by the time of a ceasefire on 17 May had risen to 159 dead and 307 missing. Talks ensued between Jumblatt's emissaries and Amin Gemayel on political reform and abrogation of the peace treaty with Israel. These reached a deadlock in late August, and the truce broke down. Violence escalated, with the Druze militia firing 3,000 shells on East Beirut and the areas to its north.

In Israel, after announcing his resignation as prime minister on 29

August, Menachem Begin shut himself up in his apartment in West Jerusalem. The move came as no surprise. Following the death of his wife, Aliza, on 14 November 1982, he had become depressive; and continuing deaths of Israeli servicemen at the hands of Lebanese Muslim guerrillas further undermined his morale. The prime ministership passed to Yitzhak Shamir, another hardline leader of the Likud bloc; and there was little change in Israel's policy towards Lebanon.

Disappointed at Amin Gemayel's failure to sign the peace treaty, and tiring of its total dependence on the Maronites, Israel withdrew its troops from the Shouf to the Awali river on the night of 3 September, without advance warning to the Beirut government. This set the scene for a major confrontation between the Druze militia and the LF. On one side were 4,000 Druze fighters, backed by about 2,000 Palestinians and the Syrian armour and artillery; and on the other were the LF units led by Samir Geagea, and a section of the Lebanese army.[21]

The combat occurred on three fronts: at Bhamdoun along the Beirut–Damascus highway, a gateway for the Shouf, between the Druze militia and the LF; at Souq al Gharb, the gate to Beirut from the east, between the Druze forces and the Lebanese army; and at Khalde, the gate to the capital from the south, between the Druze fighters and the Lebanese army. By battling as a cohesive community rooted in a small mountainous area, the Druzes performed well and prevailed over their adversaries in a conflict which was marked by mutual massacres of Christians and Druzes and the displacement of tens of thousands on both sides of the religious divide.

Along the Bhamdoun front, the Druzes claimed the capture of the town on 6 September, with some 100,000 Christians stampeding towards Beirut and about 40,000 Christians and 2,000 LF militiamen finding themselves besieged in the Christian town of Deir al Qamar. In their onslaught the Druzes killed 1,500 Christians and razed sixty-two Christian villages. Among the Christian settlements looted and burned was Beit al Din, situated across the narrow ravine from Deir al Qamar, scene of the notorious 1860 massacre.[22]

As the Druzes tightened their siege of Deir al Qamar, and threatened Beirut, President Gemayel ordered the Lebanese army into the battle. The army had by now turned communal, with General Nadim Hakim, the Druze chief of staff, absconding in the Shouf, and sixteen Druze officers and 900 troops declaring themselves conscientious objectors. The Lebanese army managed to stop the advance of the Druze militia at Souq al Gharb on 16 September. The air force used all of its eight ageing warplanes. The Druze militia shot down two, and shelled the airport from where they had taken off. By the next day they had encircled Souq al Gharb. The hard-pressed Gemayel administration appealed for help to the Multi-National Force – consisting of 1,200 US marines and 2,000 French Foreign Legion troops deployed in West Beirut, and another 2,100 Italians and 1,500 British soldiers in West Beirut's southern suburbs, measuring about 28 square kilometres and housing between 600,000 and 700,000 poor Shias.

President Reagan declared that Souq al Gharb was of strategic significance to the United States, and turned it into a test of American resolve to support the Gemayel government. The Pentagon sent its officers to Souq al Gharb to direct the defences of the Lebanese army. On 17 September and again on 19 September warplanes from the US Sixth Fleet, deployed in the eastern Mediterranean, hit Druze and Palestinian artillery emplacements in the Shouf. Thus bolstered, on 19 September the Lebanese army defeated a Druze militia unit that had managed to infiltrate Souq al Gharb. On 21 September the battleship *New Jersey*, the cruiser *Virginia* and the destroyer *John Rogers* fired 600 rounds of 70 lb shells at the Druze villages in the Shouf. French aircraft followed the shelling in an aerial mop-up operation, thus enabling the Lebanese army to hang on to Souq al Gharb as well as Khalde. While Washington achieved its immediate military objective of saving the Lebanese army from defeat, it paid a heavy political price. It demonstrated to the Lebanese Muslims that it had intervened in Lebanon as the guardian of the Lebanese Christians – just as the French had done in 1860.

On 21 September the religious leaders of the Sunni, Shia and Druze communities issued a ten-point charter which coupled its demand for an end to political sectarianism with administrative decentralization. The charter was a public adjunct to their private efforts to bring about peace.

Washington, working in conjunction with Riyadh, was also busily trying to bring about cessation of hostilities. By now it had dawned on US policy-makers that by corralling Lebanon into an unequal treaty with Israel, they had exposed its government to a grave danger, and that the Israeli pull-back to the Awali river had burdened them with the tricky task of protecting the Gemayel administration. On 23 September an American envoy visited Damascus to meet Assad, ostensibly to obtain his approval for a truce. Assad gave it, but only after securing an undertaking from the USA that, following the ceasefire, a national reconciliation conference would be convened on the basis of the charter issued by the Muslim religious leaders.

The next day the Druze militia, backed by the Syrian artillery, succeeded in linking up with the Amal fighters in the southern suburbs of Beirut. By so doing they demonstrated that the allies of Syria were militarily more powerful then those of Israel.

The ceasefire came into effect on 25 September after Jumblatt and his allies abandoned their demand for an immediate change of government and President Gemayel gave up his plan to deploy the Lebanese army in the Shouf. A National Reconciliation Committee was formed under the chairmanship of the president. Seven of its ten members were old, traditional sectarian figures – Camille Chamoun, Pierre Gemayel, Suleiman Franjieh, Raymond Edde (who was in self-exile in Paris and refused to participate), Rashid Karami, Saeb Salam and Adil Osserian, a Shia – the rest being younger leaders: Amin Gemayel, Nabih Berri and Walid Jumblatt. Its main task was to organize a reconciliation conference composed of the leaders of all sects.

The lull in the fighting did not lead to the Druzes and Shias forgetting the US and French military intervention that President Gemayel had invited. The intense American and French shelling and bombing of Souq al Gharb had left a deep mark on the collective pysche of these Muslim communities. The image of embattled Muslims encountering the might of a powerful enemy was especially potent for Shias, who viewed their own history as a series of imbalanced contests. Such indeed was the story of their revered Imam Hussein, whose death in an unequal battle in Karbala, Iraq, in AD 681 was the occasion for an annual demonstration of grief, called Ashura. When some 150,000 Shias assembled for Ashura in the south Lebanese town of Nabatiya on 16 October 1983, they clashed with their Israeli occupiers. IDF troops fired on the mourners, and killed several. In return the Shias escalated their guerrilla activity against the IDF. The result was forty more Israeli soldiers dead in the south during the next couple of months.

But the Israelis were not the only non-Arab occupiers of Lebanon killing and maiming the Lebanese. The Americans and the French too had joined the league. 'If America kills my people', said Hussein Musavi, leader of the Islamic Amal Movement, 'then my people must kill Americans.'[23]

This happened on 23 October 1983. Early that morning a truck carrying 2,000 pounds of explosives rammed into the four-storey quarters of the American marines at Beirut international airport, and demolished it, killing 241 troops. This was the single largest death toll inflicted on the US military since the Vietnam War. Some minutes later the French paratroopers quartered in the seafront district of Bir Hassan suffered a similar fate, with fifty-nine soldiers dead. On 11 November the IDF headquarters in an eight-storey building in Tyre were truck-bombed. Sixty people, half of them Israeli, were killed. The suicide bombers were members of the Islamic Jihad Organization allied with the Islamic Amal Movement. They carried out their mission in the name of protecting Islam and Muslims, and were inspired by the verse in the Quran: 'Count not those who are slain in God's way as dead, but rather living with their Lord, by Him provided, rejoicing in the bounty that God has given them'.[24] Their actions had the expected effect of creating public pressure in the USA, Western Europe and Israel to recall Western and Israeli forces from Lebanon. But Western leaders held firm. 'Stability in Lebanon is central to [US] credibility on a global scale', declared President Reagan. 'By attempting to bomb the Multi-National Force out of Lebanon, the extremists . . . have in a perverse way confirmed the success of the force in helping to stabilize the country', said British prime minister Margaret Thatcher.[25]

It was against the background of truck bombings that the National Reconciliation Committee (NRC) convened a conference in Geneva on 31 October. By publicly embracing Camille Chamoun and Amin Gemayel, Suleiman Franjieh was supposed to have ended his feuds with them. The gathering ended on 8 November with a communiqué which declared Lebanon to be 'an Arab country, a founder-member of the Arab League [which] is bound by all the obligations of that membership'. It stated that the 17 May 1983 accord with Israel should be neither ratified nor abrogated, and called on President Gemayel to devise 'a replacement document which would lead to the withdrawal of Israeli troops'.[26] While the Syrian delegation, led by foreign minister Abdul Halim Khaddam, played an active role behind the scenes, it noted that David Kimche, the official Israeli specialist on Lebanon, was also in Geneva to pull strings, and that the Lebanese Forces, Israel's ally, rejected the conference resolutions.

On his return to Beirut, President Gemayel began working on devising an alternative to the 17 May 1983 Lebanese accord with Israel. With this in view, he arranged to meet Assad in Damascus on

14 November. However, Assad suffered a heart attack on 12 November, and had to cancel the talks.

An important meeting that did take place in mid-November was that between Shamir, the Israeli prime minister, and President Reagan. The latter agreed to increase US military aid to Israel, and assured Shamir that there would be no tinkering with the text of the Israeli–Lebanese accord.

When President Gemayel visited Washington in early December, Reagan and his secretary of state, Shultz, told him that the 17 May 1983 treaty would not be modified. This undercut Gemayel's position at home, and spiked his attempts to establish a government of national unity. Jumblatt and Berri began demanding his resignation. This raised tension between the Christian-dominated Lebanese army and the Druze and Shia militias. When it erupted into armed conflict, the USA again intervened against the Muslim forces with warplanes and warships. On 4 December the Muslim militias succeeded in shooting down two American warplanes; and attacks on US marines at the Beirut airport resulted in eight American deaths. The Pentagon retaliated by shelling Druze targets in the Shouf mountains from the battleship *New Jersey*. This proved ineffective. But the battle between the joint forces of the Druze and Shia militias and their adversaries, the Lebanese army and the LF, intensified – with the latter bombarding the Shia suburbs of Beirut and killing 300.

The opposition reiterated its demands for Amin Gemayel's resignation and an end to political sectarianism, as well as to the presence of Western forces on Lebanese soil. Gemayel decided to get tough and use the army units recently expelled from the poorer districts of East Beirut (by the Lebanese Forces) and south Lebanon (by the Israeli-backed militia of Saad Haddad) to suppress opposition. The result was an escalation of conflict between the Druze militia and the Lebanese army in the Shouf, and Amal and the army in West Beirut and it southern suburbs.

On 3 February 1984 hostilities erupted between the Lebanese army and the anti-Amin Gemayel forces consisting of various Muslim militias and groups, including the Druze militia, Amal and Hizbollah (literally, Party of Allah), a militant Islamist force that had allied with the Islamic Amal Movement and Islamic Jihad Organization at the behest of Ali Akbar Mohtashemi, Iran's ambassador to Syria in 1982–3 and later its interior minister at home. President Gemayel ordered the units of the Lebanese army and the LF to take control of the southern suburbs of West Beirut. Their fierce offensive destroyed whole districts, left more than 600 dead, deprived about 400,000 inhabitants of water, electricity and food for several days, and caused the exodus of a quarter of a million of them.

Washington intervened on the side of Amin Gemayel. Its warships shelled Druze and Syrian positions in the Shouf, and its marines exchanged artillery fire with the Muslim militias. The American position was criticized by *inter alia* Sandro Pertini, the president of Italy, which had contributed troops to the Multi-National Force. 'If the US had the political will to force the Israelis to withdraw in accordance with UN Resolutions 508 and 509, there would be no need for [US] marines', he said on 6 February.[27] But Washington's intervention proved insufficient to stop the Amal leader, Nabih Berri, from issuing an appeal on 4 February to his fellow Muslims in the army to defy the combat orders.

The large-scale defections that followed caused a virtual collapse of the 33,000-strong army, 40 per cent Muslim, organized in eleven brigades. The overwhelmingly Druze 4th Brigade in Aley disintegrated, allowing the Druze militia to advance to the port of Damour. The desertion of most Muslim troops from the 6th Brigade posted in West Beirut improved the chances of the Druze–Amal alliance to capture the city. On 5 February the Christian section of the army intensely bombarded the southern suburbs, parts of West Beirut, and the Shouf mountains, thus softening its adversaries. But its battle with Amal for the control of the strategic corridor linking the southern suburbs with the Syrian-controlled countryside went badly. The army's failure brought about the downfall of the Shafiq Wazzan government. On 6 February, aided by the Druze militia, Amal expelled the Lebanese army from West Beirut, and re-established the Green Line which separated it from East Beirut.

On 7 February President Reagan suddenly announced that US marines in Lebanon were being immediately 'redeployed' to the American warships in the eastern Mediterranean. Within days the Western partners of America in the Multi-National Force – France, Britain and Italy – followed Washington's lead, and departed unceremoniously. A week later the Druze and Amal militias joined up at Khalde, thus securing control of all access roads between Beirut and the south, and the supply road connecting the Shouf with the southern suburbs and West Beirut, and confining the Lebanese army to the Souq al Gharb enclave. On 17 February the Muslim militias shelled the presidential palace in Baabda. It was effective. 'If I have to choose between the [17 May] agreement and national unity, for sure I shall choose national unity', declared President Gemayel.[28] By 25 February the Druzes had expelled the Lebanese army from Souq al Gharb, thus establishing control over the whole region. This, and the hasty departure of his Western protectors, left Amin Gemayel no option but to conciliate the opposition at home and Syria abroad.

He visited Damascus on 29 February to felicitate President Assad on his complete recovery from the severe heart attack he had suffered in mid-November. He also declared himself 'ready' to annul the Lebanese–Israeli treaty. Five days later the Lebanese cabinet decided to abrogate the treaty and 'all the effects' that 'could have resulted from it'.[29] Predictably, the LF Command Council condemned the abrogation; so did the Guardians of the Cedar and the Christian Leagues' Union. However, Pierre Gemayel refrained from doing so, content to describe the accord as 'still-born'.

The abrogation of the Lebanese–Israeli treaty was an outstanding triumph for Assad. He had other reasons to be pleased. His troops controlled north Lebanon as well as the Beqaa valley in eastern Lebanon; the Druze militia had expelled the Lebanese army and the Maronite forces from the Shouf, and shared the control of West Beirut with Amal; and the Shias in the south were making life increasingly unbearable for the Israeli occupiers.

The ignominious retreat by the US marines as well as other Western forces, followed by the collapse of the Lebanese–Israeli accord, underlined certain basic geopolitical and historical facts about Lebanon which had been ignored first by Maronite Christians, then by France as the mandate power, and latterly by Israel and America. Lebanon is an Arab country in more ways than one, with Syria as its most significant neighbour; and the woes of Lebanon can be dissipated only within the larger framework of the Arab world. The Israeli plan to turn Lebanon into a client state governed by the Phalange Party only made matters worse. Ignoring Syria was a futile and dangerous policy, as Washington was made to realize by Assad.

A member of the Alawi sub-sect (within Shiaism), Assad watched approvingly the growing politicization and radicalization of Lebanese Shias, who had grown from a quarter of a million in 1956 to a million in 1981, forming nearly a third of the national Lebanese populataion, without securing any commensurate gain in the government or any other public institution. Politically, Assad felt at ease with Nabih Berri, a constitutional lawyer, who led Amal, the most powerful Shia organization. Yet, conscious of his alliance with Iran in the latter's war with Iraq, Assad allowed the Iranian revolutionary guards to function actively in Baalbek in the Syrian-occupied Beqaa valley, and to provide inspiration and training to the militant Shia groups which came to be classified under the generic label of Hizbollah: the Islamic Jihad Organization, the Revolutionary Justice Organization, Holy Strugglers for Justice, etc.

By early 1984 the Hizbollah, guided by Shaikh Muhammad Hussein Fadlallah, had emerged as an independent force, especially in West Beirut and the south, where it had filled the political-military vacuum created by the expulsion of the PLO by the Israelis. Fadlallah argued that, by offering active resistance to Israel, the Lebanese Muslims, particularly the Shias among them, would be able to overcome their traditional sense of inferiority. The IDF's actions since its invasion of June 1982 provided enough fuel to turn Shias into an active anti-Israeli force. By allowing Saad Haddad's Christian militia to move up to the Awali river, and the Phalangists to sweep down to the Sidon area, Israel alienated the Shias in the south. And by staging extensive air raids and closing the bridge over the Awali connecting the south with Beirut, in retribution for the truck-bombing of the IDF headquarters in November 1983, Israel damaged the local economy and fuelled anti-Israeli feeling among the Shias. Soon the Shias in the south were in the forefront of the Lebanese resistance against the Israeli occupiers.

The rise of the Shia factor in Lebanon's politics coincided with the declining influence of the Sunnis, who had so far been the dominant sect in the Muslim community, sharing power and prestige with Maronite Christians. Due to the migration of hundreds of thousands of Shias during the 1970s from the south into West Beirut, the traditional base of influential Sunni families, the southern suburbs of West Beirut became a counterpoint to the Sunni centre of power. The concentration of Shias, whether in West Beirut or south Lebanon, contrasted with the scattered distribution of Sunnis – in West Beirut, Sidon, Tripoli and a few towns in the Beqaa. Second, unlike the Shias, the Sunnis had failed to create a powerful fighting force. The only Sunni militia in West Beirut, the Murabitoun, the military arm of the Independent Nasserite Movement, never attracted more than 3,000 recruits. Due to its close ties with the PLO, it was expelled from Beirut along with the PLO by the Israelis. (Its attempt to return to West Beirut in late February 1984 was frustrated by the Druze and Amal militias.) Third, the expulsion of the predominantly Sunni PLO damaged Sunni interests. Fourth, the failure of Saeb Salam, a traditional, pro-Riyadh Sunni leader, to mobilize Muslims behind President Amin Gemayel highlighted the virtual collapse of Sunni power. Finally, as a group, Sunnis did not wield much influence in Damascus, governed by an Alawi president.

Having frustrated the Israeli plan to sign a peace accord with Lebanon, and having witnessed the unceremonious departure of the Western-manned Multi-National Force from Beirut, Assad was on his way to re-establishing Syrian dominance in Lebanon.

6

Return of Syrian hegemony

March 1984 — January 1986

Once President Assad had regained Syrian dominance in Lebanon, he accelerated the process of national reconciliation. The result was a week-long Second National Reconciliation Conference in Lausanne from 12 March 1984, under the guidance of Abdul Halim Khaddam, recently promoted to the vice-presidency of Syria. The participants presented twenty-three position papers and seven manifestos.

The joint paper by Pierre Gemayel and Camille Chamoun proposed developing Lebanon's institutions towards a federal system composed of several cantons. Suleiman Franjieh's proposals included a strong policy to end Israel's occupation of south Lebanon, and new electoral and citizenship laws. Rashid Karami opposed the proposal for a federal structure. Nabih Berri demanded an end to political sectarianism, the establishment of a senate as the upper house of parliament, and a change in the electoral law to have the president elected by 55 per cent majority vote in parliament for a three-year term, renewable once. In his position paper, speaking on behalf of all Muslim groups, Walid Jumblatt endorsed Berri's proposals and went on to combine his call for political parity between Muslims and Christians with the demand for reforms in administrative, military, economic, cultural and judicial fields. President Amin Gemayel focused on a strict observance of the truce between the warring factions, and the forming of a national unity government as a prelude to securing Lebanon's unity and liberation.

Following the rejection of Jumblatt's paper by all Christian leaders, including Franjieh and Amin Gemayel, Khaddam mediated between those supporting and opposing the Lebanese president. As a result, President Gemayel offered a nine-point plan, including an end to confessionalism in the civil service except at the highest level, parity between Muslims and Christians in parliament, some curtailing of presidential authority, and various economic, social and educational reforms. It got nowhere, primarily because Suleiman Franjieh, intent on maintaining the traditional Maronite dominance as encapsulated in presidential powers, rejected it. In the end Khaddam spoke vaguely in favour of reform, and urged the formation of a national unity government. Since President Gemayel, having lost the active backing of Israel and the West, had now turned to Syria for support, Assad decided to stabilize his administration. Accordingly, the conference confirmed the truce and appointed a Constituent Committee of thirty-two members (later expanded to forty) to draft a new constitution within six months.

Taking its cue from the Lausanne conference, the political-military committee of the various Lebanese factions declared a total ceasefire on 9 April 1984, after nine years of intermittent fighting.

President Gemayel travelled to Damascus to meet Assad. There, reversing his previous position, he joined his Syrian counterpart in describing Walid Jumblatt's paper at Lausanne as a foundation for the new constitution. Once the Gemayel–Assad statement was accepted by Lebanon's leading politicians, the ground was laid for the formation of a national unity government, a task assigned to Rashid Karami.

On 30 April Karami announced his council of ministers but without first consulting its members. Whereas Pierre Gemayel, Camille Chamoun, Salim Hoss and Adil Osserian (a traditional Shia leader given the defence ministry) accepted, Nabih Berri and Walid Jumblatt refused to do so unless they were also appointed to the Higher Defence Council, with Berri also declining the justice portfolio he was offered. Later he accepted the ministry of South Lebanon and Reconstruction. But it was not until mid-June that the parliament assembled and approved the cabinet.

In late June 1984, a national concord reached at Bikfaya, the home-base of the Gemayel family, included reforming the military, an overall security plan for the capital, and a speedy implementation of the constitutional amendments proposed at the First National Reconciliation Conference in November 1983. The Lebanese Forces Command Council, which on the eve of the Second National Reconciliation Conference had established control over East Beirut as well as the Christian hinterland and set up a liaison mission in Jerusalem, rejected the Bikfaya agreement. But yielding to pressure from the Gemayel family, it later reversed its decision and on 25 July let the Lebanese government shut down the Israeli liaison mission set up at Dubaya, just north of the capital, in the aftermath of the IDF invasion.

In West Beirut, the streets were cleared of militiamen by early July, with the Lebanese army bulldozing the barricades along the Green Line, and the international airport reopening after a gap of five months. However, the Druze militia commanders succeeded in blocking the army's entry into the Shouf by insisting on stiff conditions. And in Tripoli, fighting broke out between pro- and anti-Syrian factions.

Even peace in Beirut proved brittle, chiefly because President Gemayel and his followers were basically at odds with the Muslim militias. The Gemayel camp wanted to consolidate and extend security to all parts of Lebanon, thus depriving its Muslim rivals of a military option, before proceeding with political reform, whereas the Shia and Druze leaders wanted to press ahead with immediate reform while their militias enjoyed military superiority. Thus a vicious circle was created, with security dependent on political reform, which could not be realized as security deteriorated. The circle could only be broken by an outside agency – more specifically, Syria.

By the end of July, West Beirut began witnessing sporadic fighting between the Druze, Shia and Sunni militias. Soon artillery exchanges between the Druze militia and the Maronite Lebanese Forces revived in the Shouf. Security in West Beirut deteriorated, with Shia militiamen burning down the Saudi consulate on 24 August in protest at Riyadh's alleged failure to grant visas for the hajj pilgrimage to Mecca, and Salim Hoss, a senior Sunni minister, narrowly escaping an assassination attempt in early September. The death of Pierre Gemayel, a 79-year-old patriarch, on 29 August 1984 left his son, Amin, weakened, even though the president seemingly improved his position in the immediate aftermath of the event. Amin Gemayel purged the Phalange Party of the unruly members who had joined in the course of the civil strife. But when, on 6 September, he called on the Lebanese Forces to remove the road blocks on the Beirut–Tripoli coastal highway, Samir Geagea, the LF Command Council member who controlled them, refused. This defiance was to prove the first step into the bloody internecine fighting that was to develop following the election in mid-October of Fuad Abu Nadr, a loyalist nephew of Amin Gemayel, as the chairman of the LF Command Council, to replace Fadi Afram, who had opposed Amin Gemayel.

As for the present, President Assad intervened to stablilize the situation in West Beirut, and succeeded in arranging a ceasefire. On 12 September the Lebanese government decided to conduct a series of conclaves to settle outstanding political issues. This activated the moribund Constituent Committee, formed in the wake of the Second National Reconciliation Conference and charged with drafting a new constitution to distribute power more fairly among the various sects. A fortnight later, on 26 September, the Committee recommended raising the size of the parliament from 99 to 112, divided equally between Muslims and Christians, thus reducing the 6:5 Christian majority to parity with Muslims. Since the Committee lacked the authority to implement its decisions, its recommendation got nowhere.

In contrast, President Gemayel had the active command of the military. He used it to give the army a greater say in controlling the coastal road connecting the capital with the south, part of which was occupied by the Druze militia. Jumblatt, the Druze commander, insisted that his surrender of the road or the entry of the army into the Shouf had to be part of an overall political settlement which he judged satisfactory. Later, however, he gave in to pressure from Assad – who met Amin Gemayel in Damascus on 27 December – and softened his position. Following the Assad–Gemayel talks, the Lebanese army undertook a two-stage operation to take full control of the coastal highway.

Meanwhile, Muslim Lebanese resistance against the USA and Israel stiffened. On 20 September, following the American veto of a UN Security Council resolution condemning Israel's policy in south Lebanon, a car-bomb exploded inside the US embassy compound in East Beirut, killing eight people. The Islamic Jihad Organization claimed responsibility. In the south, several political and religious bodies in Sidon decided to form the National Resistance Front. They had to take into account the fact that they had no backing from the Christians who occupied the eastern part of Sidon, which linked up with Jezzine, 20 km to the east, through a chain of Christian villages.[1]

In late October there were reports of various PLO constituents rebuilding their military strength in West Beirut. While the small Sunni militia, Murabitoun, welcomed this, Amal opposed it, afraid that it would lose the primacy it had gained in the wake of the PLO's expulsion two years earlier.

In the south, Amal and other Shia organizations had escalated their violent harassment of the Israeli occupiers. The political situation in Israel had changed in mid-September 1984 following the general election, which led to the formation of a national unity government headed by the Labour leader Shimon Peres. Aware of the growing unpopularity of Israel's occupation of Lebanon due to the rising casualties inflicted by the Lebanese resistance, the joint programme adopted by both Labour and Likud, enjoying almost equal support in parliament, included Israel's evacuation of Lebanon. In January the government decided to withdraw its troops to the international frontier in three phases: from Sidon on 16 February, from Tyre and south-eastern Lebanon in late April, and from the rest of the area in early June. This was to be done in conjunction with the Israeli-backed Lebanese Christian militia, now named the South Lebanon Army (SLA). Following the death of Saad Haddad in January 1984, Israel had appointed Antoine Lahad, a retired major of the Lebanese army, as the commander of the SLA, and enlarged it to 2,500 troops and re-equipped them.

Once Israel had carried out the first phase of its evacuation on 16 February, its remaining soldiers came under increasing attacks by the Shias. A Shia suicide car hit an Israeli troop carrier on 10 March, and killed a dozen troops. The IDF retaliated by attacking the Shia village of Zarriya, killing thirty-five civilians, injuring many more, and taking a large number of male prisoners. The IDF's iron-fist policy stoked further Shia hatred and resolve. The level of Israeli–Shia violence declined only towards the end of April, after the IDF had withdrawn from Tyre as well as from their strategic positions in south-eastern Lebanon facing the Syrians.

By then the conflict between President Gemayel and Samir Geagea had escalated in the wake of Gemayel taking control of the LF's financial management through the leadership of the Phalange Party. Samir Geagea, an important member of the LF Command Council, responded in early February 1985 by declaring the LF independent of the Phalange Party in the fields of security, policing, finance and information, thus depriving the party of much of its influence. This came at a time when, eager to support Amin Gemayel's efforts at *rapprochement* with Syria, the Phalange had consented to handing over to the legitimate government various public departments it had usurped and run in the Christian enclave for the past several years. Gemayel could not afford to let Geagea's action go unchallenged. He expelled Geagea from the Phalange Party on 11 March on the ground that he held extremist views. The next day Geagea met Fuad Abu Nadr, the chairman of the LF Command Council, and demanded that the LF be declared independent of the Phalange Party. Abu

Nadr hesitated. Overnight, Geagea assumed control of the entire militia by nominating four of his loyalist supporters and five members of the National Liberal Party to the LF Command Council of ten. The units loyal to Geagea took control of most of the areas inside the Christian enclave. There was no resistance from the anti-Geagea forces.

Tension between the mainly lower-middle-class ranks of the LF and the upper-class leadership of the Phalange Party was as old as the militia itself. Bashir Gemayel, a charismatic figure, and then his father, Pierre, an authoritarian patriarch, had managed to contain it. With both of them gone, the long-simmering tension boiled over and resulted in a formal split, with the vast majority of the ranks going with Geagea, a commander with whom they shared a similar social background. Allied to this phenomenon was the fact that the Syrian intelligence chief in Lebanon, General Ghazi Kanaan, controlling 500 operators, had through elaborate cloak-and-dagger effort engendered a lobby within the LF which advocated the militia acquiring an identity, military and political, apart from the Phalange Party.[2]

To consolidate his newly acquired position, Geagea provoked fighting between his units deployed in the Christian villages east of Sidon and the Muslim militia in Sidon, reckoning that he would draw the support of the Lebanese army and/or the IDF, and defeat his foes. Nothing of the sort happened. Instead, the Shia and Druze militias began approaching Sidon from the Shouf and West Beirut to help the local Muslim militia. Thus pressured, Geagea signed a truce. This led to the migration of the Christian villagers to the north, and lowered his prestige in the community.

On 9 May 1985 the LF Command Council assembled to elect the chairman. The candidates were: Elie Hobeika, aged 29, chief of intelligence and security since 1980; the incumbent chairman, Samir Geagea; and Fadi Afram. Hobeika reportedly produced evidence to show that behind his anti-Damascus rhetoric Geagea proposed to yield to Syrian pressures. But after he had won the chairmanship, Hobeika appointed Geagea as his chief of staff. Hobeika's rise to the top had been meteoric. When the civil war erupted a decade ago, he belonged to the élite BJ (Bashir Jemayal) unit in the Lebanese Forces. Five years later, as the chief of intelligence and security, Hobeika was put in charge of Bashir Gemayel's personal safety – a job which, according to the moderate Christian leader Raymond Edde, led him to forge ties with the CIA and Mossad.[3] Following Bashir Gemayel's assassination on 14 September 1982, Hobeika led the LF units which massacred the Palestinians in Sabra and Shatila camps. As a member of the lower middle class, Hobeika lacked social standing in a community which valued good breeding and revered its traditional upper-class leaders. However, the turbulence of the civil war and its aftermath, especially after the June 1982 Israeli invasion, had given impetus to social mobility as well as to the rise of leadership based more on merit than social class. Yet it was not all smooth sailing for such militant Maronites as Hobeika and Geagea.

To consolidate his chairmanship of the LF Command Council, Hobeika attempted to isolate Amin Gemayel loyalists in north Metn and East Beirut. To placate Syria, he declared his commitment to national reconciliation, Christian unity, the dissipation of non-Arab influences in Lebanon, and the severing of all links with Israel. In July he shut down the Lebanese Forces' liaison office in Jerusalem, a year after the Israeli mission in Dubaya had been closed. In return he won an invitation to meet Assad, who relaxed the Syrian blockade of the Christian enclave.

On the other side of the divide, as the infiltration of PLO fighters into West Beirut's Palestinian camps increased, relations soured between the Palestinians and the Amal militia, believed to be 14,000 strong.[4] On 20 May 1985 Amal mounted the War of the Camps, with attacks on the Sabra, Shatila and Burj al Barajina camps. Fighting was bitter. On 2 June Amal overran Sabra, but at a heavy human cost. Elsewhere, the outgunned and outmanned Palestinians held out, thanks mainly to the artillery shelling of Amal by the Druze militia, which had a policy of welcoming Palestinian volunteers into its ranks. The death toll in the Amal militia, running into several hundreds at 7:2 against the Palestinians, made its leadership rethink its tactics.[5]

In early June, on the third anniversary of its invasion of Lebanon, having suffered a total loss of 750 soldiers, Israel withdrew from the rest of south Lebanon. However, it handed over its positions in the self-declared 'security zone' to its surrogate force, the 3,000-strong South Lebanon Army, and left 1,000 IDF troops behind as a back-up to the SLA.

Allowing for this exception, the overall situation in Lebanon returned to the one prevailing in the late 1970s – with Syria the only foreign power deploying its troops in Lebanon on a large scale, and exercising powerful influence over the Maronite president.

While the Palestinian–Amal struggle remained unresolved, tem-peratures rose sharply in the region as a result of the hijacking on 14

June by Shia militants of a Trans World Airways plane carrying 145 passengers on its flight from Athens to Rome. The hijackers wanted the release of seventeen Shias imprisoned in Kuwait – following bomb attacks on US and French targets in the emirate on 10 December 1983 – and 753 Lebanese Shias detained by Israel in its gaols. After the aircraft was taken to Beirut, it was made to shuttle between Beirut and Algiers as negotiations between the hijackers and the authorities dragged on, with different categories of passenger being released in instalments. It was not until 30 June that, thanks to intervention by Assad, the last thirty-nine passengers were freed.

Against this dramatic backcloth, the Lebanese and Syrian governments worked on improving the package of political and military solutions, called the Damascus Plan, that Gemayel and Assad had devised in late May to tackle deteriorating security in West Beirut through the joint efforts of the Lebanese and Syrian armies. In late June some steps were taken to implement the Damascus Plan. Syria intervened, successfully, to stop Amal's War of the Camps, which had by then cost Amal 500 militiamen.

To bolster the peace process, the Syrian government sponsored a Lebanese Muslim summit in Damascus from 7 to 10 July. Chaired by Lebanon's prime minister, Rashid Karami, it was attended by Nabih Berri, Walid Jumblatt and Adil Osserian as well as the spiritual leaders of the Shias and Druzes and the grand mufti of the Sunnis, Shaikh Hassan Khalid. While naming a committee to supervise the implementation of the latest security plan, Karami promised to clear the streets of militias and to shut their offices.[6]

In the political field, the initiative taken independently by Berri and Jumblatt on 2 July to launch the National Union Front (NUF) – committed to ending the Maronite hegemony and sectarian structures and to creating a democratic, secular system – made some progress. The NUF won the support of the Baathists, Socialists, Communists and Nasserites. Its inaugural meeting at Shtura on 6 August was attended by fifteen political party leaders and sixty-seven MPs and other leading politicians. It demanded electoral reform and a special relationship with Syria, and urged escalation of attacks on the IDF in the south. However, at the next meeting Jumblatt's proposal of a presidential council of six, drawn from the major six Muslim and Christian sects, with each member to rule for one year, was not endorsed by the NUF.

Conscious of his deteriorating political support, Gemayel spent most of August in Bikfaya, his native village. Assad, by contrast, was active. Having failed to get Lebanon's politicians to adopt a reconciliation plan and fulfil it, he focused on the leading militia leaders: Berri, Jumblatt and Hobeika. In September he arranged a reconciliation meeting between them in Damascus. By so doing, Assad bolstered the status of Hobeika, enabling him to take the political initiative away from Amin Gemayel, and thus deprive the traditional Maronite leadership of any role in shaping major policies.

On 17 October the LF Radio broadcast a two-part draft document called the Damascus Agreement. Its military section envisaged the withdrawal of the Lebanese army to the barracks as a prelude to its restructuring and re-equipment, with security being taken over by the Syrian army and the Lebanese internal security forces. All militias were to be disbanded and their arms confiscated. The political section of the Agreement specified a three-year transitional period for abolishing political sectarianism, during which the system of a Maronite president, a Sunni prime minister and a Shia speaker was to be retained. The number of parliamentary deputies was to be raised from 99 to 142, and divided equally among Christians and Muslims. A broad-based cabinet was to be appointed to enforce the Agreement.

Given Samir Geagea's opposition to the negotiations which led to the drafting of the Damascus Agreement, it came as no surprise when his fighters clashed with Hobeika's supporters in late October. Criticizing the document, primarily because it specified curtailing of presidential powers, Amin Gemayel demanded a broad-based participation in fresh negotiations to hammer out a new accord. The Agreement was opposed, predictably, by Camille Chamoun and, unexpectedly, by Suleiman Franjieh. The proposed signing of the document on 11 November failed to materialize due to the LF Command Council's insistence that the three-year transition period from the present sectarian system to a secular system be extended to twenty years. The resulting stalemate raised tensions.

Later that month Amal and the army's predominantly Shia 6th Brigade launched fresh attacks on the Palestinian camps, but these proved inconclusive. In early December East Beirut came under heavy shelling. Meanwhile, Assad kept up pressure on Hobeika, Berri and Jumblatt to end the stalemate, while a desperate Amin Gemayel approached Franjieh to oppose the imminent agreement among the three militia leaders, and won his backing on 24 December. But that made no difference to Assad's plans.

On 28 December, after the differences over the length of the transition period had been resolved, Hobeika, Berri and Jumblatt signed a detailed document, entitled the National Agreement to Solve the Lebanese Crisis. Reiterating Lebanon's Arab identity and its unity, it rejected all plans for partition or political decentralization. Its main proposals were as follows:

1 The establishment of a senate charged with legislating such important issues as amending the constitution, declaring war and peace, and ratifying international treaties and agreements.
2 The immediate appointment of a new cabinet.
3 The application of all legal and constitutional texts about implementing the transitional reforms within a year.
4 The government was to propose a plan for abrogating sectarianism during the second half of the four-year term of the first elected parliament. In case the plan failed to win approval, the issue of sectarianism was to be decided by legislation during the first half of the term of the third parliament: that is, during years nine and ten.
5 The number of votes required for the election of president during the first ballot was to be reduced from two-thirds to 55 per cent.
6 In case the president withheld approval of the cabinet chosen by the prime minister, the latter was to be authorized to present the list to the parliament; and if it won the approval of 55 per cent of the deputies, then the president was to be obliged to accept the government.
7 If, during the thirty-day period after the passing of a bill, the president refused to approve it, the government could compel him to do so.
8 During the transitional period to the new constitution, the parliament was to double in size to 198 – to be shared on an equitable basis within the framework of parity between Muslims and Christians, and of equality between Maronites, Shias and Sunnis.
9 The army was to be withdrawn from its current positions, and restructured to harmonize Lebanon's pursuit of strategic co-ordination and integration with Syria.
10 The most important aspect of Lebanon's Arabism was to be its special relationship with Syria in foreign policy and in the security, economic, educational and informational fields.
11 Syria was to maintain its important role without entering into

formal diplomatic relations with Lebanon as had been the case since the creation of the two states.[7]

This was the most detailed and comprehensive reconciliation document, popularly known as the Tripartite Agreement, that had yet been drafted.

At the time of the formal signing of the Tripartite Agreement in Damascus on 30 December 1985, Karim Bakraduni, an aide of Hobeika, called for its ratification by parliament. This was one way to confer legitimacy on it, something it lacked due to the absence of the signature of either the Lebanese president or the prime minister.

As it was, Hobeika did not have sufficient authority himself to sign the document, since only half of the LF Command Council backed it. Outside of the LF, objections were raised by Camille Chamoun and the Maronite Church. Anxious to retain influence over the Maronite community, various groups and individuals switched sides dramatically, with Gemayel and Franjieh, hitherto allied to Damascus, lining up against a Syrian-brokered agreement, and the Hobeika loyalists, traditional enemies of Syria, backing it.

On 8 January 1986 the pro-Geagea elements within the LF attacked Hobeika's men, thus initiating a further round of intra-Maronite fighting. Five days later, the pro-Hobeika forces assaulted President Gemayel's strongholds in Metn and East Beirut, while he was in Damascus to tell Assad that he needed time to study the Tripartite Agreement. On his return to East Beirut, Gemayel allied with his erstwhile adversary, Geagea, in an anti-Hobeika coup within the Lebanese Forces, which resulted in Hobeika and his close aides escaping the Christian enclave in a helicopter. The internecine Maronite conflict claimed 800 to 1,000 casualties. But more significantly, with the fleeing of Hobeika from the Christian territory, the Tripartite Agreement lost its crucial Maronite component. Despite violent disunity in the Maronite ranks and declining influence of the community as a whole, there could be no lasting reconciliation in Lebanon without Maronite participation. Assad knew this, and was disappointed at Hobeika's ousting.

Assad's failure to make the reform package stick once again underlined the essential nature of Lebanese state and society. So fractured was the internal power structure – with each component allied to an external force, big or small – that no single Lebanese group or coalition of groups, buttressed by one or more foreign powers, could have its way. The Israeli–American–Maronite combine, created in the wake of the 1982 Israeli victory, failed to impose the Christian–Western hegemony on Lebanon. Equally, the Syrian–Iranian–Muslim coalition did not succeed in altering the 1943 power-sharing formula to reflect the current population estimates of various sects. This failure highlighted the limits of Syrian power.

7

Limits of Syrian power

February 1986 — September 1988

In his overall strategy of controlling various factions and militias in Lebanon, President Assad had not overlooked 300,000-plus Palestinians living in a dozen camps in Beirut, Tripoli, the Beqaa valley and the Sidon–Tyre area,[1] who in the main supported the PLO. The latter, following its expulsion from Beirut in September 1982, had set up its headquarters in Tunis, Tunisia. In the spring of 1983 Assad triggered a struggle against Yasser Arafat's leadership of the PLO by encouraging Colonels Abu Musa and Abu Salih of Fatah – the foremost constituent of the PLO and headed by Arafat – to confront the pro-Arafat fighters in the Beqaa. They did so, and defeated them.

Three years later, in April 1986, as reports of the clandestine return of the Palestinian fighters to the West Beirut camps resurfaced, the Syrian leader instigated Amal to revive its attacks on the camps, the strongholds of the PLO. By so doing he made real the Palestinian commandos' fear of violence against their unprotected families, which had been the main reason for their surreptitious return to the camps in the first place. Now they fought back valiantly. Assisted once again by the artillery attacks on the Amal forces by the Druze militia of Walid Jumblatt, who opposed an anti-Palestinian onslaught, they thwarted Amal's plan to overrun their camps. The result was a stalemate, followed by a formal ceasefire in July.

Soon Syria strengthened the Lebanese internal security forces by deploying several hundred of its troops in West Beirut. The Syrians cleared the streets of militiamen and shut down their offices, a move decried as illegal, ironically, by the Maronite leaders, who feared a similar move against them by Damascus. In any case, peace proved short-lived, and was shattered by a bloody campaign of car bombs.

This led to a meeting of the national unity government in September, the first in 1986. It went through an essentially sterile exercise of discussing political reform as a means of putting a permanent end to violence. Predictably, the new truce proved as brittle as many of its predecessors. It broke down around the time when the Gemayel–Assad talks at the Arab summit in Amman from 8 to 11 November were proving fruitless, chiefly because Gemayel refused to endorse major amendments to the Lebanese constitution. Amal, allied with the predominantly Shia 6th Brigade of the Lebanese army, resumed attacks on the Palestinian camps in West Beirut.

On 3 November 1986 *Al Shira* (The Sail), a Beirut-based magazine, disclosed that America had sold arms to Iran clandestinely and that Robert McFarlane, former US National Security Adviser, had visited Tehran earlier in the year to meet Iranian officials. The news stunned the world.

Two elements were involved. Aware of the geostrategic importance of Iran, Washington wanted to end the extreme hostility that Tehran had shown towards it since the February 1979 Islamic revolution there. Second, at a more mundane level, it was intent on securing the release of the American hostages taken by pro-Iranian groups in Lebanon.

Significantly, the abduction of William Buckley, the CIA station chief in Beirut, occurred on 16 March 1984 – two months after the US state department included Iran in its list of nations supporting international terrorism and vigorously pursued its policy of blocking arms supplies to the country, which had been engaged in a war with Iraq since September 1980. The Islamic Jihad Organization, which kidnapped Buckley, coupled its demand for the release of seventeen Shias, who had been convicted in Kuwait on charges of bombing the US and French embassies and other targets, with a call on Washington and Paris to alter their policies towards Tehran, including ending their arms embargo against Iran. By 20 May the number of American hostages held by pro-Iranian groups in Lebanon had risen to five.

Following a successful end to the TWA hijacking in late June 1985, President Ronald Reagan sent a secret message to the Iranian parliamentary speaker, Ali Akbar Hashemi Rafsanjani, then on a visit to Tokyo, via the Japanese premier Yasuhiro Nakasone. In it he thanked Rafsanjani for the release of American hostages aboard the TWA airliner, and expressed hope for better US–Iranian relations. About then, the first week of July, Reagan allowed his National Security Adviser, McFarlane, to explore the proposal that Tehran might influence the Lebanese Islamic Jihad Organization to free their American captives, now numbering seven, in a 'probable' exchange for US-made weapon supplies to Iran.

In early August, after McFarlane had briefed Reagan on Israel's proposal to sell US-made TOW (tube-launched optically-tracked wire-guided) anti-tank missiles to Iran from its stocks, he secured the president's approval. On 13 September, 508 TOWs arrived in Iran. The next day one American hostage was freed. US officials were directly involved in the second deal on 22 November, involving an exchange of 120 Hawk anti-aircraft missiles for the remaining five American hostages, the sixth, William Buckley, having died of illness by then. Three days later the CIA arranged for a shipment of eighteen Hawk missiles from Israel to Iran aboard a plane of one of its front companies. On 17 January 1986 Reagan signed an order authorizing the CIA to purchase 4,000 TOWs from the US defense department and sell them to Iran, with Israel making the necessary arrangements for the transaction. Thus the USA became a direct supplier of weapons to Iran.

American officials were anxious to hold high-level talks with the Iranian government. Vice-Admiral John Poindexter, the newly appointed US National Security Adviser, instructed his predecessor, McFarlane, to pursue the matter along with Lieutenant-Colonel Oliver North, deputy director for political-military affairs on the National Security Council. On 23 May 1986 the USA sent 508 TOW missiles and Hawk spare parts to Israel for trans-shipment to Iran. Two days later an American delegation, including McFarlane and North, arrived in Tehran. It stayed for four days. It failed in its mission to forge friendly ties with Iran at the highest level. Also, the promised release of four American hostages did not take place. Therefore, next month the USA solicited Israel's assistance in securing the freedom of the American captives. In early July 7 tonnes of US-made arms and spares were delivered to Iran via Spain and Yugoslavia, most probably by Israeli agents. On 26 July one American hostage was freed.

It was obvious that the USA was getting nowhere in achieving its objective of improving relations with Iran, and that its dealings with the Iranian regime through intermediaries had ended up as straight 'arms for hostages' swaps. This ran contrary to Washington's much trumpeted policy of not dealing with hostage-takers and terrorists. Moreover, it encouraged the pro-Iranian groups in Lebanon to engage in hostage-taking. In mid-September 1986 they kidnapped two more Americans.

Meanwhile, US officials had succeeded in establishing a fresh channel to the Tehran regime, the new contact being a 'relative' of

Rafsanjani. Oliver North and his team met him in West Germany in early October. As a result, 500 TOWs were taken from stocks in Israel and shipped to Iran through a third country on 29 October. Four days later, on the eve of US congressional elections, an American hostage, David Jacobsen, was released, with the Islamic Jihad Organization, his captor, stating that it was freeing him in response to 'overtures' by America.[2] On the whole, the Iranians had managed to make their American negotiators appear poor bargainers in private as they were later to do in public, by extracting more than they gave in return.

The disclosure of clandestine US arms sales to Iran, popularly labelled the Irangate Scandal, had a devastating impact upon American public and world opinion. It showed Washington acting against its professed policy of 'no deals' with terrorist individuals or states, and dramatically undermined the popular standing of President Reagan. While it paralysed the Reagan administration at home and abroad for several months, it raised the spirit not only of such anti-American forces in Lebanon as the Hizbollah and the Islamic Jihad Organization, but also of Amal.

In January 1987, following the refusal of the Palestinian commandos to evacuate the strategic village of Maghdusha near Sidon, Amal imposed a blockade against the Palestinian camps. By the end of the month, artillery and tank fire by Amal and its ally had made uninhabitable 90 per cent of the dwellings in Shatila and 60 per cent in Burj al Barajina.[3]

To relieve pressure on the Palestinians, Walid Jumblatt initiated skirmishes between his Druze fighters and Amal. This was not difficult to do. The joint takeover of West Beirut by the two militias had been vitiated by intermittent tension between them over such matters as the control of the streets and neighbourhoods where roadblocks were used to collect tolls: it had erupted in armed clashes in the second half of 1985 and continued throughout the following year. In early February 1987 these sporadic fights escalated into a more serious confrontation between Amal and the leftist forces, consisting of the militias of the Druze-dominated Progressive Socialist Party, the Lebanese Communist Party and the Syrian Social Nationalist Party.[4] Resenting the rapid rise of Amal, and its alliance with the predominantly Shia 6th Brigade of the army, the leftists combined to challenge it before it grew even bigger. They found the time opportune as Amal was also being challenged by the pro-Iranian Hizbollah in the southern suburbs of West Beirut.

Finding Amal under attack by the leftists and the Hizbollah, Syria decided to intervene actively. It specified 18 February as the deadline for a ceasefire. Its ultimatum was ignored by the warring factions even though the latest round of violence had claimed 150 men, with Amal and its allies in the army being the worse sufferers. As before, possessing both high motivation and superior martial skills, the Druze fighters performed well, the militias of the SSNP and the Communist Party being too small to matter very much. The continuing bloodshed led the prominent Muslim politicians to travel to Damascus and request Assad's assistance in restoring law and order in West Beirut. Agreeing to help, on 22 February Assad despatched Syria's 85th Brigade to West Beirut, equipped with tanks, armoured cars and artillery. This brigade had been withdrawn four and a half years before under Israeli pressure. Assad's action went uncriticized by both President Gemayel and his chief of staff, General Michel Aoun. The previous month, Gemayel had met Assad (unofficially) at the summit of the Islamic Conference Organization in Kuwait, and had praised Syria's help to Lebanon in his speech to the summit.

The Syrian troops went into action immediately, and were ruthless. When they encountered resistance from the Hizbollah militiamen in the southern suburbs of West Beirut, they instantly killed twenty-three of them. The end result was restoration of peace in the city, and a breathing space for the beleaguered Amal.

But there was no respite from terrorism and assassinations on both sides of the religious divide. Since the start of the civil war twelve years before, 14,000 people had been kidnapped, of whom some 10,000 had been killed. The actual fighting had claimed another 120,000 deaths and inflicted injuries on 150,000.[5]

In early January 1987 an attempt on the life of Camille Chamoun by 'The Free Bashirites – the Forces of Vengeance' led to the deaths of his bodyguards and injuries to Chamoun himself. There were two unsuccessful attempts to assassinate Samir Geagea on 20 January and 14 March 1987, bringing the total of such endeavours to twenty-six since January 1986. These terrorist actions occurred against the backdrop of continued divisions within the Maronite camp, which was divided into eight factions: President Amin Gemayel and his militia called Force 75; the Lebanese Forces led by Samir Geagea; the dissident Lebanese Forces loyal to Elie Hobeika; the Phalangist Party; the National Liberal Party of Camille Chamoun; the Guardians of the Cedars; the followers of Suleiman Franjieh; and Maronite Church leaders.

Samir Geagea and his Lebanese Forces were close to Israel and America, with Geagea receiving US-made weapons and encouraging young Maronites to join the Israeli-backed South Lebanon Army. American arms began arriving in East Beirut in early 1987. Following a letter from Pope John Paul II in March 1987 advising the disbandment of militias and urging political dialogue, Nasrallah Boutros Sfier, the Maronite patriarch, devised a plan stressing national unity and offering comprehensive social and political reform. This did not endear him to Samir Geagea. With the death on 7 August 1987 of Camille Chamoun, the nominal leader of the Lebanese Front and the last of the traditional, patriarchal figures in the Christian community, the star of Geagea rose further.

On the Muslim side, all the important Druze and Shia leaders – Walid Jumblatt, Nabih Berri, Shaikh Muhammad Mahdi Shams al Din, a Shia religious figure, and Shaikh Muhammad Hussein Fadlallah, the spiritual leader of Hizbollah – had been targets of assassination. Of these Fadlallah was targeted by the CIA working in conjunction with Saudi Arabia, which reportedly provided $3 million for the job. He was alleged by the USA to have been involved with the three bombings of American premises, including the embassy and the marine headquarters. The job was subcontracted to a Briton who had worked with a British commando organization, the Special Air Services, and involved the Lebanese intelligence agency hiring local men to execute the plan. As a result, on 8 March 1985 a car bomb exploded near Fadlallah's high-rise residence, killing eighty people and injuring 200, but leaving the Hizbollah leader unscathed.[6]

The prime minister, Rashid Karami, who had held the post since April 1984, was not so fortunate. On 1 June 1987 he was assassinated by an explosive device put under his seat in a military helicopter. The operation was carried out by three men from the army intelligence and the air force. Two months later the Swedish government arrested Private Elie Louis Salibi for allegedly planting the explosive.[7] Karami's murder damaged not only the standing of Syria but also the overall prospects of a political resolution of the Lebanese crisis.

President Gemayel appointed Salim Hoss, a Sunni leader then running the ministry of labour and education, as acting premier. But he lacked the prestige that Karami, the son of an eminent religious figure from a leading family, enjoyed among Sunnis. Karami's death accelerated the overall decline of the Sunnis as a political force. This was highlighted by the fact that, of the several traditional Sunni strongholds, only Sidon was controlled to some degree by a local Sunni militia.

This force sided with the Palestinians when hostilities broke out in the Sidon area in late June 1987 in the wake of Amal's encirclement of a Palestinian camp near Tyre. The Palestinians' legal status had suffered due to the abrogation, on 21 May 1987, of the 1969 Lebanon–PLO agreement as part of the package by which the (unratified) May 1983 Lebanese–Israeli treaty had been anulled earlier. However, the Amal–PLO fighting did not last long. Damascus soon discovered that an onslaught against the Palestinians, involving the Amal in besieging their camps, had tarnished its image in the Arab world. Arabs at large sympathized with Palestinian women and children and their protectors, the PLO commandos. Moreover, Syria realized the futility of having Amal, one of its leading proxies in Lebanon, fritter away its military power on maintaining sieges that had not yet yielded clear-cut victory. Therefore Syria brokered a ceasefire, with Amal lifting the blockade, and the PLO evacuating a strategic village east of Sidon, thus enabling Amal to re-establish access to the coastal road and allowing the Shias in the south and Beirut to be relinked.

To compensate for the loss of Rashid Karami in the Muslim camp, President Assad actively encouraged seven nationalist and progressive parties – Amal, the Arab Democratic Party (based in Tripoli), the pro-Syrian Baath Party, the Communist Party, the Popular Nasserite Organization (based in Sidon), the (Druze) Progressive Socialist Party, and the Syrian Social Nationalist Party – to form an umbrella body. They did so on 23 July 1987 and called it the Unification and Liberation Front. Assad then pressured Salim Hoss to lead the Front but, to his disappointment, Hoss refused.

However, Assad was cheered by a split in the Phalange in October which weakened the position of President Gemayel. Force 75, the militia loyal to Gemayel and based in north Metn, came under repeated attacks by the LF, now led indisputably by Samir Geagea. To withstand these it sought, and received, emergency aid from the Lebanese military commanded by General Michel Aoun.

Mirroring the internecine conflict among Maronites was the split among Shias, represented by the escalating hostility between the Hizbollah and Amal, with the former showed increasing signs of becoming a serious rival to the latter. At its parades in southern Beirut, Baalbek, Sidon and Tyre on 14 May, anti-Zionist day, and on 22 May, Jerusalem Day, the Hizbollah mounted displays of cannons, and anti-tank and anti-aircraft missiles. Its subsequent establishment of a naval unit showed that it was combining guerrilla-style warfare with classic military precepts. It had emerged as the major recipient of financial assistance from Iran, which was spending about $5 million a month on Lebanon, funding health, education and other public services through its Martyrs Foundation. With Tehran's assistance, the Hizbollah set up a television station in the Beqaa.[8]

Nonetheless, the Hizbollah's main area of armed action was in the south. There, its militia often attacked targets inside Israel's self-declared security zone within Lebanon as well as the Israeli-backed SLA, which patrolled it. The radical Palestinian groups, based in the south, did the same. In one instance, a Palestinian infiltrating Israel on a motorized hang glider on 25 November 1987 killed six IDF soldiers near Kriyat Shmona. Israel responded with unprecedented severity. Its air raid on PLO positions near Sidon killed forty-six and injured 186, the highest toll in a single raid since its June 1982 invasion of Lebanon. The fighting between the Hizbollah and the SLA too became quite vicious, with the Hizbollah losing forty men in their attacks on the SLA in the first two months of 1988.

Behind the Hizbollah militancy lay the cunning hand of President Assad. Just as he had tapped the resources of Amal to enfeeble the pro-PLO Palestinians, he saw much virtue in using the militantly anti-Israeli and anti-American stance of the Hizbollah to put the heat on the IDF and its surrogate, the SLA, inside Lebanon. This policy, pursued actively throughout 1987, also had the advantage of diverting public attention away from the intractable problems of West Beirut and restressing Syria's confrontational credentials. Yet this had to be done within the larger parameters defined by Assad's long-standing regional policy : none of the Palestinian or Lebanese militias should be allowed to act so independently and recklessly in its attacks on Israel as to trigger a major confrontation between Damascus and Tel Aviv for which Syria was not ready. An unplanned war between Syria and Israel was a nightmare Assad was determined to avoid at all costs. In the case of south Lebanon, Damascus relied on its loyal ally, Amal, to rein in the Hizbollah when it seemed to be going too far in its anti-Israeli crusade.

The kidnapping on 17 February 1988 of the US marine officer Colonel William Higgins, serving with Unifil, by the Hizbollah in the Amal-controlled area stretched the patience of Amal's southern command. Its wish to act against the Hizbollah coincided with the mood in Damascus, which had by then turned conciliatory towards Washington.

Disturbed by the destabilizing impact of the Palestinian intifada (uprising) against Israeli occupation, which erupted on 9 December 1987, the US undersecretary for the Near East, Richard Murphy, toured the region. In early February he visited Damascus to ensure that the stepping down of President Amin Gemayel on 23 September 1988 would not create another major unpheaval in the area. Sharing Murphy's wish, President Assad encouraged him to mediate between East Beirut and Damascus.

In early March Murphy returned from East Beirut with a package of political reform that had been agreed by all Christian politicians, thanks to the intercession of the Maronite Patriarch Sfier. While it included equality between Muslim and Christian parliamentary deputies, reduction in confessionalism in the state apparatus over a period of twenty years, and some adjustment of powers between the president and the cabinet, it insisted on having the Maronite president continue as the central political authority.[9]

This was clearly unsatisfactory to Assad, but he decided to continue his constructive dialogue with the USA on the Lebanese and other Middle Eastern problems. He offered to control Islamic fundamentalist forces and terrorism, secure the release of eighteen Western hostages held in Lebanon and discourage attacks against Israeli targets, if Washington agreed to accept, tacitly, Syrian influence in Lebanon above the Zahrani river, support only those Lebanese presidential hopefuls who subscribed to a political platform acceptable to Syria, and pressure Israel to limit its area of manoeuvre in south Lebanon.

At the same time Assad was keen to keep the Lebanese crisis separate from the overall Arab–Israeli conflict of which the Palestinian intifada was the latest manifestation. He said as much to the US secretary of state, George Shultz, when the latter visited Damascus soon after Richard Murphy. It now suited the Syrian leader to show Washington that he was intent on curbing Shia extremism, as practised by the Hizbollah, which had been in the forefront *inter alia* of taking Western hostages using such labels as the Islamic Jihad Organization, the Revolutionary Justice Organization and the Organization of the Oppressed of the Earth. Shultz was reportedly non-committal. During their meeting in mid-April in the Syrian capital, Assad warned Shultz that US hesitation in agreeing to a Lebanese settlement with Syria would put constitutional developments – concerning the presidency, East Beirut and Damascus – into the hands of the Islamic fundamentalists.[10] Shultz seems to have heeded the warning and decided to co-operate with the Syrian leader.

The subsequent negotiations between Assad and Murphy led to the adoption of a common stance on political reform in Lebanon to be implemented by the next president. However, the Assad–Murphy proposals were rejected by President Gemayel as well as Samir Geagea, the LF chief, who – following the split in the Phalange and the constant hammering of Gemayel's militia by the LF – had emerged as the more powerful figure. Gemayel and Geagea described the Assad–Murphy package as a device for a graduated imposition of the Syrian-sponsored Tripartite Agreement of December 1985, which had proved still-born.[11] The failure of the US–Syrian package cooled relations between Washington and Damascus. Yet Assad went on to implement his side of the bargain with America.

Indeed, by then Assad had activated his plan to curb the Hizbollah by making use of Amal. Enjoying a break in its skirmishes with the Palestinians in March 1988, Amal found itself in a better state to hit the Hizbollah in the south. On 4 April it attacked Hizbollah positions in the Nabatiya area and captured the territory after three days' bitter fighting which left fifty people dead. Once Amal had consolidated its hold over the district, it expelled scores of Hizbollah activists, laymen and clerics to Beqaa.

As if this were not enough for the Hizbollah, in early May the IDF mounted a major land operation to destroy its bases in May-fadun and elsewhere. Smelling a 'conspiracy' to annihilate their organization, Hizbollah leaders decided to go on the offensive. On 6 May their militia hit Amal in the southern suburbs of West Beirut, beyond the pale of the city's security plan, where the Hizbollah enjoyed wide latitude and had the active support of the Palestinian guerrillas based in Shatila and Burj al Barajina camps. In the fighting that followed, Amal leaders discovered that their militia had been infiltrated by the Hizbollah. Within a period of three days, which produced 525 casualties on both sides, Amal lost the central and southern parts of the suburbs. On 13 May weary Amal units evacuated the outer perimeter, allowing their rivals to advance to the airport autostrade and incite street violence in the Ouzai district next to a Syrian encampment. In Damascus the Syrian vice-president, Abdul Halim Khaddam, drew parallels between the situations in the eastern and western sectors of Beirut, with the extremists gaining ground in both parts.

Syria decided to despatch its soldiers into the southern suburbs of West Beirut. While not opposed in principle to the Syrian military presence with the specific objective of separating the warring parties, both the Hizbollah and its foreign backer, Iran, tried to gain time in order to secure favourable truce terms. When Damascus threatened to act speedily and unilaterally, the Hizbollah retaliated by threatening to kill the Western hostages its supporters held, thus subverting Syria's bridge-building with the West. There was intensified violence on 15 May, followed by a succession of brief halts in fighting. In between these ceasefires, the Hizbollah succeeded in expelling Amal from the northern areas of the suburbs. Muhammad Ali Besharati, the Iranian member of the four-member peace committee, proposed a joint Syrian–Iranian security force, but was overruled by Syria. 'We greatly value our alliance with Iran, but our regional allies must respect our position', said Vice-President Khaddam. 'Our role [in Lebanon] is above all other considerations. In their operations our allies should pay attention to our interests and to those of our [Lebanese] friends. The movements of some [Lebanese] have become a threat to the Syrian role. We shall not allow the creation of complications in the Lebanese arena.'[12]

To keep the matter strictly within the Syrian orbit, Assad summoned a Hizbollah delegation to Latakia (in Syria). Talks between the two sides led to a five-point agreement on 26 May. It provided for the Syrian troops to be deployed throughout the southern suburbs; all 'armed manifestations' in the streets were to be stopped; all militia offices were to be converted into political offices; the Hizbollah was to be allowed to stay armed and maintain its Hay al Madi barracks and military presence along the Green Line with East Beirut; and the bulk of the Syrian forces were to be withdrawn within a few weeks to be replaced by the Lebanese internal security forces.[13]

By 28 May 1988, when the ceasefire came into effect following the entry of 3,500 Syrian troops into the southern suburbs, 500 people had been killed and 2,000 injured in three weeks of intermittent fighting, with extensive damage to property due to bombardments and looting. It was the bloodiest episode since the inter-militia violence in West Beirut of fifteen months back.

Just as in February 1987, so now the vicious bloodletting underlined the indispensability of Syria as the final arbiter and interlocutor. Damascus came to exercise increased authority in the southern Shia suburbs without hurting its strategic alliance with Tehran. At the same time its forceful behaviour and success in ending the inter-Shia violence made the West, particularly the United States, more interested in conducting fruitful dialogue with it.

Having extended the Syrian presence in the southern suburbs of West Beirut, Assad encouraged the pro-Damascus Palestinian guerrillas – part of the Palestine National Salvation Front (PNSF) formed in March 1984 – to attack the PLO fighters in the Shatila and Burj al Barajina camps. After a month of intermittent fighting, the pro-Syrian partisans prevailed in Shatila, but only after most of its civilian residents had fled and most of its dwellings had been made uninhabitable. On 8 July 1988 an agreement was reached to let 175 PLO fighters and their families leave for Sidon.

By then the Syrian troops in the southern suburbs had thinned out, handing over their positions to the Lebanese internal security forces. The Hizbollah too had reduced its military manpower in the area and turned its attention and energy to south Lebanon, by despatching many of its militiamen to Sidon with a view to challenging Amal's supremacy in the region.

All in all, therefore, by mid-July the Syrians had consolidated their position in West Beirut as a prelude to tackling East Beirut in order to influence the presidential election due before 23 September 1988.

However, the East Beirut authorities too were in a strong position not only economically but also politically, diplomatically and militarily. They controlled the country's main sources of water and electricity, the important ports of Beirut and Jounieh, and a military airport at Halat capable of being transformed into a civilian facility; and they ruled an area that contained a majority of the nation's business establishments. In contrast, Muslim West Beirut possessed the international airport and, more significantly, the Central Bank, virtually the only source of funds for the government.

Politically, the internecine violence among the Shias had the effect of improving the morale of the Christians. The three centres of power – the president's office at Baabda, the army command at Yarze and the Lebanese Forces in East Beirut – were currently united against West Beirut and Syria. Most of the one million residents of the Christian mini-state were opposed to West Beirut (thought to be nurturing undefined threats to the Christian community) and Syria (considered arrogant and sly), even though a majority of them were also resentful of the Lebanese Forces' aggressive behaviour and 'taxes and levies', sceptical about the bona fides of their self-appointed leaders, and uneasy about the virtual partition of the country that had been imposed on them. In any case, since twenty-five of the seventy-seven surviving members of parliament (which had, on 1 December 1987, extended its term of office by three more years) were based in the Christian enclave, the Christian notables were confident that Syria could not impose its nominee as president.

Externally, they were backed in their anti-Syrian stance by not only Israel but also Iraq, whose president, Saddam Hussein, was intent on getting even with Assad for allying with Iran in the Iran–Iraq War, which ended in August 1988. Saddam Hussein promised to supply weapons to the Christian camp. As it was, militarily, the aggregate size of the army brigades in East Beirut and the LF militia was larger than any combination their opponents could muster. Therefore, the only way Syria could prevail was by mounting a full-scale war against the Christian enclave – something that was not on the cards given the regional and international realities. The prospect of Lebanon finding itself without a president did not worry certain sections of the Christian community. Indeed, the LF welcomed it, seeing in it the making of a partitioned Lebanon, which was its political objective.

In early August 1988 Suleiman Franjieh formally entered the electoral arena. On 10 August, General Michel Aoun, the military chief of staff, rounded upon the LF, predicting that the army would take charge of the security of East Beirut, thus tacitly offering himself as a presidential candidate. This manoeuvre backfired. It led to an alliance between President Gemayel and Samir Geagea, who was also interested in the presidency; and it elicited a distinctly cool reaction from Damascus. Aoun then joined other Christian leaders in urging a boycott of the parliamentary session on 18 August to elect the president. Their ploy worked. In the absence of the quorum of two-thirds of the surviving deputies, the session could not be held. President Assad took particular note of Aoun's stance, and virtually declared him *persona non grata* in Damascus. Assad persevered and pressed Franjieh's candidacy while the Lebanese prime minister, Hoss, withdrew his year-old resignation, thus paving the way for the continuation of his government to fill the vacuum created by the absence of the president.

The prospect of Lebanon lapsing into a condition where it lacked a head of state disturbed not only Saudi Arabia and the Vatican but also the Soviet Union. They all pressed America to act. It did. Richard Murphy arrived in Damascus on 13 September. Following three days of talks with the Syrian vice-president, Khaddam, Murphy reiterated Washington's backing for the broad principles of political reform in Lebanon, but withheld support for Franjieh's presidency. Syria then named Mikhail Dahir, a Maronite member of parliament, as its choice. Concurring with this, Murphy carried the Syrian proposal to East Beirut. This move needed to be viewed in a larger context. After years of pursuing anti-Syrian policies, Washington seemed to have come around to accepting two basic facts of life in the Middle East: only Assad had the cunning, stamina, insight, talent and strong motivation to control, suppress or manipulate the various forces operating in a fractured Lebanon; and Syria was a key player in the resolution of the Arab–Israeli conflict. Moreover, the USA needed Assad's active co-operation to secure the release of many Western hostages, including several Americans, held in Lebanon.

However, the Maronite leaders had different perceptions. To Murphy's surprise and consternation, President Gemayel, General Aoun, Geagea and Patriarch Sfier condemned the Syrian–American nominee for president. They regarded Dahir as worse than Franjieh since the latter, a seasoned politician of long standing, was strong enough to stand up to Damascus, if need be. The same could not be said of Dahir. They berated Murphy for attempting to rig the presidential election and selecting a candidate without taking into account Maronite views and preferences, and described the US–Syrian behaviour as amounting to curtailing Lebanon's sovereignty. The last argument overlooked recent history: the election of Elias Sarkis and Bashir Gemayel as president had been steered respectively by Syria and Israel. Given his own presidential ambitions, General Aoun was quick to criticize Syria and America publicly. The Maronite defiance derived partly from the fact that weapons from Iraq had begun arriving in their enclave, with the first shipment of rocket launchers and twenty tanks having been unloaded at Beirut port on 16 August, and partly from the prevalent perception that, following the end of the Iran–Iraq War, the regional importance of Assad would decline rapidly.

Of Gemayel, Aoun and Geagea, the top political-military leaders in the Christian enclave, only Gemayel, concerned about how posterity would judge his presidency, showed some interest in finding a solution to the presidential crisis that was acceptable to Damascus. The latter was working hard to get the Lebanese parliament to meet on 22 September, the day before the end of Gemayel's tenure.

On 21 September 1988 Gemayel travelled to Damascus to meet

Assad. Later, Syrian officials said that the Lebanese leader had accepted Mikhail Dahir's nomination for presidency before being received by Assad, whereas Gemayel's aides said that the purpose of the meeting was to let him propose a transitional government headed by Dahir as a compromise between the positions of Damascus and the East Beirut leaders. Assad viewed Gemayel's proposal with suspicion; and most of the Christian leaders, particularly Aoun and Geagea (who forged an alliance on 21 September), reacted negatively to his initiative.

A parliamentary session on 22 September failed to materialize. The Christian deputies made a point of objecting to the venue proposed by Syria – the old parliamenary building in Nijma Square in West Beirut – as insecure, insisting on meeting at the temporary parliamentary building at the Museum crossing point, considered neutral territory.

Until the last few hours of his office, President Gemayel tried to sell the idea of a transitional government to the Christian leaders as well as to Prime Minister Hoss, but failed. Some minutes before midnight he asked General Aoun, aged 52, to form a 'temporary military administration'. Aoun did so by appointing a military council of six, including three Muslim officers. So Lebanon, lacking a president, acquired two competing cabinets. The Hoss government argued that Gemayel's decree appointing Aoun violated both custom and the constitution. The 1943 National Pact required the prime minister to be a Sunni Muslim; and it was unconstitutional for a president either to create a government by decree or to have the military chief of staff also act as the prime minister. The refusal of the three Muslim army officers to take up their places in the Aoun cabinet reinforced the argument of the Hoss government.[14] In contrast, Colonel Antoine Lahad, the commander of the Israeli-backed South Lebanon Army, pledged his loyalty to Aoun.

Syria was openly hostile to the Aoun government. On 26 September its official newspaper, *Al Thawra* (The Revolution), called on the Lebanese to 'overthrow this government and so destroy the Zionist project it is carrying and working to implement'. It ignored Aoun's request that it receive his envoy.

During the six years of Gemayel's presidency the Lebanese economy declined rapidly: this manifested itself in shabbily dressed citizens, increasingly filthy shops, and streets filled with beggars. Per capita income fell from about $1,800 in 1982 to $250 in 1987, the official gross domestic product (GDP) decreasing from $5.1 billion in 1982 to $1.5 billion in 1986. The minimum monthly wage of $14 in 1987 was one-third its level in 1974, and the average wage only a quarter of the 1974 figure.[15] While East Beirut received six hours of uninterrupted electricity daily, the supplies to West Beirut were constantly interrupted. Unclean streets had become carpeted with grass; and as public hygiene deteriorated, disease spread.

Several factors contributed to this state of affairs. First, by the mid-1980s the public and private economic reserves were exhausted. Lebanon's foreign reserves went down from $4 billion in 1975 to $2.5 billion in 1982 to $500 million in August 1987, just enough to cover imports for twenty-five months. As a result of rebuilding and re-equipping the Lebanese army according to an American plan, there was a further loss of $1.2 billion during 1982–4.

Second, the country's economic infrastructure was damaged severely. The 1982 Israeli invasion, the War of the Shouf in 1983, the War of the Camps in 1985, and the confrontations of the radical Palestinian and Lebanese groups with Israel in the south during 1985–6 caused widespread destruction, dislocation of people, disruption of economic and other activities and a debilitating fragmentation of the economy.

Third, due to a sharp decline in the oil price in 1985–6, the number of Lebanese working in the Gulf states fell from 150,000 in 1982, providing $1,906 million in remittances, to 65,000 in 1987, sending home only $300 million. The return of migrant workers further increased unemployment in Lebanon, pushing it to 30 per cent in 1987 from a base of 12 per cent in 1980.

Fourth, the removal of the PLO from West Beirut wiped out the contribution it made to the national GDP, estimated to be 15 per cent of the total in the early 1980s. In the wake of this expulsion, the major foreign paymasters – Saudi Arabia, Libya and Iraq – lost interest in the Lebanese civil war. The input of political funds into Lebanon declined, from $300 million in 1982 to $150 million in 1987, most of it coming from Iran, a newcomer. Following the 1982 IDF invasion, Israel began to invest regularly in Lebanon by financing and training the 3,000-strong South Lebanon Army, but the size of the investment was small.

Fifth, there was a precipitate fall in state income due to a massive failure of the government to collect electricity and telephone bills. As for customs revenue, it declined from 97 per cent of the potential income in 1980 to 10 per cent in 1986, due to the emergence of fifteen private sea and airports managed illegally by various militias. This happened against the background of a steep rise in public expenditure due to increased subsidies on energy and bread, especially from 1984 onwards. The 90 per cent jump in the annual budget deficit in 1986 led to an increase in inflation from 60 per cent to 425 per cent during 1985–7. The exchange rate fell from L£3.40 to the US dollar to L£500 between 1980 and 1987.[16]

Sixth, there was a sharp expansion in the parallel economy based on smuggling; illegal ports and private customs duties; forced taxation, protection money and racketeering; drugs cultivation and trade; and arms and ammunition trade. From a modest start in 1975, the parallel economy had built up to 20 per cent of the total economic activity by 1982, and to 50 per cent by the mid-1980s. By 1987, when the official GDP had shrunk to $3 billion, the value of hashish and opium production alone was put at $1 billion.[17]

This was the economic legacy that the two parallel governments of Hoss and Aoun inherited.

8

War of liberation, Aoun style

October 1988 — September 1989

A man of humble origin and a professional soldier all his adult life, General Michel Aoun lacked both political skills and experience, a major handicap in running the prime minister's office. His cabinet of two other Christian artillery officers was complemented by an inner circle of seven, all of them professional military men.[1] Like Aoun, they were untutored in the Byzantine ways of Lebanon's domestic politics and the complexities of the Middle East and international diplomacy. Aoun matched his lack of understanding or sympathy with the traditional Maronite leadership with scorn for all parliamentary deputies and members of the Hoss government, whom he viewed as present or potential agents of foreign powers.

The only concession Aoun made to his purist, simplistic views was to ally himself with Samir Geagea, a young politician turned commander of the Lebanese Forces. If nothing else, this move enabled Aoun to consolidate his power base in the Christian enclave in his confrontation with West Beirut and Damascus. This power base stemmed from the intense loyalty he aroused among his supporters, military and civilian, due to his charisma and refreshingly blunt style. Because of its opposition to Syria, the Aoun–Geagea alliance received the active support of Iraq and Israel, although for different reasons. By rushing to pledge his loyalty to Aoun, Colonel Lahad of the Israeli-financed South Lebanon Army showed unmistakably that Israel stood behind the Maronite general occupying the presidential palace in Baabda. Iraq manifested its backing for the Maronite camp by providing sixty-eight tanks and armoured personnel carriers to the Lebanese Forces.

But the alliance of Aoun and Geagea was inherently unstable. Beyond the immediate need of presenting a united front to their adversaries, their interests and ambitions diverged. As a political-military entity, the Maronite Lebanese Forces had certain advantages over the Lebanese army. Besides being a fighting force, the LF collected taxes and levies, and administered the Christian enclave. It had sympathizers among the ranks and officers of the Lebanese army; and by a combination of aggressiveness and subversion it had established its superiority over regular troops in several confrontations since 1986. Aoun was aware of this, but did not know how to rectify the imbalance.

There were also serious political differences between Aoun and Geagea. Like the Maronite patriach and other Christian leaders, Aoun favoured adjusting the present unitary system in order to preserve Christian supremacy while gaining acceptance from West Beirut and Damascus. In contrast, Geagea was a federalist. He wanted to create a federal Lebanon composed of cantons. He had realized that, having been reduced to a numerical minority, Christians could no longer exercise supreme authority nationally: they could do so only at the canton level. He was therefore not overly concerned about the absence of a president, a situation he considered conducive to creating a federal Lebanon.

However, Geagea did not wish to challenge Aoun for the time being. His immediate target was Amin Gemayel. In fact, the LF had begun squeezing Gemayel's militia, Force 75, in north Metn even before Gemayel stepped down as president on 23 September 1988. After that day the LF put him under virtual house arrest. In early October Geagea ordered the formal integration of Force 75 into the LF, and succeeded. He took over the Gemayel family's ancestral palace in Bikfaya, two radio stations and the newspapers *Al Aamal* and *Le Réveille*. When the ex-president complained to Aoun's military cabinet, it replied that the dispute was an internal matter for the Phalange Party and was irrelevant to the army. When Gemayel appealed to the Maronite patriarch for help, the latter too turned a deaf ear. What damaged the reputation of the former president, a businessman, were the rumours that he had made financial gains by misusing his office. Following this, and the death threats he received, Gemayel decided to emigrate to France. Aoun allowed him to do so on 22 October after he had paid a large sum in tax to the East Beirut government.

Elimination of the Gemayel clan's base reduced the number of power centres in the Christian enclave from three to two: the Lebanese army under Aoun and the LF. Both Aoun and Geagea benefited. Yet Aoun, determined to emerge as the powerful commander of the united Lebanese military and/or the internationally recognized president of the republic, had reason to fret as he watched the LF increasing its armed strength and turning itself into a professional force with a well-defined hierarchy. The LF's rising pre-eminence made mockery of the Aoun cabinet's claims that it was the sole legitimate authority for all of Lebanon. The fact was that even in the Christian enclave it had to share power with the LF, which continued to operate ports, collect taxes and run radio stations as before. What worried Aoun even more was Geagea's scenario of a federal Lebanon, where the army brigades were ultimately to be downgraded to the status of appendages to the LF, which was being transformed into a professional fighting force with its own military academy.

All along, however, the opposition of Aoun and Geagea to Damascus remained solid, and succeeded in spiking the latter's plan to get the Lebanese parliament to assemble in mid-October to elect its speaker: the one-year term of the current speaker, Hussein Husseini, was due to expire on 19 October 1988. With this, Syria gave up any hope of causing a wedge between the moderate and militant Christian leaders, Patriarch Sfier being an example of moderation.

Sfier continued his efforts to dissipate the crisis caused by the absence of the president. He travelled to the Vatican to consult the Pope. On his return home in early November, he initiated a discussion on preparing a list of presidential candidates to be forwarded to West Beirut and Damascus. He was encouraged in this endeavour by Geagea, who was confident that nothing would come of it. But Sfier's initiative infuriated Aoun: he saw it as a move meant primarily to sabotage his own presidential ambitions. The initiative did not take off mainly because Damascus insisted on a programme of political reform as a precondition to considering any names recomended by the Christian side.

Soon Syria encouraged the Hoss government in West Beirut to create a 'nationalist' (as against sectarian) army, and make a beginning by appointing General Sami Khatib, a Sunni, as the provisional army commander to fill the job of General Aoun. The rival government of Aoun retaliated by announcing a series of high-level appointments. The cleavage between the two administrations widened as the Central Bank haggled over financing the activities of the Aoun-led defence ministry at Yarze in the Christian enclave. Damascus too hardened its policy towards Aoun as he began putting the Syrian and Israeli occupations of Lebanon on a par.

But this growing hostility of West Beirut and Damascus did not help Aoun or Geagea to ignore the fact that the Christian enclave, taking up only about one-tenth of Lebanon, was too small to allow the LF and the army to co-exist peacefully, particularly when the army command was unprepared to treat the LF as an equal. The inherent incompatibility of the two forces was sharpened by the injection of arms into the enclave by Iraq following the truce in the Iran–Iraq War. While continuing to supply the LF with military equipment, Baghdad began sending weapons to Aoun as well with a view to encouraging him to bait Assad. But the LF's increased fire power made Aoun nervous about losing control of East Beirut altogether, while his growing military strength made Geagea more determined to assert his position.

Aoun had a Gaullist view of himself, and saw a need for swift, sweeping action to save Lebanon from the malaise he attributed to unruly miltias and foreign powers. His plain, no-nonsense style combined with fervent nationalism appealed to the ranks and officers in the army units under his command. He had a mystical faith in the military as the institution to revive nationalist feelings among all Lebanese irrespective of their sectarian loyalties. 'Only [the military] together with the living force of our people can shatter the cell bars and release our captive country from the prison of foreign interests', Aoun told *Al Nahar* on 5 January 1989.[2]

Whatever the views of Aoun about foreign elements, the Arab League was genuinely concerned about the prospect of a formal partition of Lebanon, which, by illustrating the failure of Arab nationalism to hold together two different religious groups inside a single state, would harm the Arab world at large, and benefit Israel. The Arab League foreign ministers met in Tunis on 12 January to consider the problem. They set up a Committee of Six – Algeria, Jordan, Kuwait, Sudan, Tunisia and the UAE – chaired by Kuwait (represented by its foreign minister, Shaikh Sabah al Sabah) to bring peace to Lebanon. Opposed to the Arabization of the Lebanese problem, Syria insisted that the Committee must be consultative and not executive. It also refused to discuss the problem of either the Palestinian camps or the foreign presence in Lebanon, except that of Israel. About a month later, on 10 February, General Aoun, Prime Minister Hoss and the parliamentary speaker Hussein Husseini met the Committee of Six in Tunis. Much to the chagrin of Damascus, Aoun reportedly urged the immediate withdrawal of the Syrians in order to free the Lebanese decision-making process.

On his return to East Beirut, Aoun failed to brief the LF leadership on his diplomatic activity in Tunis. This, and the delay in giving the LF seats in the East Beirut government, upset Geagea. To get even, he set up a parallel LF cabinet, called the National Development Council.

Aoun regarded this step as provocative, and contemplated moving against the LF. He was reportedly encouraged to do so by the envoys of General Ghazi Kanaan, the Syrian military intelligence chief in West Beirut, who commanded a network which had built up an enviable record. If Aoun expelled the LF – much hated by West Beirut and Damascus – from East Beirut and accepted Syria's strategic role in Lebanon, the Syrians would withdraw from West Beirut and allow reunification of the Lebanese army in a security plan for Greater Beirut and a 'national' role for Aoun.[3]

On 14 February, calling LF militiamen 'criminals and racketeers', Aoun attacked them in East Beirut and north Metn. Commanding four fully mobilized brigades of 15,000 soldiers,[4] and possessing 90 per cent of the heavy military hardware purchased from America in the mid-1980s, Aoun was in a strong position to defeat the LF, which had barely 10,000 men under arms. Two days of intense fighting – during which General Sami Khatib, the army commander based in West Beirut, ordered his men to assist Aoun's soldiers – resulted in a humiliation of the LF, whose commander, Geagea, unilaterally accepted the ceasefire call made by Patriarch Sfier. The casualty toll was eighty people dead and 165 injured. While refusing to subordinate his militia to the army, Geagea conceded Aoun's demands. He handed over Beirut port to the Aoun government, ended LF taxation, vacated some LF military barracks in East Beirut, disbanded the LF National Development Council and formally acknowledged Aoun's political supremacy.

West Beirut politicians applauded Aoun's attack on the LF. But their applause proved premature. Instead of consolidating his supremacy over the LF and strenthening his base in the Christian enclave, the impetuous Aoun rushed to announce on 24 February his decision to close 'all illegal ports' and to compel all incoming and outgoing ships to use only Beirut port controlled by his men.[5] However, he refrained from executing his decision in order not to pre-empt the result of the impending meeting of Lebanon's religious leaders called by the Arab League Committee of Six. At this gathering at the end of February, Patriarch Sfier opposed suggestions for the curtailment of presidential authority and stressed the importance of holding presidential elections. This was resisted by the Muslim clerics. Reflecting the view prevalent in their community, they stated that even a partial acceptance of Aoun was out of the question until there was an *a priori* agreement on political reform, a position unacceptable to Aoun.

On 6 March Aoun imposed a blockade of all West Beirut militia ports: Khalde and Jiye of the Druze Progressive Socialist Party and the landing point at Ouzai, West Beirut, controlled by Amal. Three days later Aoun's coastguard seized two tankers bound for Jiye. This triggered fighting between the Aoun loyalists and the Druze units based in Souq al Gharb, with the Druze artillery targeting Beirut port. On 11 March, General Khatib, the chief of staff of the West Beirut government, declared that the Lebanese coast was open to all; and his gunners joined the Druzes in shelling Beirut port. Aoun retaliated by ordering the closure of the international airport in West Beirut. Following this, the insurance companies refused to cover the flights of the state-owned Middle East Airlines, which accounted for 90 per cent of the total traffic, thus causing the closure of the airport.

Heavy artillery exchanges on both sides on 14 March resulted in forty deaths. These salvos ended three years of agreement between the two sectors of Beirut to refrain from indiscriminate bombing of residential areas, and heralded the start of an active war which lasted six months and which could be divided into two parts: from March to May, and from June to September.

The main difference between this bout of fighting and the previous ones was political – with Aoun claiming to have mounted a 'war of liberation' against the occupying Syrian troops and promising to take 'all steps necessary' to force the Syrians out. 'Today we have one target: we shall liberate our land', he declared on 14 March 1989. 'The depth of difference, material and moral, is with Syria, not between Lebanese.'[6]

A week later, retaliating to Aoun's sea blockade, the West Beirut government imposed a land blockade of the 350 square mile Christian enclave, populated by about a million Christians. That day shelling by Aoun's men killed forty people in West Beirut. The equally vicious retaliation by the Muslim side led Aoun to vow on 24 March to drive out the Syrian occupiers 'even if Beirut were razed in the process', to call Syria a 'terrorist' state 'holding 4 million Lebanese as its hostages', and to declare that any truce had to be negotiated between the Lebanese and Syrian armies.[7]

On the night of 25–6 March, 5,000 shells crashed on East Beirut and the Christian heartland, with the defence ministry headquarters at Yarze and the nearby presidential palace at Baaba receiving 1,000 hits. This made the Christians realize that in the era of long-range artillery – with the Syrian 180 mm field guns being able to fling 200 pounds of high explosives 27 miles away – there was not a single square yard in their enclave which was safe, and that their traditional refuge in the mountains had been transformed into a vast cage. All they could do was to retaliate with their own long-range artillery. They did. They fired some 1,500 rounds at the Muslim sector – from the southern suburbs of West Beirut to Baalbek in northern Beqaa, including the Druze-dominated Shouf mountains, aiming primarily at the Syrian strongholds in West Beirut and the surrounding mountains and the Beqaa valley. On 28 March, artillery duels reached such intensity that a total of 8,000 shells were fired in Lebanon, with the Christians being the targets of phosphorus shells and 240 mm mortars, carrying 1,000 pounds of high explosives. Every night, as shelling intensified, hundreds of thousands of civilians sought refuge in the basements of apartment blocks and cinemas, church cellars and mountain caves.

With the Muslim side pouring 4,000 to 5,000 shells a night into the Christian enclave, mainly on the army and militia encampments but also on fuel tanks and power stations, Aoun's will to fight weakened considerably. He responded positively to the appeal of the Arab League Committee of Six on 27 March for cessation of hostilities, and agreed to an immediate truce. By late March, the burning of 4 million gallons of petrol and 3 million gallons of fuel oil at Dora in East Beirut, and the explosion of a gas storage tank, had compelled the Christian authorities to restrict fuel oil supplies only to hospitals and bakeries, and electricity supplies to five hours a day.[8]

Shelling intensified over the weekend of 1–2 April. When the Aoun loyalists attacked the Druze port of Jiye from speedboats on 3 April, the Druze shore batteries responded vigorously. Finding Aoun on the ropes, the Lebanese Forces came to his rescue by issuing a statement of support on 4 April. This meant that 15,000 soldiers and 5,000 army auxiliaries under Aoun were to receive the active backing of some 10,000 Christian militiamen, the joint forces altogether possessing 300 tanks and 300 heavy artillery guns. These were pitted against some 20,000 Muslim troops and militiamen backed by 35,000 Syrian troops, occupying two-thirds of Lebanon and armed with a far larger arsenal of tanks and artillery pieces.[9]

Following a meeting of the Arab League Committee of Six with

West Beirut leaders in Damascus on 5 April, there was an immediate truce for about a week. Then, on 12 April, three Syrian frigates equipped with sea-to-sea missiles docked at the port of Tripoli, and were joined by several armed speedboats. The unprecedented Syrian move was apparently designed to impose a sea blockade of the Christian enclave. The warring factions celebrated the fifteenth anniversary of the civil war on 14 April by exchanging fire for twelve hours, involving forty towns and villages.

The next day, ignoring the explicit orders of Aoun, who now wanted the UN to intervene in the fighting, the Phalange Party president Georges Saade and other Maronite leaders met the Arab League Committee of Six in Kuwait in order to end the suffering of the Lebanese people, who were now *inter alia* completely deprived of electricity. Following the heavy shelling of 15 April, which claimed the lives of a Maronite member of parliament, a leading Lebanese novelist and the Spanish ambassador to Lebanon, and which continued for three days non-stop, Aoun stepped up his invective against Syria. But instead of arousing sympathy for his cause, he succeeded only in further alienating moderate opinion in his territory.

As pragmatists at heart, the Christian members of parliament (MPs) based in East Beirut attempted to distance themselves from Aoun. Meeting under the auspices of Patriarch Sfier at his home in Bkirke on 18 April, twenty-three Christian MPs called for an immediate truce and the lifting of the blockade on ports. Their appeal was immediately picked up by the Muslim MPs of West Beirut and others, including Shaikh Hassan Khalid, the grand mufti of the Sunnis, as well as the head of the Islamic Alignment. Since the Christian MPs' communiqué did not endorse Aoun's demand for the Syrian withdrawal, Aoun was angry. He dismissed the parliamentary deputies as 'irrelevant and unrepresentative', adding that the moribund parliament was illegitimate. 'Don't be afraid if presidential elections don't take place', he declared. 'If there is no [elected] president, there is always a commander imposed by the people.'[10] He combined this declaration with a defiance of Syria and a personal attack on President Assad. 'We have reached a point where shells do not hurt us any more', he said in an interview with Voice of Lebanon on 18 April 1989. 'Only one head will be broken, the head of Hafiz Assad. How long will this criminal continue his bombardment? Nevertheless, Lebanon will be his grave and that of his regime.'[11] With this, he destroyed any chance of compromise with the powerful Syrian leader.

There was brief truce from 20 to 25 April as a prelude to the meeting of the Arab League Committee of Six to address the crisis. On 27 April the Committee called for an immediate ceasefire, the opening of all ports and transit points to the outside world, and the presence of an Arab Observer Force for three months during which political issues could be discussed. The Arab Observer Force was to consist of 312 officers from the armies of Algeria, Jordan, Kuwait, North Yemen, Sudan and Tunisia. While Prime Minister Hoss accepted the peace plan, the justice minister, Nabih Berri, rejected it, and Walid Jumblatt demanded that all ships docking at the ports inside the Christian enclave be searched for arms. Aoun gave his consent to the plan because the introduction of an Arab Observer Force meant Arabizing the Lebanese crisis, which he visualized as paving the way for Syria's expulsion from his country. Unsurprisingly, Damascus, which routinely described Lebanon as a strategic extension of Syria, took unkindly to the idea of an Arab Observer Force, which it regarded as a challenge to its claim of maintaining exclusive influence in Lebanon. It therefore set out quietly to sabotage the scheme.

On 2 May, two representatives of the Committee of Six arrived in the Lebanese capital for talks. Thanks to their mediation, General Aoun agreed to let the 'illegal' Muslim militia ports reopen, and the two rival governments consented to suspend land, sea and air blockades for three months. On 7 May, the Muslim festival of Eid al Fitr, the ten-day-old truce broke down because Aoun used the lifting of the sea blockade to bring in Iraqi arms, thus upsetting West Beirut and Damascus.

A week later, the representatives of the Committee of Six left for Kuwait with a four-point plan to be placed before the forthcoming Arab summit in Casablanca on 23 May. There, Iraq, Egypt and Jordan demanded a timetable for the withdrawal of all foreign troops from Lebanon. Assad stood his ground. 'The relationship between Syria and Lebanon has a special historical, geographical and human character without parallel in Lebanon's relations with any other Arab state', he said. 'Syrian forces will not leave Lebanon except by a Lebanese agreement in a national referendum or by a request from a unified central government.'[12] There were bitter exchanges between the Iraqi and Syrian presidents, with Saddam Hussein berating Assad for letting the (non-Arab) Iranians into Lebanon, and Assad wondering aloud if those calling for an Arab peacekeeping force could turn it into an effective instrument. In the end, given the presence of

35,000 Syrian troops in Lebanon, the summit, which lacked any representative of Lebanon, shied away from pressing for the withdrawal of the Syrian force. A disappointed Saddam Hussein left Casablanca a day before the summit ended.

However, the summit upgraded its interest in the issue by replacing the Committee of Six with the Tripartite Committee of King Fahd ibn Abdul Aziz of Saudi Arabia, King Hassan II of Morocco and President Chadli Benjadid of Algeria. The new Committee was given six months to settle the Lebanese crisis with the assistance of the Lebanese MPs, since they were the only popular representatives with authority to approve any proposals for political reform. The Committee's specific task was to consolidate the truce and the lifting of the sea and land blockades, and to facilitate discussion of reform leading to the election of a new president and the formation of a fresh government – to pave the way for the withdrawal of all foreign forces. Significantly, while demanding the withdrawal of Israel from Lebanon, the summit resolution made no mention either of an Arab peacekeeping force or any reduction in the Syrian military presence in Lebanon. (This was at variance with the demands of Aoun who, while pressing for the Syrian pull-back, wanted the UN to tackle the Israeli occupation of south Lebanon. By and large, the Maronites regarded the Israeli troops and their Lebanese surrogates as useful in containing the Shia and Palestinian militias in the south.) The summit decisions were welcomed in Lebanon by among others Prime Minister Hoss.

By the time the ceasefire took hold in late May, 480 people had lost their lives and another 2,850 had received injuries,[13] hundreds of millions of Lebanese pounds worth of property and earnings had been lost, and tens of thousands of Lebanese had fled the country with their capital. However, following the lifting of the sea blockade, maritime activity had increased sharply, with the number of ships calling at the Christian port of Jounieh jumping from one in March to forty-one in April and ninety-three in May, and the tonnage handled rising nearly eighteenfold during the period, from 1,156 tons to 20,505 tons.[14]

The Arab League Tripartite Committee met in Rabat on 4 June, and then flew to Damascus to meet Assad on 8 June. After that its representative, Lakhdar Ibrahimi, an Algerian diplomat, kept up the momentum for peace by shuttling between Damascus and Beirut.

Ibrahimi's diplomacy was needed. Following the successful unloading of 1.3 million gallons of fuel from a ship that had docked in a port in the Christian enclave on 4 June, the Druze and Syrian troops stepped up attacks on the Christian ports and residential areas. The shelling continued for several days, with the Christian sector suffering acute shortages of petrol, fuel oil and other necessities due to the reimposed sea and land blockades. Over the weekend of 10–11 June, the fighting spread to the Souq al Gharb front.

Regional tensions shot up in mid-June as President Assad raised the stakes when he discovered that Iraq was shipping Soviet-made Frog-7 surface-to-surface missiles (with a range of 120 km) to Aoun through the Jordanian port of Aqaba – thus placing Damascus within the firing range of Aoun's army. On 17 June Assad asked King Hussein of Jordan to stop the loading of Frog-7 missiles at Aqaba. When King Hussein refused to stop the departure of a Greek-flagged freighter loaded with the missiles, Assad approached Moscow to intervene, and sent a message to President Hosni Mubarak of Egypt to turn the vessel back in the Gulf of Suez. (In the past, the Egyptian president had turned back Iraqi shipments of arms at least twice.) When Mubarak failed to act, partly because by now his country had joined Iraq, Jordan and North Yemen to form the Arab Co-operation Council, Assad informed the Soviets that Syria would attack the arms ship destined for Aoun. On 28 June Assad repeated the warning to the US embassy in Damascus, saying he would order an attack on the freighter if it continued sailing towards its destination.

Since Syrian gunboats had hit two ships heading for Jounieh over the past four weeks, Assad's threat was taken seriously. On 29 June Moscow sent a special envoy to Baghdad. About then the US embassy in Baghdad asked the Iraqis to avoid confrontation with Syria on the high seas, on the ground that an armed clash near the Israeli coast might get out of hand and escalate into a full-scale war. Washington also contacted Moscow. Thus pressured, on 2 July the Iraqi president ordered the arms freighter to turn back.

Soon after, Baghdad announced that it would cease arms shipments to the Lebanese Christians.[15] But, distrustful of Saddam Hussein's word, Assad insisted that Aoun return to Iraq any Frog-7 missiles he might have received earlier, and tightened the sea blockade of the Christian enclave by adding two Syrian frigates to the six gunboats that had already been cruising offshore. On 9 July, Syrian shells hit a Maltese-flagged oil tanker heading for the Christian sector; and the following day the Syrian gunboats hit a Jounieh–Larnaca ferry. While an oil tanker managed to break the embargo on 14 July, the Syrian artillery hit a Greek-flagged tanker on 23 July, with the Syrian navy towing the damaged vessel to a port in northern Lebanon. Little wonder that the number of ships calling at Jounieh dropped from ninety-seven in June to sixteen in July.[16]

By then Aoun had also experienced a diplomatic setback. On 28 June the Arab League Tripartite Committee, meeting in Oran, Algeria, announced its plans for securing peace in Lebanon, including the convening of a parliamentary session in a foreign Arab country. As an ultra-nationalist, Aoun objected vehemently to the idea of the Lebanese parliament meeting outside Lebanon. But his stand proved unpopular among Arab diplomats: it ignored the fact that in 1983 and 1984 Christian notables participated in a debate on political reform at two reconciliation conferences held in Switzerland.

Equally, Syria's diplomatic standing suffered when it found itself at odds with the Tripartite Committee's recommendations. Following its meeting in Rabat on 22 July, the Committee declared that it had reached an impasse. Nine days later the foreign ministers of the three countries issued an interim report, which concluded that the situation in Lebanon was grim 'even beyond our most pessimistic expectations'. The document was critical of Damascus in two areas: (a) Syrian–Lebanese relations, and (b) the Lebanese government's aim to extend its authority over all of Lebanon. On (a), the Committee favoured close Syrian–Lebanese co-ordination in the Beqaa valley to face the Israeli threat, and a looser arrangement elsewhere. On (b), it recommended a comprehensive security plan to be implemented in conjunction with political reform and elections tied to a graduated withdrawal of Syrian soldiers, who were to be replaced by Lebanese troops. Damascus criticized the latest Arab League report, and stuck to its concept of Syrian–Lebanese co-operation and co-ordination encompassing 'strategic, economic, social and other aspects' as outlined in the December 1985 Tripartite Agreement, which was signed by Berri, Jumblatt and Hobeika.

Heavy shelling from both sides, which started on the eve of the 22 July meeting of the Arab League Troika, continued for several days, reaching a peak on 27 July with eight hours of non-stop exchanges, with the Christian camp using Israeli-made phosphorus bombs and 240 mm mortars.[17] That day Geagea agreed to co-ordinate the artillery salvos of his LF militia with Aon's troops so as to create a belt of artillery fire to enable the incoming ships to enter Jounieh and Beirut ports. The intermittent but intense fighting since March had considerably reduced the 1.5 million population of the two sectors of Beirut.

For the first time in fourteen years of warfare, there was no organization able to reinstate broken ceasefires because Aoun had rejected the traditional all-Lebanese truce committees, insisting that these must contain Syrian representatives. This demand was rejected by Prime Minister Hoss, who viewed it as a ploy on Aoun's part to strike a direct deal with Damascus, bypassing the West Beirut government.

On 28 July events in southern Lebanon grabbed front-page newspaper headlines and leads in television news bulletins in the West. On that day the IDF abducted an eminent Shia cleric, Shaikh Abdul Karim Obeid, and two of his aides from a village in south Lebanon using airborne commandos. This refocused the Western world's attention on its sixteen hostages in Lebanon: nine Americans, five Britons and two Germans.

Taking of local hostages for political reasons or ransom had been part of the civil war since the beginning. But a foreign element was introduced in mid-March 1982 by the Maronite militiamen. They kidnapped four Iranian diplomats: Kazem Akhvan Allaf, Ahmad Motevaselian, Muhsin Musavi and Muhammad Taqi Muqadam. Since the Iranians were never released, it was widely believed that they were killed by their captors. In retaliation, the Islamic Jihad Organization abducted David Dodge, the acting president of the American University in Beirut (AUB), on 19 July 1982.[18] Periodic kidnapping of Western nationals by Lebanese and Palestinian groups bearing various names, but controlled overall by the Hizbollah leadership, continued. By mid-1989 the Islamic Jihad Organization (IJO) held two US citizens – Terry Anderson, a journalist, and Thomas Sutherland, an academic – taken captive respectively in March and June 1985. The Islamic Jihad for the Liberation of Palestine (IJLP), which had abducted three American academics – Robert Polhill, Jesse Turner and Allan Steen – in January 1987 wanted to exchange them for the hundreds of Palestinians detained without charges in Israeli gaols. The Revolutionary Justice Organization (RJO) held two US citizens, including Joseph Ciccipio, deputy comptroller at the American University in Beirut, who had converted to Islam to marry a Lebanese Muslim. The IJO had also been holding a British television journalist, John McCarthy, since mid-April 1986. He had been seized on his way to Beirut airport in the wake of air raids on Libya by US F-111s, based in Britain, when feelings against the United States and Britain were running high among militant Lebanese and Palestinians. Soon after, purportedly acting on behalf of the Libyan leader,

Muammar Qadhafi, the Revolutionary Organization of Socialist Muslims, a Palestinian group led by Abu Nidal, killed Peter Kilburn, an American librarian at the AUB, and Alec Collett, a British freelance writer.[19] Terry Waite, an envoy of the British Archbishop of Canterbury, Robert Runcie, who had been negotiating with the IJO for the release of the Western hostages, was himself taken captive in January 1987. Later, a group calling itself the Organization of the Oppressed of the Earth (OOTOOTE) claimed to be holding him.

It was the OOTOOTE which had kidnapped Lt-Colonel William Higgins, a US marine officer serving with Unifil, as an alleged agent of the CIA, in early 1988. Following the Israeli abduction of Shaikh Obeid, the OOTOOTE threatened to hang Higgins unless Obeid and his two aides were freed by Israel within twenty-four hours. Israel refused to do so. The next day, 31 July, the OOTOOTE released a video showing Higgins hanging by a rope.

Next the RJO threatened to kill Joseph Ciccipio if Shaikh Obeid was not released. Ciccipio's wife made a plea for her husband. In response, on 1 August the RJO announced forty-eight hours' stay of his execution. As the USA flexed its military muscle, with the Pentagon assembling a fleet of fourteen ships in the eastern Mediterranean, the Hizbollah, the umbrella organization of the militant Shia groups, threatened retaliation. While offering to help secure the release of the Western hostages in Lebanon, the recently elected Iranian president, Rafsanjani, issued a friendly but strong warning to President George Bush against using military means.[20] Damascus argued that any solution to the latest crisis over the hostages should take into account the larger problem of Lebanon.

On 6 August the RJO offered to free Ciccipio if Israel released Obeid and 450 Arab captives: 150 Lebanese prisoners belonging to the national and Islamic resistance, and 300 Palestinians gaoled for participating in the intifada, divided equally between Hamas, an Islamic organization inside the Occupied Territories, the Islamic Jihad, and the United Leadership of the Uprising. On 9 August, Shaikh Assad Berro, a friend of Obeid, mounted a suicide attack on an Israeli convoy in south Lebanon, injuring six Israeli soldiers. Once the hostage-takers had refrained from killing any captives and the USA had reciprocated by not using force, tension subsided, leading to a decline in Western media interest in the hostage issue.

Fighting between the warring Lebanese factions, now abundantly equipped with multiple-rocket launchers firing forty to sixty rockets at a time, resumed in the Beirut area and elsewhere with greater ferocity than before due to Aoun's decision to escalate the conflict. In order to internationalize the conflict he resorted to *inter alia* commando actions. The resulting violence, which led to 500 deaths – coupled with perilous living conditions typified by barely two hours of running water every four or five days[21] and one hour of electricity daily – caused a large-scale exodus. By early August, when up to 350,000 people, about 40 per cent of the population of West Beirut, had fled to the south,[22] a similar proportion of the residents of East Beirut had escaped to the mountains or emigrated altogether.

On 10 and 11 August, some 10,500 shells were fired by both sides, with the Druze militia in the Souq al Gharb coming under heavy fire from the Christian side. Syria responded by despatching tank columns to the fronts across Dahr al Baidar pass, and by increasing shell fire, using among others 240 mm mortars, more to depress civilian morale than to destroy military targets. On 13 August a force of 1,200 men – consisting of the Druze militia, the pro-Syrian Palestinian guerrillas and the Syrian Special Forces commandos – staged a dawn assault on the Souq al Gharb ridge, which formed a major demarcation between Christian and Muslim camps, thus lessening Christian pressure on West Beirut. The fierce combat left eighty people dead in four days, and raised sectarian passions so sharply that the 2,000 Muslim troops, who formed part of the four brigades under Aoun, defected and travelled to Tripoli under the control of the Syrians.[23] However, since the Muslim side failed to capture the Souq al Gharb ridge, Aoun claimed victory.

Overall, since March 1989 three major factors had contributed to the ferocity of combat: the audacity of Aoun in challenging Syria's might and making repeated personal attacks on its president; the end of the Iran–Iraq War, which had allowed Saddam Hussein to turn his attention to stoking up trouble for his long-standing Arab rival, Assad, by intensifying trouble in his back yard, Lebanon; and the rise of intifada in the Occupied Territories, which had deprived Assad of his Palestinian card, thus making him more determined to succeed in Lebanon.

The murderous intensity of fighting activated various capitals: Paris, the Vatican, Washington, Moscow and New York (the headquarters of the UN). The US administration issued a statement condemning 'slaughter of innocent people and renewed use of heavy calibre weapons'. The French president despatched envoys to Damascus, Riyadh, Washington, Moscow, the Vatican and Tunis, the headquarters of the Arab League. In the main they concentrated on getting Syria to stop bombarding the Christian enclave.

Finding his rival, Assad, under pressure, Saddam Hussein publicly renewed his support for General Aoun. On 14 August the Iraqi News Agency reported that President Hussein had telephoned Aoun saying that Iraq would continue to back his forces, and that Assad was 'implementing an evil conspiracy in Lebanon that is aimed at dividing up the Arab world and sowing discord among its people'.[24]

That day fourteen Lebanese and four Lebanon-based Palestinian groups, meeting in Damascus, decided to form the Lebanese National Front with the following aims: to scrap the confessional system; to end the Israeli presence; to defeat Aoun's political and military programme; and to banish the concept of 'red lines', meaning understandings reached between various foreign powers regarding the limits in Lebanon which were not to be crossed. Unprecedentedly, the Front included both secular and religious groups: Amal, Islamic Amal, Hizbollah, the Druze-dominated Progressive Socialist Party, the pro-Syrian Arab Baath Socialist Party, the Lebanese Communist Party, the Syrian Social Nationalist Party (Emergency Council), the Syrian Social Nationalist Party (Supreme Council), and the Tawheed (based in Tripoli). Among the Palestinian groups were the Popular Front for the Liberation of Palestine – General Command (PFLP–GC), headed by Ahmad Jibril, and Fatah Intifada (also known as the Fatah Provisional Command) led by Abu Musa.

The next day the Lebanese groups decided to form an alliance of their militias having an aggregate strength of 18,000, with 10,000 men belonging to the secular parties and 8,000 to the Islamic – a move which showed that Aoun's continued obduracy had succeeded in cementing differing elements in the opposing camp to an extent considered unlikely before. 'There are no more "red lines"', said George Hawi of the Lebanese Communist Party. 'Syria and Iran will support the war against Aoun materially and in every other way. The Hizbollah will participate in the war. A unified front will emerge to rally all material and human resources to topple the agent regime led by Aoun's clique.' This was confirmed by General Mustafa Tlas, the defence minister of Syria. 'Under no circumstances will we permit a defeat of the Lebanese patriotic forces', he said in an interview with a Kuwaiti newspaper.[25]

To underline the point, on 15 August the Syrian troops, assisted by Suleiman Franjieh's militia, launched an attack at Maad, southeast of Batroun, opening a new front, and gathered along the

Christian enclave's northern front. Severe fighting broke out in the Beirut and Batroun regions, including heavy shelling of Jounieh by the Syrians. Pope John Paul II intervened. 'In the name of God, I appeal to the Syrian authorities to stop the bombardments which threaten to destroy the capital of Lebanon, and the whole country', he said. 'Do not take on the mantle of Cain, he who was guilty of the death of his brother.'[26] That day, on his own initiative, the UN secretary-general, Javier Perez de Cuellar, convened an extraordinary Security Council meeting on Lebanon.

On 16 August the Security Council issued a statement, not a resolution. 'The Council reaffirms its statement of 24 April 1989 and urgently appeals to all the parties to put an end to all operations and to all firing and shelling on land and at sea', it said. 'It firmly appeals to all the parties to observe a total and immediate ceasefire. It also appeals to them to secure the consolidation of the ceasefire, the opening of the lines of communication, and the lifting of the sieges.' The Council expressed its full support for the Arab League Troika in the efforts it was making with a view to putting an end to the trials of the Lebanese people through the establishment of an effective and definitive ceasefire.[27]

Following this, and following Moscow's appeal to Damascus to stop the bloodshed, warfare subsided, but only briefly. Indeed, on 19 August the armed militias returned to West Beirut's streets. As a French aircraft carrier and a frigate steamed towards Lebanon, the Revolutionary Justice Organization threatened retaliation – by killing its American hostages – if France intervened. Jumblatt vowed 'to repel France as we did before', alluding to the truck-bombings of October 1983 and their aftermath.[28] In his interview with the Paris-based *Journal du Dimanche* (Sunday Journal), published on 20 August, Aoun said that he 'would like a French military intervention' but did not want 'to compromise France with a Lebanese request'. In response the Hizbollah said: 'The era of the Crusaders' invasion has gone, following the spread of the spirit of martyrdom that forced the [US] marines and the French to retreat in 1983.'[29]

On 22 August, Syria accused France of complicating the Lebanese crisis. Prime Minister Hoss said that the sole purpose of the French fleet was 'a possible evacuation of French nationals', amounting to 7,000, of whom 5,700 had dual nationality.[30] However, Aoun expected the French warships to break the Syrian sea blockade of the Christian enclave. Most foreign observers thought that the French purpose was to deter a full-scale Syrian attack on the Christian enclave. Paris set the record straight by declaring that its flotilla was 200 miles from Lebanon and not 12 miles (as had been rumoured), and that the nearest any French warship had reached was Larnaca, 120 miles from Lebanon. Nonetheless, the French military move inhibited a fresh Syrian assault, and put pressure on Moscow to lean on Damascus.

Britain lacked ties with Damascus, broken off in April 1986 following an attempt by a London-based Jordanian, Nizar Hindawi, who was believed to be connected with the Syrian embassy, to blow up an Israeli airliner in mid-air. With France behaving in an openly anti-Syrian fashion, America lacking interest in the Lebanese predicament, and China too deeply immersed in its internal problems to be interested in any foreign crisis, the Soviet Union was therefore the only permanent member of the UN Security Council inclined to act positively in the diplomatic arena. It did. On 25 August the Soviet envoy Gennady Tarasov met Aoun, Hoss and Patriarch Sfier, who was openly dissatisfied with Aoun's war of liberation. Tarasov left Beirut to meet President Saddam Hussein in Baghdad. He tried to encourage the resumption of the Arab League's peacemaking efforts. In the end Syria refrained from attacking the Christian territory.

There were three main reasons why Assad did not order his troops into the Christian enclave: he did not want his troops to suffer casualties since Syria's involvement in Lebanon was unpopular with his armed forces; the Syrian soldiers inside the Christian sector would have been open to terrorist attacks, which would have made their stay problematic, to say the least; and Syria's direct, large-scale intervention would have been condemned not only by the West but also by leading Arab countries.

On 28 August the French envoy, François Scheer, offered a peace plan: a ceasefire; a halt to arms deliveries to all parties; political reform to end Christian dominance; and a phased withdrawal of the Syrian troops starting with West Beirut. It secured the endorsement of the Soviet Union, but was turned down by the warring Lebanese camps.

The Syrian success in shelling a Maltese-flagged oil tanker off Jounieh on 29 August upset General Aoun, who was getting increasingly angry with Washington, whom he accused of pressuring 'friendly states [such as France] to stop them giving military assistance to the Lebanese', and of 'selling Lebanon to Syria'. Despite repeated appeals by the general, John McCarthy, the US ambassador who had arrived at the American mission in East Beirut in late 1988, had refused to present his credentials to the Aoun government. (Nor had he done so to the Hoss administration.) In an interview with the French newspaper *Le Figaro*, published in early September, Aoun alluded to the US envoy's failure to present his credentials to the government in East Beirut, thus denying his mission diplomatic protection, and warned that American diplomats might be kidnapped.

On 5 September pro-Aoun Christians demonstrated outside the US embassy to express their anger at Washington's policies. Surrounded by a mob that seemed to have besieged the mission, the American ambassador called on General Aoun to help. Aoun refused to act because, he argued, Washington had not recognized his administration. The next day, following the US state department's instructions, the ambassador closed the mission instantly; and he and his American staff of twenty-nine left for Cyprus. This convinced Aoun that he could not count on international help to expel the Syrians, and that he needed to intensify the violence. There was heavy bombardment in the Beirut region on 7 September, followed by the escalation of fighting on the Madfoun and upper Metn fronts for four days.

On 14 September, exactly six months after the launching of the war of liberation by Aoun, the Arab League Troika presented a seven-point plan. It included: a Lebanese Joint Security Committee to be set up under Lakhdar Ibrahimi, an Algerian diplomat; the Syrian naval blockade to be lifted; the Joint Security Committee to have the right to inspect any ship alleged to be carrying arms; Beirut's international airport to be reopened; all states to work to stop arms inflow into Lebanon; and the Lebanese parliamentary deputies to meet outside Lebanon (on 30 September) and discuss a 'charter of national reconciliation'.

Aoun turned down the plan, partly because it contained a Joint Security Committee, which was exclusively Lebanese, ignoring his demand for the inclusion of Syria in it; and partly because the Lebanese parliamentarians were to meet outside the country, an idea he had rejected before on nationalistic grounds. His stance could be summarized thus: first Lebanon must be free of all occupations, then reform could be worked out.

Aoun's adversaries, particularly Syria, found the plan satisfactory. The change in the Troika's position towards Damascus from the one adopted in late July reflected the change in the Saudi stance. This stemmed from Riyadh's fear of the rise in Iraqi influence in the region, and Washington's pressure on it to appease Damascus as a *quid pro quo* for the latter's promise to help in the release of Western hostages, a subject which continued to interest the Western media and public.

On 17 September the Arab League Troika published a draft National Reconciliation Charter for discussion by the Lebanese parliamentarians at their session in Taif, Saudi Arabia, starting on 30 September. It included among other things a plan for gradual Syrian military redeployment in Lebanon, with written guarantees, following the formation of a new government.

The next day, King Hussein of Jordan endorsed the Arab League Troika's peace package, which implied that he had either stopped trans-shipment of Iraqi arms or was about to do so. The next day a meeting of the Christian leaders urged Aoun to accept the Troika's proposals. Washington and Moscow issued a joint statement urging all parties to do so; as did Paris.

Reversing his position, Aoun accepted the Troika plan on the night of Friday, 22 September, thus creating the basis for a truce. The change in the Aoun camp was brought about by its military inferiority, its weakness on the domestic front, and weather. Despite the fact that Syria had deployed in Lebanon only about 10 per cent of its total 300,000 army troops, most of them in the Beqaa valley, they were so well equipped that in the six months of fighting their 600 artillery guns had fired 300,000 shells at the Christian enclave, a performance the Aoun loyalists could not match, especially when, given the geography of the region, their military supplies from Iraq were at best erratic. The civilian morale in the Christian territory, already low due to the shortages of basic necessities caused by Syria's land and sea blockades, plummeted as the deadly 240 mm mortars of the Syrian military began to fall. Finally, Aoun realized that the approaching rains and cold weather were not conducive to fighting.

The intermittent six-month war, which encompassed one-third to a half of Lebanon, from Damour, south of Beirut, to Batroun in the north, and the Beqaa in the east, caused the deaths of over 1,000 people and injuries to 4,600, and the displacement of a staggering 90 per cent of Beirut's population of 1.5 million, with 600,000 going south, and some 200,000 fleeing Lebanon altogether.[31]

On 23 September the Joint Security Committee, headed by Lakhdar Ibrahimi, began daily meetings to consolidate the ceasefire. The next day Beirut airport resumed business. The lifting of blockades enabled sea ports to reopen. More and more displaced residents returned to the two sectors of Beirut. But there was no change in the political positions of Aoun and his adversaries, with Aoun insisting that there could be no reform before a Syrian withdrawal, and his opponents reiterating that there would be no such pull-back until reforms were instituted.

This, in short, was the situation as the Lebanese parliamentarians prepared to leave for Taif to shape the future of their long-suffering country.

9

The Taif Accord, a trigger for inter-Christian conflict

October 1989 — October 1990

On 30 September 1989, sixty-two Lebanese parliamentarians, half of them Christian and the other half Muslim, plus the speaker, Hussein Husseini, gathered in Taif accounting for all but nine of the surviving MPs.

On the eve of their departure from East Beirut, twenty-four Christian deputies were instructed by General Michel Aoun not to discuss reform until there were firm guarantees of a Syrian withdrawal. Aoun's effort, however, was in vain. At the outset, Muslim MPs refused to link a phased Syrian evacuation to political reform – confident that reform was favoured by both the USA and the Soviet Union, with Washington depatching two envoys to Taif to convey this message to the parliamentary speaker.

Deliberations of the Lebanese assembly were overseen by Saud al Faisal, the foreign minister of Saudi Arabia, the leading member of the Tripartite Committee. He also played an important mediating role, and shuttled between Taif and Damascus. On 9 October the parliament appointed a Formulations Committee of seventeen MPs – including the leader of the Maronite Lebanese Front, Georges Saade – headed by Husseini, to discuss the National Reconciliation Charter which had been drafted by the Tripartite Committee after consultations with Syria. The document proved contentious, with Saade walking out on 12 October, objecting to setting a deadline for ending the confessional system in the administration. To placate him, other members of the Formulations Committee agreed to describe the proposal to staff the government machinery on the basis of Muslim–Christian parity as a 'temporary measure', to be abolished at a rate to be set by a future Committee of the Notables, consisting of former presidents, prime ministers and speakers. Once Saade was mollified, the way was open for the Formulations Committee to recommend to the full house its endorsement of the National Reconciliation Charter.

On 22 October all of the thirty-one Christian MPs and twenty-seven of the thirty-one Muslim deputies signed the Charter. It encompassed political reform – requiring amendment of the 1926 constitution and the 1943 National Pact – as well as the issues of Lebanese sovereignty, the liberation of south Lebanon, and Lebanese–Syrian relations. The agreed reform conciliated the diverse communal demands. By consenting to limit abolition of confessionalism only to the administration (and that too over a long period), and allowing Christians to keep the presidency albeit with reduced powers, Muslim deputies showed a spirit of compromise. Retaining the confessional system also meant that a Sunni Muslim would continue to be the prime minister, which King Fahd of Saudi Arabia, who was inclined to further Sunni interests, found satisfactory. In the sphere of Lebanese–Syrian relations, by accepting Syria's presence for at least two more years after a national unity government had agreed on constitutional reform, Christian deputies provided Syria with legitimacy – something it had lost with the expiry of the 1976 Arab League mandate in the early 1980s[1] – and conceded Syria's strategic concerns in Lebanon. The Charter they and their Muslim colleagues signed soon gained currency, nationally and internationally, as the Taif Accord/Agreement.

The political reform included amending Articles 17 (concerning executive power), 52 (regarding international treaties) and 53 (concerning presidential powers) of the 1926 Constitution. The original Article 17, which read 'The executive power should be vested in the President of the Republic', was to become 'Executive power is assigned to the Council of Ministers'. This Council was to consist of an equal number of Muslim and Christian ministers. The venue of the cabinet meetings was to be moved from the presidential palace to the prime minister's office or a separate cabinet room. The president's attendance at the cabinet meetings was to be optional, and he was not to be allowed to vote. The original Article 53, which empowered the president to designate the prime minister for approval by parliament, and to appoint or dismiss ministers, was to be amended. The number of parliamentary deputies was to be raised from 99 to 108, divided equally between Muslims and Christians. The Taif Accord required the president to consult the speaker and senior MPs before designating the prime minister, who was authorized to appoint ministers in consultation with the president, with the right to dismiss a minister being exercised only by the cabinet. Likewise, Article 52, which empowered the president to 'negotiate and ratify international treaties' was to be modified to require the president to secure the consent of the prime minister as well as the approval of the cabinet before an international treaty could become operative. On the whole the agreed reform favoured the cabinet, which, as a collective, emerged more powerful than the prime minister. But to guard against the possibility of Muslim or Christian ministers acting as a bloc and constantly getting their way, a two-thirds majority was specified for cabinet decisions.[2]

Concerning 'establishment of Lebanese state sovereignty over all of the Lebanese soil', which seemingly required foreign assistance to the central authority to extend its jurisdiction, Syria was asked to provide such aid if 'requested' by the Lebanese government. As for Syria's military presence in Lebanon, redeployment was to begin within two years of the formation of a national unity government under a properly elected president, with the Syrian troops undertaking phased withdrawal from Beirut to the Beqaa valley, the new Syrian line being at Hammana, 20 km from the eastern outskirts of Beirut. The details were to be specified by a joint Lebanese–Syrian Committee, and the Arab League Troika guaranteed Syrian compliance. Prince Saud al Faisal pledged Arab League support for the National Reconciliation Charter; and the Troika promised an Arab League summit after the Syrian redeployment in Beqaa to encourage Beirut and Damascus to agree on a date for complete Syrian withdrawal.

However, General Aoun immediately denounced the National Reconciliation Charter, saying that it failed to meet his precondition about setting a timetable for the Syrian withdrawal first. A strike in the Christian enclave on 24 October closed down businesses, banks, schools and colleges, allowing the students to mount a large, pro-Aoun demonstration outside the presidential palace. His young, enthusiastic followers made a habit of staging noisy demonstrations and rallies daily. Addressing supporters who had gathered for the third day running outside his palace, Aoun demanded 'severe punishment' for the parliamentarians who had voted for the Taif Accord, which he described as 'an unforgivable crime' committed by people who had lost their identity and were traitors.[3] He called for a referendum on the Accord. Given the prevalent feeling among Muslims that, despite the fact that they formed 57 to 60 per cent of the national population, their leaders had settled for parity with Christians, and that Maronites had surrendered too little of their privilege, the Taif Accord would have probably failed to win a majority vote. But in the light of prevalent civil disorder and lack of security, holding a national referendum was out of the question.

In any case Aoun's idea was shot down by none other than the Lebanese Front – composed among others of the Phalange Party, the Lebanese Forces and the National Liberal Party (led by Danny Chamoun) – which on 25 October backed the Taif Accord. It urged the nation's leaders 'to treat the Arab and international resolutions with flexibility in order to take advantage of their positive elements and limit their negative elements'.[4] Patriarch Sfier, who was in the Vatican while the parliament met in Taif, applauded the agreement, urging the Christian MPs to vote for it at a parliamentary session inside Lebanon, thus transforming it into a legal document, and to co-operate with the West Beirut government in electing the next head of state. 'We have no interest in electing a president who is against Syria', he declared. Sfier found himself backed by most of the traditional Christian politicians. Together, they warned that rejecting the Taif Accord would lead to a new round of warfare in which the Christian side would find itself abandoned by all its past foreign allies, a very realistic prediction. On 28 October the Phalange Party reaffirmed its support for holding an election for president, and urged Aoun to choose a path of peace. The following Sunday Sfier delivered a sermon from the pulpit in East Beirut in which he described Aoun's stand as 'illegal and unconstitutional'.[5]

General Aoun turned to the United Nations, lodging a formal protest with the UN secretary-general against the presence of foreign troops, particularly those from Syria, who occupied the largest part of Lebanon. He accused Damascus of 'inhuman and amoral practices, the assassinations of political and religious personalities, bombardments, blockades, the destruction of the entire Lebanese infrastructure'. On 1 November, having considered Aoun's letter, the Security Council endorsed the Taif Accord, already backed by the USA, the USSR, Britain, France and the Vatican.

Fearing reprisals from the Aoun government and its supporters, the Christian MPs had decided not to return home, and had flown instead to Paris from Taif. There they awaited a call for a parliamentary session inside Lebanon to vote on the Taif Accord and to elect the president. Lakhdar Ibrahimi, the Arab League Troika's representative, soon arrived in Damascus to discuss convening the Lebanese parliament, a step actively supported by both Riyadh and Washington.

As Aoun threatened to dissolve parliament – the last key institutional embodiment of the theory of a unified Lebanon, along with the Central Bank, headed by Edmond Naim, a Maronite – the Council of Maronite Bishops issued a statement insisting on 'the preservation of democracy'. The Phalange Party warned that the dissolution of parliament would undermine the foundations of the republic.

On 3 November, General Aoun issued a final call to the Christian MPs in Paris to return to the Lebanese capital to 'explain' their treacherous action to the people. At the same time, bombs went off at the homes of three of them in East Beirut and Jounieh. The parliamentarians ignored his call. The next day Aoun dissolved the parliament, arguing that political authority had passed on to his 'transitional government' from President Gemayel, and that any move made by the 'former' MPs would therefore be null and void. Prime Minister Hoss described Aoun's action as illegal.

Ignoring Michel Aoun's moves, the Lebanese parliament met on Saturday, 4 November, at the Qulayaat airstrip in the Syrian-controlled northern Lebanon, four miles from the Syrian border. Thirty of the thirty-one Christian MPs flew in from Paris; and twenty-seven Muslim parliamentarians and the speaker, Husseini, arrived from West Beirut, bringing the voting total to fifty-eight or four-fifths of the surviving MPs. They ratified the National Reconciliation Charter adopted earlier at Taif. Then fifty-two of them voted Rene Muawad, a 64-year-old Maronite, as president. He had been an MP for his home town of Zgharta, the power base of Suleiman Franjieh, a long-standing ally of Syria. In 1958 Muawad had disagreed with President Chamoun's calling of US marines and had gone to Damascus, where he had cultivated good relations with the Syrian leadership. Now, recognizing the importance of the Syrian presence in Lebanon, he said: 'There is no solution to the Lebanese ordeal without the active help of Syria, to which Lebanon is bound geographically, historically and nationally.'[6] A conciliator, Muawad promised to form a broad-based national unity government.

On Sunday, 5 November, while Patriarch Sfier backed Muawad in his sermon, describing Aoun's actions as illegal and unconstitutional, Aoun dismissed the parliamentary session as illegal. His supporters demonstrated outside his palace in Baabda. Later, at night, several thousands of them attacked the residence of Sfier in Bkirke, 7 miles east of Beirut. They beat the 70-year-old patriarch and forced him to kiss a portrait of Aoun. Sfier fled to his summer residence in Diman, a village 52 miles north of Bkirke, inside the Syrian-controlled territory.

Both the Lebanese Front and the Lebanese Forces condemned the assault on the Maronite patriarch. But this had little impact on the popular support for General Aoun. His followers organized a successful general strike on 6 November in East Beirut as well as other parts of the Christian enclave. Buoyed by this, and the attack by his supporters on the Voice of Lebanon Radio station run by the Phalange Party, the leading political constituent of the Lebanese Front, Aoun threatened to occupy the Phalange headquarters. Samir Geagea, who agreed with the Phalange's policy on the Taif Accord, ordered his Lebanese Forces militia into the streets to protect Phalange offices and property. This dissuaded Aoun from implementing his threat against the Phalange. But he kept up his attacks on the Taif Accord. 'Do you believe in a Syrian withdrawal in the presence of a government and a parliament formed by Syria?' he asked in the course of an interview with the Beirut-based *Al Anwar* (The Light) on 17 November. 'Why was I absent from [i.e. not invited to] Taif? Why were the key Lebanese figures, who represent the Lebanese people, ignored?'

On the other side, whatever reservations Amal's Berri, or the Progressive Socialist Party's Jumblatt, or even the Hizbollah leaders had about the Taif Accord were dropped under pressure from Damascus. Jumblatt had criticized the agreement for its failure to address the questions of the role, size and political orientation of the army, and proposed the convening of a constituent assembly to deal with constitutional reform. Among Shias, even the pro-Damascus Amal was angry. Once again, despite their position as the largest community, the Shias – numbering 1.1 million among 3.6 million Lebanese citizens – had been abandoned by the government, which was dominated by Maronites (estimated to be 900,000 strong) and Sunnis (numbering 750,000).[7] But Amal blamed the Saudi king, the most powerful figure in the Arab League Troika, for the unsatisfactory result of the parliamentary deliberations. The Hizbollah saw the Taif Accord as perpetuating the old system and acting as a barrier to creating an Islamic republic in Lebanon, its ultimate goal. The other major reason for the Druze and Shia dissatisfaction with the Accord was that their militias (as well as those of the Maronites) were to be disbanded within six months of the national unity government being sworn in.

Externally, however, the Taif Agreement, now stamped with parliamentary approval, was well received both in the Arab world and beyond. Unsurprisingly, Abdul Halim Khaddam, the Syrian vice-president, said: 'Syria will give any assistance requested by the national unity government for the extension of its authority to every part of Lebanon.'[8] Even Iraq acquiesced. It promised to stop shipping arms to Aoun, and not to oppose the Muawad administration. Its chargé d'affaires was one of the senior diplomats from the fifty-plus embassies based in West and East Beirut who were received by Muawad within a week of his assuming office.[9] Unable to move into the presidential palace at Baabda, which Aoun refused to vacate, Muawad had set up office in an apartment block in West Beirut.

On 13 November he asked Salim Hoss, who had been the prime minister since June 1987, to form a national unity government to implement the Taif Accord. But before he could do so, the president was assassinated. On 22 November he and twenty-two others, forming part of the presidential motorcade returning from an Independence Day reception, were killed by a huge bomb which exploded on a West Beirut road as the motorcade passed. Prime Minister Hoss and Speaker Husseini narrowly escaped. As always, there were various theories as to who had engineered the explosion. Since Muawad was Syria's nominee, Damascus and other capitals friendly to it – such as Riyadh, which worked in close conjunction with Washington – were ruled out. That narrowed the field to those internal and external parties which stood to lose either their political/diplomatic power or their ability to manoeuvre Lebanese factions due to a gradual return to normality in Lebanon – the Aoun camp being foremost among them, followed by Israel, the Hizbollah and Iran.[10] If Israel was behind this explosion, then it got even with Syria for the blowing up of its presidential nominee, Bashir Gemayel, seven years earlier.

Although shocked, the leaders in West Beirut and Damascus, acting in conjunction with Riyadh and Washington, moved swiftly to fill the power vacuum. On 24 November fifty-two Lebanese parliamentarians, forming three-quarters of the surviving MPs, first assembled in Baalbek, and then moved to a hotel in Shtura, a Syrian military centre. They extended the parliament's life by further three years, until 1993. Then forty-seven of them voted for Elias Hrawi (b. 1930), a Maronite MP from Zahle, as president. Hrawi called for special ties between Lebanon and Syria, and asked Salim Hoss to form a new government.

The next day Prime Minister Hoss announced a cabinet of fourteen, divided equally between Muslims (three Sunni, three Shia and one Druze) and Christians (three Maronites, two Greek Orthodox, one Greek Catholic and one Armenian Orthodox), and including Saade, Berri and Jumblatt. President Hrawi dismissed General Aoun's cabinet on 26 November, and ordered him to vacate the Baabda palace. Refusing to recognize Hrawi's election, Aoun rejected his call to leave the official headquarters.

On 28 November the Hrawi–Hoss government dismissed General Aoun as the military chief of staff, and replaced him with the acting chief of staff, General Emile Lahoud, who had abandoned Aoun some months earlier. Lahoud urged the four army brigades based in the Christian sector to transfer their loyalty to him, but in vain. Indeed, Lahoud's action had the contrary effect of intensifying the Aoun loyalists' commitment to their leader.

East Beirut observed a general strike in solidarity with Aoun, whose supporters took to demonstrating outside the shell-blasted presidential palace in Baabda. Each day crowds around the Aoun headquarters grew bigger and noisier. They were addressed by among others Shaikh Imad Hassan Najar, leader of the Muslim Solidarity delegation from the Sunni quarters of West Beirut. He accused the Syrians of murdering five leading religious and political personalities, the latest being Nazim Qadri, a Muslim MP, in May on the day he was to have lunch with Aoun. Earlier Qadri had called on the Lebanese people to 'revolt, to say "No" to the Syrians, to all occupiers and foreigners who seek to divide us'. Now Shaikh Najar concluded his speech outside the Baabda palace with the cry 'God is Great – and Aoun is the beloved of God'. The Christian crowd took up the slogan.[11]

President Assad decided to act, militarily, before the incipient division within the Muslim camp solidified and weakened his base in Lebanon. He bolstered Syria's military strength in Lebanon to 45,000 by despatching three more Syrian brigades through the Dahr al Baidar pass into the Beirut zone, and amassed other Syrian units on the edges of the Christian enclave, putting them all on high alert. Finding the full Syrian military might poised against him, Aoun temporized. In an interview on French radio on 29 November he said: 'I am ready to compromise and respect the vital interests of Syria, but not to cede the fundamental rights of the Lebanese people, above all their right to self-determination.'[12]

His apparent reasonableness increased Aoun's popularity, with even more people coming out in the streets to demonstrate for him. Aware of the Syrian troops poised to attack, they staged a twenty-four-hour sit-in around the Baabda palace, thus providing Aoun with a perpetual human shield. This tactic, which involved tens of thousands of civilians and continued for the next four weeks, proved effective.

Admitting that fear of a civilian bloodbath had so far prevented an attack on Baabda, President Hrawi said on 1 December that he was prepared to give more time for diplomacy to resolve the crisis. He appealed to Washington, Moscow and Paris to help in evicting Aoun from the presidential palace. While the Americans pressured France to ease out Aoun, they and the Saudis urged the Syrians not to attack the Christian enclave.

Aoun needed to devise a plan to resist the Syrians if they carried out their threat. He appealed to the Israelis through the commander of the Israeli-run Southern Lebanon Army, Antoine Lahad, for military support in case of a Syrian offensive. At home he turned to his erstwhile rival, Samir Geagea, the LF commander, who had recognized the presidency of Hrawi, whom he described as 'the son of the Christian area'. Finding Aoun pleading for his assistance as a fellow-Christian, Geagea declared that in case of a Syrian attack, the LF would stand with Aoun's units to 'defend the Christian area'.[13]

On 3 December, Sunday, as Syria readied its troops for an all-out assault on the Christian territory, President Hrawi gave Aoun two days to leave the presidential palace. 'In case Aoun wants to force us it will be an operation of a few hours,' he predicted.[14]

The Aoun camp rallied its foreign supporters. A delegation of 30 French parliamentarians arrived at an improvised airport near Byblos, and drove straight to Baabda to join the pro-Aoun crowds, thus providing fresh impetus to Paris and Washington to restrain Damascus.

America combined its diplomatic pressure on Syria with a public call to General Aoun to step down; and President George Bush joined President Mikhail Gorbachev of the Soviet Union at their summit in Malta in insisting that there must be no violence in Lebanon. There was also a warning from Israel, relayed by Washington, that the Syrian air deployment – an essential part of Syria's plan to overpower the Christian enclave or deliver a quick strike against Baabda – risked an Israeli military response since the Syrian move would violate one of its agreed 'red lines'.[15] Under the circumstances, Assad seemingly put off the Syrian assault against Aoun. Indeed, following Israel's shelling of Nabatiya and Kafr Rumman in the south on 2 December, Prime Minister Hoss said that an attack on the Christian region was ruled out.

Aoun was quick to interpret, vociferously, the Syrian failure to attack the Christian enclave as a victory for his side. His strident defiance and demagogy, which appeared to have succeeded, bolstered his standing, with the previously neutral or adversarial Christian notables now joining his camp. Patriarch Sfier was a case in point. 'General Aoun is a man of courage and integrity', he declared. 'Support for him has grown because his ideas are not just good but necessary . . . A country must be sovereign.' In contrast, President Hrawi was left to repeat the old argument: 'If there had not been innocent people around the former Lebanese army commander [Aoun], we would have suppressed the mutiny and finished the story.'[16]

To keep Aoun on his toes, President Assad said on 9 December that he was prepared to offer military assistance to President Hrawi to oust Aoun. However, by then the Hrawi administration had decided to intensify its economic and diplomatic drive to overthrow the general. Albert Mansur, the Greek Orthodox defence minister, declared on 15 December that the Central Bank would block salary payments to soldiers fighting for Aoun. The diplomatic isolation of the Aoun government increased as a growing number of important foreign powers declared their backing for the Taif Accord. Following the communiqué in favour of the Accord issued on 16 December by Presidents George Bush and François Mitterrand, after a meeting on the Caribbean island of Martinque, the summit conference of the Gulf Co-operation Council (consisting of the six Gulf monarchies) in Muscat, Oman, two days later put out a similar statement. On 28 December, having considered Lebanon's latest complaint against Israel for mounting two major air raids in the Beqaa and the Sidon area, resulting in twelve deaths, the UN Security Council backed the Taif Accord and the efforts of the Arab League Troika to solve the Lebanese crisis.

Whatever satisfaction Aoun derived from aborting the Syrian offensive proved short-lived. Once the Syrian threat had vanished, the simmering tension between his troops and the LF militia, which had persisted during his confrontation with Syria, came to the fore.

The immediate and paramount point of contention between the two Christian forces was the stance on the Taif Agreement. On 13 December the LF magazine, *Al Masira* (The March), stated baldly that the 'war of liberation', which was a mistake, had been lost, and that the Taif Accord should be accepted. Slowly, but surely, such instances led Aoun to a conclusion that he had reached about the LF about a year earlier: he could not function alongside an LF which, possessing an impressive infrastructure, continued as an autonomous power centre. Encouraged by the groundswell of support for him in the wake of successfully thwarting the Syrian plan for a full-scale offensive against the Christian enclave, and freshly aware of the ordinary Christians' dislike of the LF, notorious for its strong-arm methods and extortionist tactics, Aoun felt the time opportune to move against the militia. The LF Command Council, for its part, began to question openly and frequently the soundness of Aoun's political judgement. In early January 1990 it found a reason to doubt the integrity of Aoun, who had made a point of presenting himself as incorruptible and straightforward, and refreshingly different from the typical Christian politician given to compromise and corruption.

On 3 January the Paris-based *Le Canard Enchaîné* revealed that General Aoun held a large sum in a secret bank account in France. Aoun claimed that the money had been 'donated' to him to fight the 'war of liberation'. But the Hrawi–Hoss government challenged this, claiming that the money belonged to the ministry of defence and was meant for arms purchases, and that Aoun had diverted these funds to his personal account. The next day Prime Minister Hoss requested the French foreign minister, Ronald Dumas, to sequestrate these funds. He also called on the US secretary of state, James Baker, to sequestrate the funds available to the Lebanese military attaché in Washington for the purchase of American arms.

The West Beirut administration saw these moves as part of its strategy to oust its rival in East Beirut through financial and diplomatic pressures. On 5 January Aoun warned that, if the financial squeeze on him by the West Beirut government continued, he would set up his own taxation system in the Christian sector. The Hoss administration responded by suspending customs duties on everything except motor vehicles in order to deprive Aoun of a chance of siphoning off its customs revenue, a major source of government income.

With the financial screws tightening on him, Aoun tried to impose his authority more fully in the Christian sector. On 17 January, for instance, he suspended *Al Diyar* (The Houses) for defying his ban on referring to Hrawi as president. The next day two radio stations run respectively by the Phalange Party and the Lebanese Forces went on strike against Aoun's action. In the end, the dispute was settled by a compromise whereby neither Hrawi nor Aoun was to be called president.

Encouraged by the fissures in the Christian leadership, the Hrawi–Hoss administration attempted to show that it was on top of its problems and that the Taif Accord was being implemented. During their meeting with Assad in Damascus on 21 January, Hrawi, Hoss and Speaker Husseini finalized a security plan for West Beirut. It involved a withdrawal of the militias and a phased take-over of security by the Lebanese army and the internal security forces from the Syrians, who were to be concentrated in selected areas, ready to back up the Lebanese units whenever necessary.

The inter-Christian tension in East Beirut reached such a level that on 29 January the Lebanese Forces attacked a position of Aoun's army. An angry Aoun ordered the closure of all LF barracks, and declared that henceforth there would be no 'armed elements outside the framework of the army'. That is, he demanded that the LF should either dissolve itself or merge into the army command. This was summarily rejected by Geagea, who derived his power solely from the LF. Aoun's units attacked LF positions in Qarantina and Furn Shebbak.

On 31 January fighting spread to other parts of the Christian enclave: Ashrafiya in East Beirut as well as at Byblos, Halat, Dubaya, Jounieh and Yarze. The papal nuncio, Pablo Puente (who had presented his credentials to President Hrawi three weeks earlier), arranged several brief ceasefires to evacuate the dead and injured. Blaming Aoun for the latest round of hostilities, Washington called on him to step down. Aoun refused, claiming that Syria and America, with the particular involvement of the US ambassador to Damascus, Edward Djerejian, had conspired to trigger the fighting between the LF and his soldiers in order to impose Geagea on the Christian enclave.

In the battling that went on until 17 February, Aoun's troops captured the LF base at Dubaya on 6 February. A week later Aoun called on his army reservists to volunteer for an all-out assault on the LF. Together the Aoun troops and reservists seized the Christian suburbs of Ain Rummane and Furn Shebbak on 15–16 February. The LF was driven out of its positions south of the Dog river but retained part of East Beirut's Green Line, from Ashrafiya to the port, and the northern part of the Christian territory covering Kisrwan and Byblos districts – altogether forming two-thirds of the Christian enclave. Aoun's forces overpowered the LF by combining massive artillery and rocket fire with slow-moving street battles, which left the East Beirut suburbs looking as though they had been devastated by a firestorm.

To the surprise of foreign observers, neither Damascus nor West Beirut joined the fray to destroy the Aoun government. Both Damascus and West Beirut had their reasons to stay out of the latest bout of violence. Since Lebanese Muslims considered the inter-Christian fighting beneficial to them, the longer it went on the better, they reckoned. Second, the hostilities within the Christian territory led more and more Christians to emigrate, thus reducing the overall Christian percentage in the national population. Third, the longer the conflict dragged on, the greater was the chance of Aoun losing his popularity. Finally, and most important, the Damascus–West Beirut axis knew that its assault on Aoun's forces would bring about a cessation of the inter-Christian violence, with Geagea allying with Aoun to confront non-Christian fighters, repeating a pattern of the past.

While bitterly opposed to Aoun, President Assad did not want clear-cut victory for Geagea since that would have made him the sole Christian strongman, a result the Syrian leader was determined to avoid. He had all along pursued a policy of sustaining or engendering discord between various Lebanese factions in order to keep them all weak and open to manipulation, and ensuring that no single party, Muslim or Christian, became so powerful as to follow an independent path for long. So, during the current hostilities, Syria allowed food and fuel through its checkpoints into the Aoun territory to prolong the combat between him and Geagea. At the same time it allowed LF militiamen to cross over into West Beirut's southern suburbs when they found themselves battered by Aoun's army in Ain Rummane, and then to move northwards and rejoin their colleagues in the LF-controlled part of East Beirut.

The warfare between the two Christian forces was so murderous that in less than three weeks the death toll reached 770, three-quarters of the figure for Aoun's six-month war of liberation against Damascus.[17] The embarrassed Aoun loyalists called their attack on the LF in East Beirut's suburbs 'a limited operation' to open 'blocked roads', but failed to convince the traumatized inhabitants of the Christian enclave. The resulting wanton destruction lost Aoun much public support, which had been his strong card so far. Now East Beirut residents cursed both Aoun and Geagea for pursuing their power struggle at the expense of the people they claimed to represent. Aoun felt that his capture of Ain Rummane and Furn Shebbak would break the LF's morale. But he was mistaken. In fact, Geagea carried out his threat of attacking Aoun's only remaining military asset in Kisrwan – a helicopter base at Adma manned by 200 commandos. In order to evacuate the base Aoun accepted a ceasefire on the night of 17 February.

However, there were other, weightier explanations for Aoun's decision. He came under heavier diplomatic pressure from France and the Vatican to stop fighting than did Geagea. Second, he realized that within the Christian enclave opposition to intervention from the USA and the USSR had declined, thus making a joint superpower move likely – a development which would have severely curtailed his room for manoeuvre. Third, and more practical, he needed peace urgently in order to reorganize his forces, as did Geagea.

The truce was arranged by a committee comprising Bolous Naaman, a Maronite abbot; Khalil Abi Nadir, the archbishop of Beirut; and Shaker Abu Suleiman, president of the Maronite Lebanese Front. The agreement barred entry of any forces from outside the Christian sector, and established a National Committee, consisting of members of both warring camps, and presided over by Aoun, to consolidate the truce and allow normal life to resume. Geagea accepted it, since it ran counter to Aoun's claim of a monopoly of power.

However, Aoun was unwilling to normalize the new status quo since it favoured the Lebanese Forces territorially. He found himself without any sea port, except the undeveloped, illegal facility at Dubaya. More embarrassingly, all his ministries, except defence, were in the LF-controlled territory. Since he lacked sufficient manpower, he could not mount an all-out offensive against the LF immediately: if he attacked on one front, he exposed himself on others. He had therefore to be content with mounting small-scale operations.

Clashes between the LF and Aoun's troops erupted on 25 February, and escalated. In a major attack by Aoun loyalists on LF units on 1 March, seventy-four people were killed and another 170 injured. This led the Maronite patriarch, Sfier, to warn: 'Whoever gives the order to shoot and whoever obeys such orders will be excommunicated.' The next day Aoun's forces withdrew from some of the LF positions they had seized, thus facilitating the mediation efforts of the Vatican. Its special envoy, Paolo Sozzi, arrived from Rome on 4 March, and succeeded in securing a ceasefire.

But efforts to build on this truce failed because of the continued disagreement between the warring sides on their attitudes towards West Beirut, Damascus and the Taif Accord, with the mediators tilting more towards Geagea than Aoun. A Maronite conference presided over by Patriarch Sfier resolved that the Christians should recognize the Hrawi government, and called for negotiations between Geagea and Aoun. Geagea endorsed the resolution by stating on 13 March that he was prepared to join the Hrawi administration, if invited.

This angered Aoun, who renewed hostilities in the LF-controlled Kisrwan district on 19 March. Fighting then spread elsewhere in the Christian sector. By the end of the month almost all the enclave, including East Beirut, had become a theatre of war. The bitter combat led to the destruction of the economic infrastructure of East Beirut, resulting in drastic disruption of public utilities. With this, the residents of East Beirut found themselves facing the same degree of hardship and suffering as their counterparts in West Beirut. Little wonder that during a brief ceasefire on 1 April tens of thousands of Christians fled East Beirut, heading either for the hinterland in the Christian enclave or for West Beirut, now considered militarily safer than most Christian settlements.

Following his declaration of allegiance to President Hrawi on 3 April 1990, Geagea said that he accepted the Taif Accord (with reservations), and requested Hrawi to offer military assistance for the LF in its conflict with Aoun. He proposed that all civilian public buildings situated within the LF-controlled areas, and the Lebanese army barracks – which had declared 'neutrality' during the 'war of the brothers' – be placed under the command of General Emile Lahoud, the military chief of staff of the West Beirut government. Hrawi responded by putting Brigadier-General Elie Hayek, a defector from the Aoun camp, in charge of these barracks. Hayek visited them, but did little more.

Hrawi had his reasons, practical and political, for being cool in his response to Geagea's initiative. The Lebanese president lacked enough troops to make his government the unchallenged authority in the Christian enclave. He realized that by posting an insufficient force there he would end up providing an official cover to the LF to continue exercising real power. If, by any chance, LF militiamen melted away, his soldiers would find themselves pitted against the much stronger troops of Aoun. In other words, Hrawi did not wish to see his men being inferior to, or dependent on, Geagea's militia. Moreover, Hrawi needed to pay attention to Syria's political stance.

Damascus did not approve of Geagea because he had frustrated the December 1985 Tripartite Agreement between Jumblatt, Berri and Hobeika, and he continued to receive military aid from Israel as well as Iraq. Also, there was undiminished hostility between Suleiman Franjieh and Geagea, who was responsible for the murder of the former's son, Tony ; and Assad did not wish to antagonize Franjieh, a veteran politician. In any case, the Syrian leader did not want Hrawi to make a deal with Geagea, who wished, secretly, to see Hrawi installed in Baabda and then be persuaded to distance himself from Syria in the way President Sarkis had been earlier.

Clashes between the LF and Aoun loyalists continued throughout April and the first half of May, with heavy fighting erupting between them on 24 April when the LF blocked the unloading of arms destined for its adversary. In early May the LF attempted to prevent Aoun using the beach marina on the small stretch of the coastline at Dubaya that he controlled, arguing that the marina was 'illegal'.

While the LF held the upper hand on the battlefield, Aoun made gains in the political arena. In late April, Danny Chamoun and Jibran Tueni, the leaders of the Lebanese Front, reconstituted the organization at the expense of the Phalange Party, thus favouring Aoun. At its 2 May meeting, boycotted by the Phalange, the Lebanese Front leadership called on the LF to dissolve itself and transfer its military equipment to the Lebanese army commanded by General Aoun. It then conferred with the general about the possibility of talks with the West Beirut government which might lead to the formation of a national unity government outside the ambit of the Taif Accord.

As Arab leaders prepared to attend a summit on 28 May 1990, some relief came to the warring factions and suffering civilians in the Christian sector. The Arab League meeting, called at President Saddam Hussein's request, was being held in Baghdad. Since he had backed both Aoun and Geagea in their 'war of liberation' against Syria, and since he continued to arm Geagea, Saddam Hussein expected not to be embarrassed by hostilities between the two Maronite warlords on the eve of the meeting. Aoun and Geagea understood this, and were amenable to ceasing hostilities. In addition, France pressured both sides to stop the violence, and the Pope appealed for peace. Following the mediation by the papal nuncio, Pablo Puente, the warring sides announced a five-point 'permanent truce' on 26 May. It consisted of an immediate ceasefire ; the opening of the crossing points inside the Christian enclave and the reopening of schools; the release of all detainees; an end to propaganda in the media; and a halt to military manoeuvres. It came into force on 29 May, the second day of the Arab summit in Baghdad.

Puente tried to further the peace process by mediating between the three centres of power – Aoun's army, the LF and the Lebanese Front – in the Christian enclave, and between them and the Hrawi administration, and to pave the way for the formation of a national unity government. The decision of the Phalange ministers, Georges Saade and Michel Sassine, in early June to resume attending cabinet meetings, which they had been boycotting for some months, helped the process. Puente was able to get Aoun to drop his demand that political reform and the formation of a national unity government must be preceded by fresh parliamentary elections – an unrealistic proposal in the light of the prevailing chaos and violence.

On 16 June, Puente presented to the Hrawi government a package which proposed the creation of a national reconciliation cabinet by the addition of six ministers and two deputy prime ministers, with Aoun being one of the deputy premiers. (The position of Geagea was left open.) The first task of the expanded cabinet would be to re-examine the Taif Accord. Since the Hrawi administration was opposed to the idea of reconsidering the Accord, it rejected Puente's proposals.[18]

Aoun was not unhappy at this turn of events. He felt that once he engaged in talks with traditional politicians on both sides of the sectarian divide, and settled for a cabinet seat, he would lose much of the fervent backing he had received from large sections of the Maronite community for being blunt and uncompromising. At the same time, he continued to show his willingness to negotiate with any honest broker who wanted to conciliate the governments in East Beirut and West Beirut.

In mid-July he held a series of talks with Ibrahimi, the envoy of the Arab League Troika, to discuss his conditions for joining the Hrawi administration. Aoun proposed that the conciliation process should start with all the militias withdrawing from 'administrative Beirut', and the West Beirut government guaranteeing that no reprisals would be taken against his troops. Then he would hand over control of his army and the defence ministry at Yarze to General Lahoud of the West Beirut government. A new, enlarged cabinet would be formed in which he would be represented 'effectively'. The parliament would cease legislating constitutional reform as the expanded cabinet renegotiated the Taif Accord point by point. As a guarantee, he would not vacate the presidential palace in Baabda until the revised accord had been fully implemented.

Rejecting these proposals, the Hrawi government reiterated its commitment to the Taif Agreement, and demanded Aoun's evacuation of the Baabda palace, while intensifying its diplomatic and financial campaign against him. On 28 July the government urged all diplomatic missions to cease contact with Aoun. It banned delivery into the Aoun-controlled area of currency and fuel, which until then had been seeping through the Syrian checkpoints surrounding the Christian enclave. Through Ibrahimi, the Arab League envoy, the government warned Aoun that if he did not accept its proposals he would find all crossing points into and out of his territory blocked by the Syrian troops.

By then France and the Vatican had advised Aoun to hand over everything to the Hrawi administration, since he was left with only a third of the Christian enclave, amounting to a niggardly 3 per cent of Lebanon, and was deprived of any port or city. Iraq had also stopped supporting him. Yet Aoun was not prepared to throw in the towel. Following four meetings in two weeks with him, Ibrahimi concluded that Aoun was unwilling to surrender, even though he had stopped mentioning a Syrian withdrawal and instead focused on domestic reform as contained in the Taif Accord. Aoun's position suited Damascus. It was in no hurry to bring about his downfall, which would only benefit Geagea's militia. President Hrawi shared the Syrian stance. He needed Aoun's army units virtually intact if he was to have a fighting chance of controlling the LF rather than becoming its hostage.

On 2 August 1990 Iraq invaded and occupied Kuwait, thereby creating a major international crisis. The events in the Gulf were to have a direct impact on the Lebanese situation in so far as Syria – which had been distancing itself from its long-time ally, the Soviet Union, since late 1989 – benefited diplomatically and otherwise by joining the anti-Iraqi coalition that the USA forged to expel Iraq from Kuwait. As weeks passed, and the UN sanctions against Baghdad imposed on 6 August began to bite, Lebanon felt the pinch since Iraq and Kuwait were its major export markets. Due to the turbulent conditions in the region, Lebanon also lost much of its trade with Jordan and the Gulf states. Furthermore, the exodus of some 100,000 Lebanese and Lebanon-based Palestinians from Kuwait and Iraq meant an end to their remittances home. The total losses to Lebanon amounted to $150 million a month. Also much of the humanitarian aid coming from the oil-rich Gulf states to Lebanon ceased. The damage to Lebanon's economy could be gauged from the exchange rate of its currency, which sank from L£710 to the dollar on 6 August to L£1,100 three weeks later.

However, the political direction of the Hrawi government at home remained unaffected. It pressed on with the constitutional reform as laid out in the Taif Accord despite periodic hiccups. On 14 August a parliamentary session had to be adjourned since only forty-three deputies turned up, four fewer than the quorum of two-thirds of the surviving seventy MPs required to amend the constitution. Many Christian MPs from East Beirut insisted on Aoun's deposition as a precondition for attending a parliamentary session, since they feared violent repercussions from his supporters, civilian and military, for defying him. At the behest of Syria, Saudi Arabia and America intervened. They helped to assemble the Christian MPs in Ashrafiya on 20 August, and encouraged them to forge a common policy.

Consequently, on 21 August fifty-one MPs turned up at the old parliament building in Nijma Square. Of the forty-nine deputies participating in the voting, all but one opted for overhauling the 1926 Constitution by altering thirty-one articles. These amendments curtailed the power of the president and increased the authority of the cabinet, making it more autonomous from the president. The size of the parliament was raised from 99 MPs to 108, with the nine new seats going to Muslims, thus bringing about parity between them and Christians. The new share of the Islamic sects (with the old share in brackets) was: Sunni 23 (20), Shia 23 (19), Druze 7 (6), and Alawi 1 (none). The supporters of reform claimed that the parliamentary vote increased the Hrawi–Hoss government's credibility and resolve. General Aoun was unimpressed. He declared that he did not recognize any actions of the parliament since he had dissolved it ten months earlier. His stand was endorsed by the National Liberal Party, a constituent of the Lebanese Front: it said that the parliament, elected in 1972, was unrepresentative, and that its vote did not commit Lebanon to anything.

Following his success in parliament, President Hrawi tried to enhance the authority of his government. He did so in consultation with President Assad, whom he met in Damascus on 29 August. Saudi Arabia manifested its approval of the Hrawi government by providing it with emergency aid of $100 million on 19 September. Two days later the Lebanese president signed the constitutional legislation into law, and warned Aoun of the possible use of force against him.

This had become a real possibility after a successful meeting between James Baker, the US secretary of state, and President Assad in Damascus on 14 September to strengthen the anti-Iraqi coalition had sealed a *rapprochement* between their countries. Assad reportedly succeeded in securing Washington's approval to move militarily against General Aoun to resolve the overlong Lebanese crisis. Buttressed by this understanding, President Hrawi imposed a blockade on the area controlled by Aoun. He received backing from the Lebanese Forces. The Lebanese army units crossed the Green Line in Beirut to man some positions in East Beirut which were vacated by the LF militia stationed along the front line with Aoun's forces.

To avert an attack by the Hrawi troops, Aoun's followers mounted a candle-lit vigil at night on 1 October at one of the crossing points on the northern edge of their territory, close to the positions of the LF and the Hrawi loyalists. They were attacked with firearms by unknown assailants, who killed twenty-five people and injured eighty-two. Aoun and most foreign diplomats blamed the LF for firing on unarmed Aoun supporters. The LF commander, Geagea, claimed that Aoun's intelligence men had crossed over to the other side and fired in order to win international sympathy.

The Hrawi–Hoss government's economic blockade of the Aoun enclave began to bite, with petrol becoming scarce. On 3 October, France protested against the anti-Aoun blockade by refusing to issue visas to Lebanese citizens. But this had no effect on the West Beirut authorities.

In a performance reminiscent of their moves in the previous spring, the Syrian and Lebanese military units reinforced their positions on the edge of the Aoun enclave, and allowed the Hizbollah to do the same to their positions along the Green Line in the southern suburbs of West Beirut. The Syrian troops, tanks and artillery moved to the front line with the Aoun loyalists. Faced with this threat, Aoun did what he had done before: he mobilized his supporters. To raise their morale he took to addressing them outside his presidential palace. This was effective, but not to the same extent as before. More worryingly, Aoun realized that this time he had to be prepared to fight on two fronts, since the LF militia too was poised against his forces.

Friday, 12 October, started badly for the general. The LF clashed with his units at the Geen Line near the museum. In the evening, while Aoun was addressing his followers outside the palace, Habib Hilal, a young Lebanese Shia carrying an Australian passport, fired at him twice, but missed, killing a bodyguard instead. Aoun continued his speech, pledging to fight on until death.[19] Later, in private, however, he was less than defiant. For the first time he reportedly discussed his resignation with his close aides.

At 7 a.m. on 13 October, following two hours of heavy shelling and air raids by the Syrian military at dawn on targets in the Aoun-controlled enclave, the Syrian and Lebanese soldiers launched a ground assault. They encountered fiercest opposition on the Souq al Gharb front. The Syrian air force mounted two bombing raids on Aoun's palace at Baabda. This led to General Aoun and his entourage fleeing to the nearby French embassy at about 8.30 a.m., and seeking asylum there. The use of Syrian warplanes in the Lebanese conflict meant the crossing of one of the three 'red lines' that had been imposed by Israel on the eve of its final phase of withdrawal from Lebanon in June 1985.[20] However, due to the active participation of Damascus in the US-led coalition against Iraq, Washington had not only agreed to lift this 'red line' but had also persuaded Israel to do so.[21]

At about 9.30 a.m., following a telephone conversation with his opponent, General Emile Lahoud, Aoun in a radio broadcast called on his soldiers to stop fighting and obey Lahoud's orders. At the same time he reportedly contacted his officers by telephone, and ordered them to keep on battling for the next four or five hours. He thus meant to give time to Israel to intervene on his behalf – a vain hope.

The fighting continued until the afternoon. It was only at 3.15 p.m. that Lahoud's army troops managed to capture the presidential palace at Baabda. They were soon followed by the Syrian soldiers. With this, the Hrawi government became the sole political authority in Lebanon. The day-long battle, resulting in the deaths of 800 people, military and civilian, and injuries to 1,000, marked the end of a civil war that had lasted fifteen and a half years.

One of the first things that the Syrian troops did on entering the presidential palace at Baabda and the defence ministry at Yarze was to remove to Damascus the central computer and the records of military intelligence, which kept files on all Lebanese of any importance. The computer was an invaluable asset.

Following the Damascus–West Beirut victory, the Syrian troops allowed the militias of Elie Hobeika (known officially as the

Lebanese Forces Executive Command (LFEC) – the Promise) and the pro-Damascus, mainly Christian Syrian Social Nationalist Party to enter the densely populated areas of the Aoun enclave. To seek revenge for the attacks they had suffered in late 1985 and early 1986, they looted, raped and killed. But they did not stop there, for Samir Geagea soon complained that the Hobeika loyalists and SSNP militiamen had entered areas in the Christian enclave controlled by his LF militia, and had begun occupying Phalange Party offices and harassing former Phalange fighters. Later, as the Syrian troops withdrew from the Baabda area, the Lebanese army's mainly Muslim brigades entered the region with the aim of bringing it under government control. In the process they took over the former LF and Phalange Party offices now occupied by the SSNP and Hobeika's LFEC militiamen.

On 15 October the Lebanese troops started dismantling the Green Line – the barricades dividing East Beirut and West Beirut – an action as significant to Lebanon as the dismantling of the Berlin Wall in November 1989 to the two parts of Germany. At a more practical level, Lebanese citizens showed their confidence in the Hrawi government, now indisputably in charge of the nation's affairs, by depositing moneys in the banks. This improved the exchange value of the Lebanese pound by 40 per cent within a week.

Soon the Lebanese army released hundreds of prisoners held by the now defunct Aoun government, including 325 militiamen of the LFEC, twenty-three Syrians and seven Lebanese. Among them were Habib Tanios Shartuni, the assassin of Bashir Gemayel,[22] and Habib Hilal, who had tried to assassinate Michel Aoun. As Syrian troops began withdrawing from the presidential palace at Baabda, the Lebanese army started to consolidate its control of the Christian region of Metn.

On 17 October, Edmond Naim, governor of the Central Bank, issued a sequestration order covering the sums held in the names of General Michel Aoun, Brigadier-General Edgar Maluf and Colonel Issam Abu Jamra, and their families. They estimatedly held $100 million in five different Lebanese banks. The action against them was not taken too soon. On 19 October, when Edgar Maluf and Issam Abu Jamra and their families as well as Aoun's family were allowed to leave the French embassy for Paris, they were discovered to be carrying more than $200,000 in cash, which was confiscated as property of the Lebanon government.[23]

During their talks on 20–1 October, Presidents Hrawi and Assad agreed on a package of measures. These were: to form Greater Beirut by extending the capital city's boundaries to Damour in the south, Dubaya in the north, and Souq al Gharb-Aley-Bhamdoun in the east; to appoint a government of national unity; to co-operate on security matters; and ultimately to disband all militias, Christian and Muslim – first by taking over the militia offices in the Metn area by 14 November, followed by the withdrawal of all militiamen and heavy military equipment from Greater Beirut, to enable the Lebanese army to deploy throughout the region on 19 November.

On 21 October masked men, dressed in army uniforms, entered the apartment block where Danny Chamoun, the leader of the National Liberal Party, lived in Baabda, and gunned down Chamoun, his wife and two of their young children. Accusing fingers were pointed at Syria because the area was under its nominal control, and because Chamoun had backed Aoun. The killings increased the sense of insecurity among those who had once violently opposed the Syrians. Samir Geagea was one of them. During his talks with the authorities in Beirut he insisted on the removal of the Hobeika loyalists and SSNP militiamen from East Beirut in exchange for the withdrawal of his LF units from the streets. As for other Beirut-based militias, they agreed to depart from Greater Beirut by the official deadline.

Since both Amal and Hizbollah militias had bases in the Beqaa valley and the south, and since they had been fighting one another periodically in these areas as well as in the southern suburbs of West Beirut, there was a need to hammer out a truce between them. Both Syria and Iran actively pursued this aim. As a result, the leaders of the Hizbollah and Amal decided to bury the hatchet, and signed an agreement to that effect in Damascus under the supervision of Syrian and Iranian officials on 5 November 1990. It reaffirmed the principles of the earlier Damascus concord of January 1989, and laid out plans for the withdrawal of the Amal and Hizbollah militias followed by the deployment of the Lebanese army in the disputed areas. Unlike the previous occasions when similar agreements were concluded with much cynicism regarding their durability, there was optimism that the latest concord would hold. The end of the civil warfare had created an environment conducive to a peaceful conclusion of the smaller conflicts fostered by the larger, more pervasive struggle.

Overall, the civil war had consumed over 152,000 people, a quarter of them children.[24] It had led to the emigration of at least three-quarters of a million Lebanese, mostly Christian.[25] Those who remained, particularly in the two sectors of the capital, had to bear a miserable existence. In East Beirut running water had been scarce for many months. A similar situation prevailed in West Beirut, with the Syrian and UN Refugee Welfare Agency water tankers emerging as the major source of supplies. Electricity produced at a power station in East Beirut had been cut severely. To make matters worse, municipal workers had gone on strike in the summer, causing stinking garbage to pile up.

Having put the war behind them, the Lebanese people and government faced a gargantuan task of reconstruction. With whole districts in the capital and entire hillsides and valleys in the Shouf mountains and the Maronite hinterland destroyed, the scale of rebuilding to be undertaken was stupendous. In the public domain, the cost of repairing and reconstructing the roads, electric plants and water supply and sewerage systems was all the more staggering, given the parlous state of the country's foreign reserves, down to $500 million towards the final days of the conflict.[26]

However, the end of the civil war at least prepared the way for the dissipation of the numerous problems that had arisen in the course of its long duration.

10

Peace at last, Syria ascendant

Having defeated Aoun, the Hrawi government redoubled its efforts to fulfil its security plan for Greater Beirut, which included disarming the militias, an enterprise in which it received unqualified backing from Damascus. On 7 November 1990 it finalized the boundaries of Greater Beirut by incorporating a 25 km belt round the city. Two days later, taking its cue from Syria, Amal completed its withdrawal from Greater Beirut, having earlier abandoned its positions in the Shiyya district of West Beirut and its illegal ports of Ouzai and Khalde. It sent most of its militiamen to Beqaa and the south. Later, the Hizbollah was to follow suit by despatching its armed men mainly to the south. The Lebanese authorities made an exception in the case of the Palestinian camps in the southern suburbs, now firmly dominated by the pro-Damascus Palestine National Salvation Front, by letting the armed Palestinians maintain security inside the camps, but not outside.

On 9 November the cabinet's Security Commission – consisting of the defence minister, Albert Mansur, a Greek Catholic, and the agriculture minister, Muhsin Dalloul, a Shia – reached an agreement with the Lebanese Forces on the withdrawal of its men. The terms were: pull-back of all militiamen who had entered the Metn region after 13 October; withdrawal of the LF's heavy and medium weapons as well as its fighters from Greater Beirut; evacuation of the premises which had been confiscated and used as offices by the militias and political parties during the civil war; elimination of all checkpoints; return of local residents to their homes; and unhindered political activity within the law.

The speed and extent of the LF's withdrawal from East Beirut proved unsatisfactory to the government since it refused to close down its forty-five checkpoints in its stronghold of Ashrafiya,[1] in protest against the failure of the SSNP and Hobeika's LFEC to shut down their offices in the former premises of the Phalange Party and the LF. President Hrawi and the Syrian intelligence chief, General Ghazi Kanaan, intervened, with Kanaan travelling to the Kisrwan region to meet Samir Geagea at his home. Geagea insisted on the Metn district being returned to the control of 'a just and capable state', implying that the SSNP militia as well as Hobeika's men, intent on avenging the LF attacks on them four years earlier, should not be allowed to return to the area. He also wanted a say in deciding which army units and personnel were to be posted where, pointing out that the mainly Druze 11th Brigade had been deployed in the Druze neighbourhood of Greater Beirut. The Geagea–Kanaan talks went on past 19 November, the deadline for the militias to end their armed presence in the streets and for the Lebanese army to become solely responsible for security.

However, on the eve of national Independence Day on 22 November, an agreement was struck. In return for Gaegea relinquishing the remaining LF positions, the Hrawi government promised that the Phalange Party offices taken over by its rivals would be returned to the Phalange; that the abuses by the SSNP and Hobeika's LFEC would be stopped, and that they would not be allowed to enter Ashrafiya, the LF stronghold; that the Lebanese army units replacing the SSNP and LFEC militiamen would not be hostile to the LF; and, most important, that no Syrian troops would be deployed in the vacated Christian areas.[2]

The LF's evacuation started in earnest on 25 November, the first anniversary of Hrawi's presidency. Declaring Greater Beirut a symbol of national unity, Hrawi announced that the new, expanded cabinet would provide seats to militia leaders as a reward for disbanding their forces.

On 3 December, when the last piece of heavy military equipment as well as the last militiamen of the LF were removed from the capital, Greater Beirut officially came into being. All the crossing points dividing East Beirut and West Beirut along the Green Line – which ran from the Beirut port in the north through the commercial centre and then through the Shia-dominated southern outskirts – as well as those within East Beirut, were opened up. This meant the implementation of the final part of the three-part plan by Prime Minister Hoss, the first two being steering constitutional reform through parliament, and campaigning along with Syria to remove General Aoun.

Having fully accomplished his programme, Hoss resigned on 19 December, preparing the way for his successor to lead a broad-based government charged with implementing the next stage of the Taif Accord, especially the disbanding of the militias and the formalizing of relations between Lebanon and Syria.

President Hrawi asked the education minister, Omar Karami, to form a new cabinet. A brother of Rashid Karami, Omar had stepped into the shoes of Rashid, assassinated in mid-1987, so far as the leadership of their home town, Tripoli, was concerned. On 24 December he announced a thirty-member national unity cabinet, divided evenly between Muslims (Sunni, 6; Shia, 6; and Druze, 3) and Christians (Maronite, 6; Greek Orthodox, 4; Greek Catholic, 3; Armenian Catholic, 1; and Armenian Orthodox, 1). Nine of them were ministers without portfolio, seven of them being former militia leaders, including Nabih Berri, Walid Jumblatt, Samir Geagea and the heads of the militias of the SSNP and the pro-Damascus Baath Party. Of the three militias excluded, the Hizbollah refused to join in protest at the lack of any governmental plan to combat the Israeli aggression in the south. Though the leader of the Sidon-based Popular Nasserite Organization, Mustafa Saad, was kept out, Sidon's MP, Nazih Bizri, was included as a minister without portfolio. That made the Lebanese Communist Party's militia the only one to be ignored.

The LF and the Phalange Party criticized the cabinet for being 'heavily pro-Damascus', with the pro-Syrian categorization applied to the prime minister (Karami, Sunni), deputy prime minister/defence minister (Michel Murr, Greek Orthodox), interior minister (Sami Khatib, Sunni) and foreign minister (Faris Bouez, Maronite, a son-in-law of President Hrawi). Samir Geagea (minister without portfolio, Maronite), Georges Saade (post and telephone, Maronite) and Michel Sassine (labour, Maronite), belonging either to the Phalange Party or the LF, refused to join the government. Geagea was particularly incensed because the cabinet included two of his bitter enemies, both Maronite – Elie Hobeika and Suleiman Tony Franjieh, a son of Tony, assassinated by a hit team led by Geagea.

The right-wing Maronite leaders' protest adversely affected the turnout of the parliamentarians when they were summoned to vote in early January 1991 on the new government. Only forty of the surviving sixty-nine MPs showed up, the lowest attendance, both relatively and absolutely, so far. Of these, all but three ratified the cabinet.

Once the US-led coalition started war against Iraq on 17 January 1991, much of the public attention in Lebanon turned to that conflict.

The pro-Iraqi Palestinian guerrillas and their Lebanese allies declared a state of maximum alert. Zaid Wahbe, the PLO leader in Sidon, warned that the PLO would attack American and British interests from Lebanon, Amman, Cairo and Damascus. The US ambassador in Beirut, Ryan Crocker, and his staff immediately vacated the embassy for fear of an attack. As America and its allies kept up intense, round-the-clock bombing of Iraq, anti-Western feelings rose sharply. On 27 January there were large pro-Saddam Hussein demonstrations in the Palestinian camp of Rashidiya near Tyre. Two days later PLO fighters fired rockets at Israel, which responded with gunboat and helicopter attacks on Rashidiya and other camps. The exchanges between the Palestinians on one side and the IDF and the SLA militiamen on the other continued for a week, and an Israeli air raid on south Lebanon left eight people dead. On 31 January there were explosions outside the Qatari embassy and the Banco di Roma in Beirut. The other targets of explosives during the next few days were the Turkish embassy and the Libano-Kuwaiti bank.

Despite the skirmishes between the Palestinians and the Israeli-backed SLA in the south, the Lebanese army started deploying on 7 February in the disputed areas of the Iqlim al Tuffa hills, south-east of Sidon, following the PLO's withdrawal as a buffer between the feuding Hizbollah and Amal. Other army units moved south to Nabatiya and Tyre, bypassing Sidon.

On 10 February, following the continued exploding of bombs aimed at the diplomatic and other premises of the member countries of the anti-Iraq coalition, the Syrian troops raided the offices of several Lebanese and Palestinian parties : an exercise which went on until the Gulf War ended on 28 February with the Iraqis expelled from Kuwait.

In the wake of a successful end to the Gulf hostilities, the US secretary of state, James Baker, initiated several rounds of talks in the Middle East with a view to convening a peace conference to settle the 43-year-old Arab–Israeli conflict. On 15 March he met the Lebanese foreign minister, Fariz Bouez, in Damascus to persuade him to participate in these negotiations.

While the general law and order situation improved after the Greater Beirut security plan went into effect in early December, assassination attempts continued unabated. Elie Hobeika survived such an attempt on 12 March. So too did Michel Murr, the defence minister who also chaired the cabinet committee charged with disbanding the militias, on 20 March. But the car bomb which exploded at Antelia as the defence ministry motorcade passed killed nine and injured thirty-eight.

Within the administration, Samir Geagea's behaviour caused concern. Though a cabinet minister, he lost no opportunity to criticize the Hrawi government. His incompatibility with the rest of his colleagues stood out. President Assad had frowned on his inclusion in the cabinet, aware that the LF commander had yet to accept the idea of Lebanese–Syrian relations being formalized in such a way as to confer big-sister status on Syria.

So, on the eve of the first full meeting of the broad-based cabinet on 28 March, Geagea's resignation came as a relief to his colleagues. His place was taken up by Roger Deeb, secretary-general of the Phalange Party and a member of the Lebanese Forces Command Council, who had won the approval of Assad after a meeting with him in Damascus.

The cabinet took decisions on such major issues as dissolving the militias, extending central authority over all of Lebanon, implementing administrative decentralization as outlined in the Taif Accord, and nominating new MPs.

It decided that disarmament and dissolution of the militias must be completed by 30 April, an overly optimistic schedule. While the authorities had periodically collected small arms from the militias, they had not yet touched their tanks and artillery. Then there was the issue of the Palestinians bearing arms, with their leaders arguing that the 6,000 Palestinians under arms in Sidon and further south did not constitute a militia but an army fighting a war against Israel.

The second cabinet decision – to extend central authority to all of Lebanon in two steps by the end of September – also seemed unrealistic. So far, the demolition of the barricades between East and West Beirut and the clearance of mines had continued satisfactorily. But the major impediment to the extension of Lebanese sovereignty was the Israeli-run South Lebanon Army. It was known that Israel would not allow the Lebanese army to enter its self-declared security zone where 1,000 Israeli soldiers were deployed; and that the Palestinians and southern Shias would refuse to lay down their weapons, arguing that they felt unsafe with the SLA around. And, unknown to the world at large then, Syria had promised to refrain from attempting any change in the status of Israel's self-proclaimed security zone on the eve of the IDF's evacuation of the south in June 1985.[3]

Besides deciding to implement the administrative decentralization part of the Taif Accord, the cabinet resolved to present legislation to the parliament for the appointment of forty new deputies to fill thirty-one vacant seats and nine new ones until fresh elections were held. The right-wing Maronite politicians agreed with the idea of nomination, but argued that instead of the pro-Syrian cabinet appointing the new MPs, the parliament should do so. There was no chance of their proposal being accepted by others.

By now, faced with the defeat and ousting of General Michel Aoun, even the most militant Maronites had come around to accepting, albeit grudgingly, the continued Syrian presence in their country. While the Christian community felt a sense of loss at its diminished political power, it derived some comfort from the fact that despite its minority status – with its members constituting about 40 per cent of the national population[4] – it retained an equal share of the political pie.

Moreover, they could not help realizing that Lebanese society was speedily returning to normality under Syria's hegemony. By early April 1991, the dismantling of the checkpoints in Greater Beirut, coupled with discreet presence of Syrian troops in the streets, made people feel safe enough to move about freely – a stark contrast to the situation that had prevailed for the better part of sixteen years. Commercial activity too had picked up, with banks registering large deposits from abroad, and the exchange rate of the Lebanese pound improving from 1,100 to the US dollar to 700 in the last four months to 1990. Hospitals and educational institutions had returned to normal functioning. Electricity and water supplies, though limited to six hours a day, had become regular. A lot of construction and reconstruction had begun, encouraged partly by the government's announcement that it controlled all seaports and other main economic facilities, a development which augured well for its revenue.

'While Lebanese may not like the Syrian stamp on the peace, most of them accept it as better than war,' noted Jim Muir, a British journalist based in Beirut. 'It has given them an opportunity for the first time in 15 years to rediscover their own country, to cross its many psychological barriers, and to savour things that a generation of war had denied them.'[5]

There were sceptics who referred to earlier periods of relative quietude – from November 1976 to February 1978, between April 1978 and March 1980, from July 1981 to May 1982, and between October 1982 and January 1984 – which had proved transient. But the difference this time was that the root cause of violence, Muslim anger at the inequity of the political system, had been addressed. Also, the Lebanese people were utterly exhausted and fed up with sixteen nerve-racking years of warfare and insecurity, and this acted as a strong damper on those armed men who thought of firing their weapons again.

By the end of April, the Lebanese authorities had despatched army units to areas adjacent to Greater Beirut; and the militias of Amal, the Druze-dominated Progressive Socialist Party, the Arab Democratic Party and Suleiman Franjieh's party had surrendered their weapons to the Syrian army, with Amal and Druze militias claiming to return to Damascus the military equipment, including tanks and artillery, which the latter had allegedly 'loaned' them.[6] The Hizbollah was the one party whose militia had been left out of the government's drive to disarm and dissolve all privately controlled paramilitary forces. Since Iran was the mentor of the Hizbollah, and since relations between Iran and Syria were close, the matter was discussed during President Rafsanjani's meetings with Assad in Damascus on 20-1 April 1991. A few days later Rafsanjani told visiting senior Hizbollah leaders – Shaikh Muhammad Hussein Fadlallah and Shaikh Subhi Tufaili – in Tehran that he and Assad had decided to postpone disarming Hizbollah until July.

Once parliament had passed a law on 9 May giving equal parliamentary seats to Muslims and Christians, the cabinet turned to formalizing Lebanese–Syrian relations. On 15 May it approved a draft of the Treaty of Brotherhood, Co-operation and Co-ordination between Lebanon and Syria, and two days later – on the eighth anniversary of the initialling of the Lebanese–Israeli peace treaty (later annulled by Lebanon) – published its text.

The treaty consisted of six articles. Article One enjoined the parties to 'realize the highest degree of co-operation and co-ordination between them in all political, security, cultural, scientific and other concerns . . . within the framework of the sovereignty and independence of each of them'. Article Two required the parties to achieve co-operation and co-ordination in economics, agriculture, industry, commerce, transportation, communications, customs and development. 'The interrelationship of the two countries' security requires that Lebanon not be made the source of a threat to Syria's security or Syria to Lebanon's in any circumstance whatsoever', stated Article Three. 'Lebanon shall therefore not allow itself to become a passage or a base for any power or state or organization the purpose of which is the violation of Lebanon's security or Syria's security.'

Equally, Syria 'shall not allow any action that threatens Lebanon's security, independence or sovereignty'. The next article specified the formation of a Lebanese–Syrian military committee to determine the size and duration of the Syrian troops' presence in Lebanon. Article Five focused on the contracting parties' foreign policy, and required them to co-ordinate their Arab and international policies. The last article specified the formation of joint agencies at different levels to implement the treaty – from the Higher Council, consisting of the presidents, prime ministers, deputy prime ministers and parliamentary speakers, to the committees on defence and security, foreign affairs, and economic and social affairs.[7]

The treaty was signed by Presidents Hrawi and Assad in Damascus on 22 May 1991, which happened to be the first anniversary of the unification of North Yemen and South Yemen. 'What is between Syria and Lebanon is God made', said President Assad at the signing ceremony. 'What is good for Lebanon is good for Syria, and security and prosperity in one of the two countries will reflect on the other.'[8]

But there were many dissenting voices, especially in the Christian community in Lebanon. Patriarch Sfier was one such. 'Lebanon is in no position to conclude treaties before liberating its land, deploying its army across the country and restoring state authority', he said, complaining that the treaty was 'imposed by one side on the other like any accord between two unequal states'.[9]

The reality was that the latest pact formalized the new balance of power which had emerged after the convulsions which followed the Israeli aggression of 1982, including Washington's ill-fated attempt to sponsor *Pax Americana* in Lebanon and elsewhere in the region. In the course of the Gulf Crisis and War of 1990–1, Syria became part of the dominant camp in the new regional balance of forces. It therefore expected the USA to give it a large room for manoeuvre as it tried further to stabilize Lebanon under its wing. In a sense, after the débâcle of the adventurous policies of the Reagan administrations during the 1980s, Washington had returned to the friendly stance it had adopted towards Syria after its intervention in Lebanon in June 1976 – with the added incentive that Syria was no longer allied to the Soviet Union, which had, in any case, ceased to be a superpower rival to the USA. Its failure to create *Pax Americana* had given way to accepting *Pax Syriana* in Lebanon as formally represented by the latest Syrian–Lebanese treaty. This was well summed up by a leading US official. 'Given the facts on the ground – Syria's 13 million people to Lebanon's 3.5 million and the continued presence of 40,000 Syrian troops on two-thirds of Lebanon's territory – there really isn't very much we can do about the situation', he said.[10] The Bush administration's immediate hope was that the treaty would help stabilize Lebanon, thus facilitating the release of the Western hostages, including six Americans.

These sentiments were not shared by Israel, a bitter rival of Syria. According to its defence minister, Moshe Arens, the pact perpetuated the presence of the Syrian 'army of occupation' in Lebanon, allowing Damascus to reinforce its troops there by deploying heavy weapons along its border with Israel. 'The Syrians are in the process of swallowing up Lebanon and in effect putting an end to Lebanese sovereignty', he told the Israeli parliament's foreign affairs and defence committee.[11] Other politicians in Israel compared the Lebanese–Syrian pact to *Anschluss*, Nazi Germany's annexation of Austria in 1938. The hawkish housing minister, Ariel Sharon, who had masterminded Israel's 1982 invasion of Lebanon, was particularly bitter, and exaggerated the danger to his country. 'Syria's take-over of Lebanon is liable to place Haifa and its surrounding industrial and residential centres within the range of Syrian artillery', he warned. He seemed to have missed the irony that his Lebanese adventure, instead of laying the foundation for a Greater Israel, had ended up promoting the cause of a Greater Syria.

Israel warned Assad not to cross the 'red lines' – pertaining to the deployment of Syrian troops and military hardware, especially aircraft and SAMs, in certain areas of Lebanon.[12] On 3 June, the day the Lebanese and Syrian foreign ministers exchanged the instruments ratifying the new treaty following its approval by the two parliaments, Israel struck. It staged air raids on the Palestinian and Lebanese militia positions in the Sidon region for three days, killing twenty and injuring 130. These were the most severe raids by the IDF since its June 1982 invasion of Lebanon.

However, this Israeli action had no impact on the course that the Hrawi regime had resolved to follow. On 6 June the government appointed forty new MPs to fill the vacant and newly created seats, and bring the total strength of the parliament to 108. Of these nominees, thirteen were cabinet ministers, including Prime Minister Omar Karami, his deputy Michel Murr and foreign minister Fariz Bouez – as well as such ministers without portfolio as Nabih Berri, Walid Jumblatt, Elie Hobeika, Suleiman Tony Franjieh, and Abdullah Amin, head of the pro-Syria Baath Party.[13]

In mid-June the government announced that it would deploy army units in the Sidon area by early July, and use force to overpower the Palestinian and Lebanese paramilitary units there if they did not surrender their weapons. After the 1985 Israeli withdrawal the Palestinians had rebuilt their military strength in the Ain Hilwa and Miya Miya camps and the surrounding hill villages. For the next several years some 6,000 Palestinian fighters – allied to the Sunni Popular Nasserite Organization, led by Mustafa Saad, who controlled Sidon – stayed in the shadows of the Syrian- and Israeli-controlled zones of Lebanon. In 1990 the Palestinian fighters began acting as a buffer between the Hizbollah and Amal militias in the Iqlam al Tuffa hills. As the central government tried to extend its control further south, it came into conflict with the Palestinian groups. On 19 April 1991 the army arrested six guerrillas of the Popular Front for the Liberation of Palestine while they were trying to infiltrate the Israeli-occupied security zone.[14] It was the first action of its kind, and bode ill for the Palestinians in the region, since they owed their allegiance to the PLO, and not to the pro-Damascus Palestine National Salvation Front. As the Beirut government piled pressure on them in mid-June, their leaders demanded renegotiated status for more than 350,000 Palestinians living in Lebanon. The government replied that it would negotiate only Palestinians' civil and social rights, and that they would not be allowed to bear arms.

On 1 July the central government deployed 10,000 troops in the Sidon area. But the Palestinians, following the orders of the PLO chairman, Yasser Arafat, based in Tunis, refused to surrender their positions in the hill villages surrounding the camps of Ain Hilwa and Miya Miya. In the ensuing three-day combat, the Lebanese prevailed. The 6,000-strong Palestinian force lacked any plans to fight, and had poor military leadership. About sixty people, mainly Palestinian, died in the battle, which ended with the Palestinian guerrillas giving up their arms and positions to the Lebanese soldiers, and retreating to the camps. The poor morale of the Palestinians was also due to the political-military isolation in which the PLO had found itself following its pro-Iraq stance in the Gulf Crisis of August 1990–February 1991. In contrast, the morale of the newly reconstituted Lebanese army was high. It battled as a united force, with Muslims and Christians fighting side by side. This engendered a new spirit of national pride among the Lebanese people, even though it had emerged as a result of overpowering Palestinian 'brethren'.

After 7 July the Beirut government deployed its army up to the front line with the SLA at Kafr Fallus, 8 km up the hill from Sidon.

Washington worked in the background and pressed Israel not to hinder the move. Then the Hrawi administration planned to despatch its troops to the Jezzine salient, an unofficial extension of the Israeli-occupied security zone made by the SLA. Jezzine, a Christian town about 20 km east of Sidon, was linked to the security zone by a 16 km corridor patrolled by the IDF and the SLA. Opposed to the Hrawi plan, Israel attempted to dissuade the Lebanese government from deploying its troops in Jezzine by threatening to assist the SLA to resist any such move. Beirut argued that, since it had banished the PLO forces from the Sidon hills and disarmed the Palestinians in the Sidon and Tyre camps, there was no longer any chance of the Palestinians attacking Israel, and that it had therefore lost its purpose for occupying south Lebanon. This reasoning was primarily directed at Washington in the hope that it would pressure Israel to evacuate south Lebanon as demanded by Security Council Resolution 425. But Israel had no such intention.

Indeed, Israel had by now hardened its position on the issue, partly in response to Syria's success in concluding a wide-ranging pact with Lebanon. Previously it had stated that it would withdraw once a strong government was in office in Beirut. Now its foreign minister, David Levy, said that Israel would pull back only after all other foreign forces had done so, *and* an Israeli–Lebanese peace treaty had been concluded.

At a more practical level, the SLA commander, Antoine Lahad, claimed that only 10 per cent of the arms of the Palestinian guerrillas had been confiscated by the Beirut government, and that there were other militias in the area committed to hitting Israel and its local allies. Principal among these anti-Israel forces was the Hizbollah. Following the disarming of its fighters in the Beirut area in November 1990, the Hizbollah had shifted its men and weapons to the southern Beqaa valley as well as to the mountain caves adjacent to Jezzine and the Israeli-occupied security zone in the south, containing about 1,000 IDF soldiers and 3,000 SLA troops. It had increased its attacks on the Israeli and SLA patrols in the area, in the process inviting swift and heavy responses from the IDF. Following the central government's success in curbing the Palestinian and Lebanese forces in the Sidon area, the Hizbollah mounted an attack on 17 July 1991 on the edge of Israel's security zone, killing one Israeli and three SLA soldiers. As before, Israel responded by pounding Hizbollah positions with air raids and artillery fire, and used the incident to highlight the need to stay put in south Lebanon to protect its northern territory.

As for the Hizbollah, its secretary-general, Shaikh Abbas Musavi, argued that so long as Israel remained inside Lebanon, his armed men would not surrender their weapons to the Lebanese government. When he came under pressure from the Beirut–Damascus axis following the heavy Israeli raids in mid-July, he temporized a little: he provided to the Lebanese authorities a list of the 3,500 Hizbollah militiamen active in the south against Israel and the SLA. The Hrawi administration accepted this compromise because it feared that an all-out offensive against the Hizbollah would not only sour relations between Damascus and Tehran, the mentor of the Hizbollah, but also split the Lebanese cabinet. Several of the ministers approved of the strategy of guerrilla pressure on Israel until its unconditional withdrawal from south Lebanon, seeing in the Iranian-funded Hizbollah militia a valuable counterpoint to the Israeli-funded SLA.

The Lebanese government intensified its diplomatic moves to secure the Israeli pull-back. In his meetings with the US secretary of state, Baker, in Cairo during the latter's fifth tour of the region in August 1991, President Hrawi emphasized that Israel's withdrawal must not be linked to the overall Middle East peace process, since it was demanded by an independent UN Security Council resolution. But America was reluctant to pressure Israel, afraid that such a move might lead to Israel reversing its agreement to attend a peace conference with its neighbouring Arab states to conduct bilateral talks. There were also unconfirmed reports that President Assad had reached an understanding with Baker that he would not press too hard on the Israeli pull-back from south Lebanon if the USA were to back his case for the return to Syria of the Golan Heights seized by Israel in the June 1967 Arab–Israeli War.

In short, while a Washington–Damascus agreement in September 1990 leading to the overthrow of Aoun had laid a firm base for a lasting solution to the domestic aspect of the sixteen-year Lebanese crisis, only a US–Israeli understanding to link an Israeli withdrawal from south Lebanon with the signing of a Lebanese–Israeli peace treaty held a realistic promise of resolving the external aspect of the crisis. The Lebanese–Israel peace accord was expected to accommodate Israel's demands that the SLA should be integrated into the Lebanese army and given the task of maintaining security along the Lebanese–Israeli border, and that Lebanon should share the waters of the Litani with Israel.

The Hrawi government continued its efforts to return the territory under its control to normality by tackling the problems stemming from the civil strife. The rehabilitation of former militiamen was a priority. A ministerial committee charged with the task had decided earlier that of some 40,000 militiamen only 20,000 – divided equally between Christians and Muslims – would be integrated into the army and police. In the course of its selection, it came under heavy pressure, with the militia leaders, now part of the cabinet, insisting on a maximum acceptance of their men into the rehabilitation scheme. But the committee stuck to such ground rules as the age limit of twenty-five for enrolment into the military. In the end, it admitted to its scheme 6,500 men from the Lebanese Forces (with a reported size of 20,000 at its peak), 2,800 from Amal (with the highest strength of 14,000 at one point) and 2,800 from the Druze PSP (with the peak of 15,500).[15] Due to teething problems, the training of the first intake of 6,000 former militiamen, which should have started in June, was delayed by three months.

Among other priority issues was the question of war crimes. On 14 August the Lebanese cabinet approved legislation on the subject, and it was adopted by the parliament. It empowered the government to provide amnesty for war crimes committed before 28 March 1991 – except assassinations or attempted assassinations of clerics, politicians or diplomats, and the committing of massacres of civilians. Even though the Lebanese Forces Command Council was critical of the exceptions, only six Christian MPs out of fifty-four voted against the bill.

This law prepared the way for the government to deal with Michel Aoun, who had taken refuge in the French embassy since 13 October 1990, and his two aides, Edgar Maluf and Issam Abu Jamra, who had been permitted earlier to leave for France. On 27 August the government offered conditional pardons to them, the main conditions being that they had to stay abroad for a minimum period of five years, and that they had to refrain from activity, political or otherwise, which would adversely affect Lebanon's national unity or its basic interests. This smoothed the way two days later for the departure of Aoun from the French embassy in Beirut to Marseilles, France, under a French military escort,[16] a development welcomed by the Hrawi government, which grew increasingly confident during the summer.

Its mood was reflected by its citizens. The rising confidence of Lebanese, at home and abroad, manifested itself in several ways.

During summer holidays in August some 300,000 *émigrés* had booked flights to Beirut, now served by thirteen airlines; and tens of thousands of them had transferred large sums of money to the Lebanese banks. While business had revived, it could never reach the level of 1982 because the economic infrastructure, heavily damaged by the Israeli invasion, was insufficient to cope with economic activity above a certain level. The authorities had started collecting customs at the rate of $5–6 million a month. But such sums were dwarfed by the demands for urgent repairs and reconstruction, with emergency repairs to electricity generating stations alone costing $210 million. The government had yet to decide whether to finance the initial stages of reconstruction by inviting foreign capital, prefer- ably owned by Lebanese *émigrés*, or by borrowing money from the banks abroad against its foreign exchange reserves of $660 million and gold reserves of about $2.5 billion.[17] As with any other high policy, it needed to consult Damascus before reaching a decision.

As specified by the Lebanese–Syrian treaty, the defence and interior ministers of the two countries signed a security agreement on 1 September. It guaranteed exchange of intelligence and extradi- tion of fugitives. The Lebanese defence minister said that his ministry would hand over any information that could affect Syria's stability to its counterpart in Damascus.

Once again, in pursuance of the above accord, the Lebanese leaders met their Syrian counterparts in Damascus on 17 October to forge a common position for the Middle East peace conference to be conducted in Madrid on 30 October. In its talks with the USA, which acted as the honest broker, Lebanon had been demanding that UN Security Council Resolution 425 be treated independently of the main Israeli–Arab conflict, and that Resolution 425 was not negotia- ble.[18] The Lebanese–Syrian meeting turned out to be a prelude to a larger gathering of the foreign ministers of Syria, Egypt, the PLO, Jordan and Lebanon on 23 October in Damascus to hammer out a common Arab position in the talks that the respective delegations of the Syrians, Jordanians, Palestinians and Lebanese were to hold with the Israelis in Madrid.

Israel disapproved of the subservient role played by Lebanon in the inter-Arab talks and by the centrality of the Syrian role, and expressed its feelings by directing artillery salvos at the Nabatiya area from 21 October onwards. On 29 October, on the eve of the Madrid conference, Israel extended shelling to Iqlim al Tuffa, the southern Beqaa valley and the Palestinian camp of Rashidiya near Tyre.

Within Lebanon not everybody approved of Beirut's participation in the Madrid peace conference. The Hizbollah was in the forefront of the protest. On 30 October it held a mass rally in Beirut against the conference, when its leaders called for the dissolution of the Zionist state. It stepped up attacks on Israel and the SLA in south Lebanon. This brought about Israeli retribution in the Nabatiya area. Only after the USA, listening to the pleas of Lebanon at the Madrid conference, had pressured Israel to stop, did the IDF cease fire.

The freeing of Western hostages, which had begun with the release of the British journalist John McCarthy on 8 August, gathered pace. Responding to the Lebanese and Palestinian demands, on 11 September Israel released from Khiam gaol fifty-one Lebanese held as prisoners without charge for periods up to five years, and returned the bodies of nine Hizbollah militiamen. Following the wishes of McCarthy's captors, the Islamic Jihad Organization, the UN secretary-general, Javier Perez de Cuellar, became involved in securing the release of the Western hostages and some 350 to 400 Lebanese and Palestinians held without charge by Israel either at Khiam in its Lebanese security zone or at home. Israel demanded to know the whereabouts of six soldiers missing since 1986, only one of whom was believed to be alive. Following the delivery of the bodies of two dead Israeli soldiers to Israel, Terry Waite, a Briton, and Thomas Sutherland, an American, were released on 18 November. A fortnight later Israel freed twenty-five Lebanese detainees. This in turn led to the release of three more Americans: Joseph Ciccipio, Allan Steen and Terry Anderson. By Christmas 1991 all Western captives had been freed, except Heinrich Strubig and Thomas Kemptner, two German aid workers who had been kidnapped in May 1989 by the Holy Strugglers for Justice. Their fate had become interlinked with those of Muhammad Ali Hamadi and Abbas Hamadi, imprisoned in Germany for hijacking, kidnapping and murder.

In a sense, the Western hostage situation was reflective of the bigger picture: while the civil war had ended, the issue of the Israeli occupation of a border strip in the south remained unresolved.

11
Summary and conclusions

The roots of inter-religious conflict in contemporary Lebanon can be traced back to the late sixteenth century when Fakhr al Din Maan founded the Emirate of Mount Lebanon, which included both Druzes and Maronites, under the aegis of the Ottoman emperor. The simmering religious antagonism between these communities, compounded by traditional hatred between serfs and landlords, erupted into violence in 1845. The Ottoman intervention failed to suppress the conflict, which escalated into ferocious fighting during 1858–60. Finding the Druzes in a superior military position, France, recognized by the Ottomans as the Maronites' guardian, sent an expeditionary force to Lebanon to save the Maronites from a crushing defeat, and to restore peace – a pattern which was to repeat itself nearly a century later, with America taking over the role of France.

What emerged out of the ashes of the Ottoman empire in 1920 was a larger Lebanon, its expansion having been achieved by the French mandate power at the expense of Syria, a fact never forgotten by the Muslims of the region. France's intention was to create and foster a European outpost on the foundation of a Christian community which embraced a little over half of the Lebanese population. To offset the possibility of the expanding Muslim community emerging politically stronger as a result of a demographic majority, a confessionalist system, based on the census figures of 1932, was institutionalized in the form of the National Pact of 1943. It placed the all-powerful presidency into the hands of a Maronite. This locked the political system into a time warp. The only way the faster-growing Muslim population could adjust the system to reflect the demographic reality was by taking up arms.

In the wake of post-war decolonization in the region, and the rise of Arab nationalism at the expense of British and French imperial power – highlighted by the failure of the British–French–Israeli alliance to recapture Egypt's Suez Canal in late 1956 – the Muslims in Lebanon were increasingly inspired by Arab nationalism, popularly known as Nasserism. And so were a fair proportion of non-Maronite Christians. The Maronites and their leaders on the other hand, beholden to the West, swam against the popular current in the region, with President Camille Chamoun openly aligning himself with America. This, coupled with his blatant rigging of the 1957 parliamentary elections and repression of the opposition, fuelled anger in the Nasserist camp to the extent that a civil war erupted in mid-May 1958. In a significant replay of history, the Nasserist side was led by Kamal Jumblatt, a Druze, while the pro-Western, conservative side was led by Chamoun, a Maronite. To preserve the unity of the Lebanese army, its commander, General Fuad Chehab, maintained neutrality.

During the course of the conflict, the pro-Western monarchy in Iraq was overthrown by Nasserist military officers in mid-July 1958. This unnerved President Chamoun, who called for the US troops which the American president, Eisenhower, had promised to offer to any Middle East country that found itself being menaced by the aggressive intentions of a regional country 'occupied by international Communism' (in short, Egypt under Nasser). The arrival of US marines, who outnumbered the Lebanese army, enraged the opposition, which controlled about a third of Lebanon. The fighting intensified. But to expedite the departure of the foreign forces, the opposition MPs agreed to vote for General Chehab, who had disapproved of the invitation to US troops, as president. Thus the 1958 civil conflict, ending in late July, proved to be mercifully short.

Both Chehab and his successor, Charles Helou, maintained stability by aligning their external policies with those of the Arab hinterland and by co-opting the leaders of urban Muslims in ruling the country, thus blending Lebanon's Christian identity with Arab nationalism. But with more and more Palestinians being turned into refugees due to the Israeli occupation of the West Bank and Gaza, which stemmed from the June 1967 Arab–Israeli War, and to the clashes between armed Palestinians and the Jordanian military, Arab nationalism turned more radical.

The rising presence of Palestinians in Lebanon, many of them armed, had the effect of radicalizing the underprivileged Muslims, particularly in urban areas, which experienced above-normal growth as a succession of Israeli air attacks on south Lebanon in the early

1970s uprooted tens of thousands of Muslim peasants. The slowly crystallizing alliance between Palestinians and left-of-centre Lebanese was seen as a serious threat to the political system by the right-wing Maronites. In the mid-1950s President Chamoun had taken a similar view of the rise of Nasserism, which was portrayed as antithetical to Lebanese nationalism. He and other Maronite leaders had reiterated their distinctness from the Arab world by arguing that Maronite history, centred around the Church and Mount Lebanon, stood apart from the mainstream Muslim Arab experience. Indeed, militant Maronites had come to identify with Israel since its founding in 1948 as an enclave society that, like the Maronites, was surrounded by Muslims.

But there were differences too between then and now. Unlike in 1958, what emerged in the mid-1970s was a conflict in which two major camps combined to fight the third, the three protagonists being: (a) the status-quoist Lebanese Front, a confederation of predominantly Maronite parties, led by Camille Chamoun; (b) the reformist Lebanese National Movement, a confederation of mainly Muslim parties, headed by Kamal Jumblatt; and (c) the Palestinian resistance, led by Yasser Arafat. The Palestinians were a significant element in the civil conflict until the PLO's expulsion from Beirut in September 1982 by the invading Israelis.

Initially, the PLO's financial and military aid was an important factor in the victories that the LNM–PLO alliance scored over its adversary, the Maronite Lebanese Front. The left-of-centre alliance extended its control over two-thirds of the country. This alarmed Lebanon's powerful neighbours – Israel and Syria – and led to the direct military intervention of Syria, thus making the civil war a quadrilateral affair, with Damascus playing the role of a partisan arbiter.

The reason for armed intervention by the Syrian president, Assad, was as follows. A Lebanon under the LNM would allow the PLO such unfettered freedom of action that the conflict between the PLO and Israel would escalate sharply, providing Israel with an excuse to invade Lebanon, occupy part of it and threaten Syria's security. To obviate such a scenario, Assad decided to move – but only after he had assured Israel through the USA that his objective was to halt the civil war in Lebanon and that the size and deployment of his troops would not jeopardize Israel's security.

Assad's military intervention in Lebanon on 1 June 1976 against the reformist LNM–PLO alliance was a dramatic reversal of the regional policies that Syria, ruled by the Arab Baath Socialist Party since 1963, had previously pursued. Denunciation came not only from Moscow, a long-time ally of Damascus, but also from such radical Arab states as Iraq, Algeria and South Yemen. Unable to comprehend how Syria could be fighting on the side of the Lebanese camp which was being armed by Israel, the LNM–PLO alliance urged the Soviet Union to pressure Syria to pull its forces out of Lebanon. While the Soviet leaders were critical of Assad's move, they were loath to alienate Syria, aware that they had already lost Egypt as an ally four years before.

The quick success that the Syrian forces had on the battlefield allowed Assad to sign an agreement with the LNM–PLO alliance which specified an immediate ceasefire and an endorsement of the November 1969 Cairo Agreement between the Lebanese government and the PLO, which allowed the PLO certain rights inside Lebanon. On the political front, by getting Elias Sarkis, his nominee, elected as president of Lebanon, Assad made an impressive gain. Once Sarkis had assumed office on 23 September 1976, it became easier for Assad to despatch more troops into Lebanon to expel the LMN–PLO alliance from the Christian areas they had refused to vacate.

For political and strategic reasons, it did not suit Assad to annihilate the LNM–PLO alliance. Had he done so he would have ended up depending on the Maronite camp, a situation he wanted to avoid. Throughout the long Lebanese saga Assad consistently followed the policy of weakening his opposing force of the moment to the point of severely crippling its independence, and not annihilating it altogether.

Now Assad picked up the Saudi call for a truce, and backed the decision of the Arab summit on 26 October 1976 to deploy in Lebanon a 30,000-strong Arab Deterrent Force, with the bulk of the troops drawn from Syria. Thus he legitimized the Syrian military presence in Lebanon, an important achievement which silenced his critics at home and abroad. The posting of the ADF in most of Lebanon, including Beirut, by mid-November 1976 heralded the virtual end of the nineteen-month civil war.

Yet the writ of the ADF, nominally operating under the Lebanese president and deployed in large areas of northern and eastern Lebanon, did not run in the Christian enclave north of Beirut, with its capital in Jounieh; nor did it run in the proto-state, south and south-east of Beirut, administered by the radical Lebanese and their Palestinian allies, who competed for the control of south Lebanon with Saad Haddad, a former Lebanese officer now commanding a pro-Israeli militia, which had turned itself into an early warning system for Israel against attacks by the Palestinians.

Reconfirmation of the Lebanese–PLO Cairo Agreement of 1969 by the Arab summit in October 1976 left the Maronite leaders dissatisifed. They shared with Israel the common objectives of expelling all armed Palestinians from Lebanon and reducing the presence of Palestinian civilians. Their spirits rose when a right-wing Likud-led government, headed by Menachem Begin, took office in Israel in May 1977. They strengthened their links with Israel.

The precipitate visit of the Egyptian president, Anwar Sadat, to Jerusalem in November 1977 caused such revulsion elsewhere in the region that it brought all other Arab forces together. It provided Assad with a welcome opportunity to return the Syrian policy to cordial links with left-of-centre, anti-Zionist forces in the region. Relations between Syria and the LNM–PLO alliance improved dramatically, while those between Syria and the Maronite Lebanese Front turned frosty. Following a series of anti-Syrian demonstrations and strikes in the Christian enclave, there were clashes between the Maronite militias and the Syrian-dominated ADF. Assad concluded that the alliance he had forged with the Maronites in the spring of 1976 could not be sustained primarily because the latter would never accept the Syrian hegemony over Lebanon that he had in mind.

Israel had its own scenario for Lebanon. Having paved the way for a peace treaty with Egypt, following the signing of the Camp David Accords between Israel and Egypt in September 1978, its government focused on getting Lebanon to follow the Egyptian lead. But this aim could not be achieved so long as the PLO had its headquarters in Beirut and ran a state within a state under the aegis of the 1969 Cairo Agreement with the Lebanese authorities. The Israeli policy-makers concluded that the process of eliminating the PLO from the complex Lebanese equation needed to be initiated in south Lebanon, an area it used as a base for its anti-Israeli actions.

An attack by a group of Palestinians on an Israeli bus provided Israel with a rationale to invade south Lebanon in mid-March 1978. It occupied half of the territory. When it withdrew it surrendered its positions either to the United Nations Interim Force in Lebanon or to the Haddad militia, which it had brought under its control. It barred the Syrian-dominated ADF from crossing the Litani, and vetoed the proposal of the Lebanese government to deploy its Litani Brigade alongside Unifil in the south.

All told, Israel's invasion was a success. It ended the Palestinian presence and infrastructure in the immediate border region, and legitimized and strengthened Israel's relations with the Christians below the Litani. It enabled Israel to become a permanent feature of the internal Lebanese conflict, and to divide the areas of influence inside Lebanon with Syria, confining the latter to the area north of the Litani.

Israel's ties with the Maronites became stronger and less inhibited. This fuelled the ambition of Bashir Gemayel, the rising star in the Maronite camp, to become the next president. He started eliminating credible Maronite rivals. Having banished Raymond Edde, the leader of moderate Maronites, to France, armed henchmen of Bashir Gemayel assassinated Tony Franjieh, the eldest son of Suleiman Franjieh, in June 1978. These events, combined with a clandestine visit to Israel by Bashir Gemayel the following month, worried Assad. He visualized Israel establishing itself in the heartland of Lebanon by way of its growing Maronite connections, thus threatening Syria's security through the Beqaa valley and the Beirut–Damascus highway, and was determined to thwart this scenario.

Assad's strength lay in the fact that the Syrian troops in Lebanon, acting under the aegis of the Arab Deterrent Force, were a formidable fighting force capable of altering the balance of power in Lebanon, and that overall they had emerged as a stabilizing factor. Since none of the Lebanese factions dared to see complete Syrian military pull-back from Lebanon, which was certain to re-ignite the civil conflict, Assad resorted to using the threat of withdrawal as a lever to make President Sarkis or other Lebanese leaders follow his counsel.

The comparative peace that followed the Israeli withdrawal in the spring of 1978 did not prove sufficient to further national reconciliation. The Lebanese Front insisted on resolving the Palestinian and Syrian problems first, aware that this would enfeeble the Muslim position, whereas the LNM wanted immediate moves to reform the system while its Syrian and Palestinian allies were able to lend it support. Within the administration similar divisions existed. President Sarkis perceived national reconciliation as a prelude to curtailing Syria's influence in his country, whereas Prime Minister Hoss regarded it as a preamble to implementing a national security plan in conjunction with the Syrian ADF and to institutionalizing Lebanon's special relationship with Syria. This dichotomy persisted throughout the conflict and was finally to be resolved in Syria's favour.

Having consolidated his hold over the Christian enclave, Bashir Gemayel, working in co-operation with Israel, moved in April 1981 to extend his control over the strategic Christian town of Zahle in the Beqaa valley, near the Beirut–Damascus highway, with a view ultimately to connnecting up with the Christian areas in the south. Assad saw through the Maronite–Israeli game plan, and acted militarily to frustrate it. His success induced direct military involvement by Israel, which shot down two Syrian helicopters in late April. This provided Assad with a chance to disregard his 'red line' agreements with Israel, and deploy surface-to-air missiles in the Beqaa. Israel's prime minister, Begin, decided to destroy these missiles, but had to postpone the strikes due to poor weather conditions. The breathing space provided valuable time not only for the Arab states to rally round Syria – thus ending its isolation due to its siding with Iran in the Iran–Iraq War which erupted in September 1980 – but also for America to cool the tempers of its strategic ally, Israel. The result was a series of understandings between Israel, Syria and the PLO brokered by the USA which went into effect on 25 July 1981 along with a ceasefire in south Lebanon. Syria was permitted to deploy missiles in the Beqaa so long as it did not fire them; Israel was allowed to continue its reconnaissance flights over Lebanon as long as it did not target the Syrian missiles; and Israel and the PLO agreed to cease cross-border attacks, with Assad guaranteeing the PLO's compliance.

The truce held for about a year – until Israel broke it, using as its pretext the attempted assassination of its ambassador in London, Argov, to launch a full-scale invasion of Lebanon in early June 1982. For the first time the Jewish state initiated an offensive campaign when its existence was *not* at stake.

Israel's ten-week invasion, which was launched with the full knowledge of at least the US secretary of state, Alexander Haig, and which *inter alia* caused irreparable damage to Lebanon's economic infrastructure, yielded mixed results. By uprooting the PLO's headquarters and fighters from Beirut, Israel weakened its most troublesome adversary and virtually eliminated any chance of PLO members attacking targets inside Israel. It also benefited by securing the departure of the Syrian troops from West Beirut. The cumulative effect of these expulsions was to provide Israel with political opportunities in Lebanon that it had not enjoyed before. It was now in a position to rearrange the political map of Lebanon in favour of its allies, the Maronites, to install their young leader, Bashir Gemayel, as the president, and to upset the traditional Lebanese way of resolving conflicts based on the concept of 'No victor, no vanquished'.

On the other hand, by resorting to non-stop bombing of the civilian sectors of West Beirut, and cutting off supplies of water, electricity and food, Israel severely damaged its image in the Western world, and weakened its lobbies, especially in the USA. Indeed, the merciless tactics used by the Israeli defence minister, Sharon, disturbed even his own cabinet colleagues. This, and the massacre of 2,000 unarmed Palestinians in Sabra and Shatila camps by the Maronite militia in mid-September 1982 following the assassination of their commander, Bashir Gemayel, the president-elect, produced a groundswell of public opinion in Israel against Sharon and the invasion he had masterminded.

Having got even, more or less, with the Israelis by eliminating their charismatic protégé, Bashir Gemayel, Assad was amenable to accepting as president the lacklustre elder brother of Bashir, Amin Gemayel, who was uncontaminated by contacts with the US or Israeli intelligence agencies. Though Assad's backing was important in gaining Amin Gemayel the overwhelming support he received from the Lebanese MPs in his election, he was not so beholden to the Syrian leader as his predecessor, Sarkis, who was a nominee of Syria.

In any case, following the Israeli invasion, America had emerged as an important player in Lebanon, and its contribution of 1,200 marines to the Multi-National Force of four Western nations had given it a military presence it did not have before. It was committed to implementing its long-standing policy of securing peace between Israel and its Arab neighbours.

Now the United States pressured President Gemayel to negotiate directly with the Jewish state with a view to concluding a peace treaty. Aware of the hostility towards Israel in the Arab world, Gemayel offered to conduct tripartite talks with the USA acting as the mediator. These negotiations led to an agreed draft of a peace treaty between Lebanon and Israel in mid-May 1983. It formally ended the state of war between the two countries, and banned Lebanon from allowing the use of its territory or airspace for the passage of troops or military equipment from any state not having diplomatic relations with Israel. It also required Lebanon to abrogate any regulations, laws or treaties that were in conflict with the Lebanese–Israeli accord, including all the commitments that Lebanon had made as a founder-member of the Arab League since 1945. It curtailed the Lebanese government's power to station troops between the Zahrani and Awali rivers, and required it to recognize the Haddad militia as the sole force authorized to patrol the area up to Zahrani, and to allow the stationing of Lebanese–Israeli supervisory teams charged with detecting and destroying any armed guerrillas in the area.

Had this treaty been ratified and implemented, it would have enhanced the already dominant role of the Maronites in Lebanon, and moved the country away from the Arab world, thus deepening the sense of genuine grievance that the Lebanese Muslims had been nursing since the creation of modern Lebanon, and further destabilizing the state and society. As it was, the contents of the treaty confirmed the worst fears of Assad and the left-of-centre anti-Gemayel forces in Lebanon, who denounced it vehemently. The passing of the treaty by sixty-four Lebanese MPs made little difference to their stance.

The expulsion of the PLO, led in the main by Sunni Muslims, from Beirut, and the failure of the traditional Sunni leaders of Lebanon to oppose the rise of the Maronite–Israeli–US alliance, created a vacuum in the Muslim camp which the leadership of Shias, now the largest single sect, was quick to fill. This manifested itself in the growing importance that Amal, headed by lay and clerical Shias, came to acquire. It became a reliable tool of Syria, led by Assad, who belonged to a sub-sect within Shia Islam. The Hizbollah, a Shia organization which emerged in the aftermath of the Israeli invasion, remained loyal to Iran, then allied to Syria in its war with Iraq. Together, Amal and Hizbollah formed the backbone of armed resistance to the Israeli occupiers in south Lebanon, a Shia-majority region – as well as the public protest against the Lebanese–Israeli treaty in West Beirut.

By withholding his signature on the treaty, President Gemayel expected to pressure Israel to vacate the large Lebanese territories that it continued to occupy. The resulting stalemate suited Syria and its Lebanese allies more than it did other parties.

In late August 1983, working in conjunction with Damascus, the Amal and Druze militias challenged the authority of Gemayel. The resulting confrontation split the Lebanese army along communal lines, and induced US and French military intervention on the side of the Lebanese president. While Washington and Paris secured their immediate military aim of sparing the Lebanese army a humiliating defeat, they paid a heavy political price. They showed to the Lebanese Muslims that, like the French in 1860, they had intervened in Lebanon as the saviours of the Maronites.

By truck-bombing the military barracks of the USA and France in Beirut in October, and killing 300 American and French troops, militant Shias felt they had got somewhere towards settling scores with Washington and Paris. In retrospect, they paved the way for the departure of the Western Multi-National Force, which came in early February 1984 when President Gemayel's effort to cow the Shia residents of West Beirut, by deploying the army against them, backfired. Finding himself without his Western guardians, Gemayel buried the Lebanese–Israeli treaty, and with it any future Israeli plans to transform Lebanon into a client state ruled solely by the Maronites. As before in this long conflict, the winning party had stretched its power and resources beyond sustainable limits, and had to retreat.

As Assad surveyed the scene in early March 1984, he found his forces controlling northern Lebanon and the Beqaa valley in eastern Lebanon, the Druze militia controlling the Shouf, and the Druze–Amal alliance controlling West Beirut – with militant Shias in the south making life increasingly intolerable for the Israeli occupiers.

Yet when it came to national reconciliation among Lebanese, the chances were as bleak as before. The differences between Gemayel and his adversaries were similar to those between the Maronite Lebanese Front and the LNM earlier. Now, while the Gemayel camp insisted on consolidating and extending security to all parts of Lebanon, thus depriving its Muslim opponents of a military option, before introducing political reform, the Shia and Druze leaders demanded immediate reform against the backdrop of the military superiority of their militias.

In September 1984, with the installation in Israel of a national unity government committed to evacuating Lebanon and led by the Labour leader Shimon Peres, the spirits of the pro-Syrian Lebanese parties rose. The last of the three-phase Israeli withdrawal from Lebanon was carried out in early June 1985, with the IDF surrendering its positions to its surrogate force called the South Lebanon Army, leaving 1,000 troops behind in a border strip and secretly setting out a few 'red lines' for Syria.

Excluding south Lebanon, though, the general situation in Lebanon reverted to what had existed in the late 1970s – with Damascus, deploying a large force in Lebanon, possessing a powerful lever over the Maronite president. Moreover, many years of the Syrian presence in Lebanon had helped Assad to sharpen his intelligence tool to the extent of infiltrating the Maronite side, thus making his adversaries prone to the sort of manipulation that had long been a hallmark of Assad's policy towards the Muslim camp and the PLO. The Maronite camp had been weakened by the death in August 1984 of Pierre Gemayel, a highly respected, authoritarian patriarch; and Amin Gemayel, lacking his father's stature and experience, had proved ill-equipped to control such ambitious young commanders as Samir Geagea and Elie Hobeika. Indeed, in an overnight coup Geagea had hijacked the Lebanese Forces militia in March 1985, and Gemayel had found himself unable to reverse the coup. The later change of leadership at the LF, from Geagea to Hobeika (who quickly co-opted Geagea as his second-in-command), did nothing to repair the reduced prestige or power of Gemayel.

Finding Gemayel deprived of the last vestige of military power, Assad decided to concentrate on those leaders, Muslim and Christian, who commanded large militias : Berri of Amal, Jumblatt of the Druze militia, and Hobeika of the LF. The end result was the adoption by them in December of a statement called the National Agreement to Solve the Lebanese Crisis. The most detailed and comprehensive reconciliation document yet drafted, its ten points covered not only political reform but also Lebanon's special relations with Syria. However, since Hobeika failed to carry the LF Command Council with him on the issue, the agreement proved still-born.

Assad's failure in this instance illustrated again the fractured nature of Lebanon's internal power structure, with each component allied to an external force, big or small. That meant that no single Lebanese party or a coalition of parties, reinforced by one or more external powers, could dictate its terms. The Israeli–US–Maronite alliance, forged in the heat of the 1982 Israeli invasion, failed to impose the Judaeo–Christian–Western hegemony on Lebanon. Similarly, the Syrian–Iranian–Muslim coalition failed to amend the 1943 power-sharing formula to mirror the current demographic estimates of the sixteen recognized sects. This failure underlined the limits of Syrian power, just as the annulment of the 1983 Lebanese–Israeli treaty had highlighted the limits of Israel's power.

The only general consolation that Syria could derive in late 1986 was the serious blow that America's prestige suffered in the region in the wake of the Irangate Scandal when it was revealed that, contrary to the Reagan administration's much vaunted policy of not dealing with hostage-takers and terrorists, it had engaged in straight 'arms for hostages' swaps with Iran, hoping that Tehran would persuade the pro-Iranian groups in Lebanon to release the American hostages they were holding. In all the clandestine bargaining that had occurred, the USA had come out badly. By showing Iran in a better light at the expense of America 'the Great Satan', the Irangate Scandal raised the morale especially of such Lebanese Shia parties as the Hizbollah and Amal.

Though not in sympathy with the religious militancy of the Hizbollah, Assad found the party a suitable instrument to pressure the Israeli and SLA troops in the self-declared security zone of Israel in Lebanon. The pursuit of this policy during 1987 had the additional merit of diverting popular attention away from the insoluble security and other problems of West Beirut and refurbishing Syria's confrontational credentials. At the same time, the practice of militancy had to be allowed within the framework outlined by the Syrian leader thus: none of the Palestinian or Lebanese parties should be given so much latitude as to provoke Israel into starting a major confrontation with Syria for which the latter was unprepared. When Assad found the Hizbollah getting out of control in its anti-Israeli campaign in south Lebanon, he engaged Amal, his loyal protégé, to clip the Hizbollah's wings. This ploy also suited his policy of engaging in a constructive dialogue with the USA to forge the future of Lebanon.

After sulking for four years in the wake of the unceremonious withdrawal of US marines from Beirut in early 1984, the second Reagan administration's interest in Middle East politics revived following the launching of an intifada (uprising) by the Palestinians in the Occupied Territories in December 1987. Assad offered to rein in the militant Islamic forces in Lebanon, help secure the freedom of the Western hostages being held there, and discourage attacks against targets in Israel in return for an American agreement to accept Syrian influence in Lebanon above the Zahrani river, to endorse only those presidential candidates who publicly endorsed political reform, and to pressure Israel to narrow its area of manoeuvre in southern Lebanon. The US secretary of state, Shultz, overcame his initial reluctance and agreed, leading to Syrian–American co-operation. This puzzled and angered Maronite leaders: their agreement was crucial to electing the next president before 23 September. They dismissed the common Syrian–American position on reform as nothing more than the rehashing of the aborted, Syrian-sponsored Tripartite Agreement of December 1985.

But Assad kept to his promise of curtailing the power of the Hizbollah not only in south Lebanon but also in the Shia suburbs of West Beirut, using Amal as his agent for the purpose. When Amal found itself at the losing end of the fight, Assad intervened directly to save Amal. And when the foreign patron of the Hizbollah, Iran, an ally of Syria and a member of the peace committee, suggested the formation of a joint Syrian–Iranian security force, it was firmly told by Damascus to keep its hands off Lebanon: 'Our role in Lebanon is above all other considerations.' Through all the vicissitudes of this long conflict one factor remained constant: Syria's insistence on a special relationship with Lebanon, and its confrontation, overt or covert, with any and every country, big or small, Arab or non-Arab, which challenged this Syrian claim. Before the Lebanese civil war was over, Syria had successfully challenged not only Israel and America on this issue, but also Iraq and the Arab League Committee of Six on Lebanon led by Kuwait.

For now, Assad's strong-arm tactics against the fundamentalist Hizbollah improved his credibility with Washington, which came to appreciate anew his stamina, insight and cunning, and helped the two governments to agree to name Mikhail Dahir, a member of the camp of Suleiman Franjieh, a pro-Syrian Maronite politician, as their presidential nominee. But the proposal was rejected outright by the Maronite leadership.

Due to the failure of the Lebanese MPs to meet and elect the next president before 23 September 1988, Amin Gemayel ordered his chief of staff, General Aoun, to form a temporary military cabinet. Aoun's government of six military officers never met in full, since the three Muslim ministers refused to take up their posts. Nonetheless, Lebanon now acquired two governments which functioned in parallel for the next two turbulent years.

General Aoun's outspoken and populist manner was refreshingly different in Lebanese politics. Unsullied by compromise, he projected himself as a Lebanese nationalist, simple and pure. While these attributes and tactics enhanced his popularity among his military and civilian followers, they proved insufficient to control or weaken the Lebanese Forces, a political-military entity which collected taxes and levies, administered the Christian enclave, including its ports, and was led by Samir Geagea, who wanted to change a unitary Lebanon into a federal one consisting of cantons. The LF's continued pre-eminence in the Christian enclave made a mockery of the Aoun government's claims to be the sole legitimate authority in Lebanon.

Aoun therefore attacked the LF in mid-February and succeeded in establishing the supremacy of his army. But instead of consolidating his position in the Christian sector, he vowed to extend his authority to the Muslim sector, starting with the closure of *all* illegal ports.

This was the start of what Aoun called the 'war of liberation' from Syria, 'a terrorist state'. He was encouraged in this campaign by the Iraqi president, Saddam Hussein, who, having signed a truce with Iran in August 1988 after eight years of fighting, wanted to punish Assad for having sided with the Iranians during that war, by arming the Maronite camp. The combat between the warring Lebanese sides was ferocious, with thousands of shells raining on civilian areas, and Syria and the West Beirut government imposing land and sea blockades on the Christian enclave inhabited by about a million people. The suffering caused by the blockades and fighting split the Christian leaderships, with most politicians and religious leaders calling for an immediate ceasefire. Aoun, on the other hand, became more obdurate and launched a bitter personal attack on President Assad.

At the Arab summit on 23–5 May, unattended by any Lebanese representative, Assad was pressured by the leaders of Iraq, Jordan and Egypt to produce a timetable for the withdrawal of his troops. Assad replied that the Lebanese–Syrian relationship had 'a special historical, geographical and human character', and that the Syrian forces would leave either by 'a Lebanese agreement reached in a national referendum' or 'a request from a unified central government'. He knew that the presence of 35,000 Syrian troops in Lebanon spoke louder than any resolution that the Arab summit might pass on the withdrawal of all foreign forces from Lebanon. In the end, the summit expressed its sense of urgency by replacing the committee of six foreign ministers with a committee of three heads of state (Algeria, Morocco and Saudi Arabia) and giving it six months to resolve the crisis. Amazingly, the new high-powered body was to meet its deadline, albeit after the predictable ups and downs.

The interim report by the foreign ministers of Algeria, Morocco and Saudi Arabia in late July blamed Syria for the impasse they had reached on the question of linking the implementation of a comprehensive security plan for Lebanon with a timetable for a graduated withdrawal of the Syrian troops, with Damascus insisting on sticking to the concept of Lebanese–Syrian co-operation in strategic and other fields according to the December 1985 Tripartite Agreement signed by Berri, Jumblatt and Hobeika. Unsurprisingly, fighting between the Lebanese factions intensified, with both sides amply supplied with deadly shells and mortars by Damascus and Baghdad; and the living conditions of the residents of both sectors of Beirut deteriorated sharply. Calls for an immediate end to violence came from the leading Western capitals and the UN.

In mid-August the Muslim and leftist Lebanese groups gathered in Damascus, and planned an all-out offensive in conjunction with the Syrian troops. While the UN Security Council appealed to all parties to stop firing, Moscow despatched a special envoy to the region. His efforts succeeded in persuading Assad to defer a full-scale campaign to overthrow Aoun. He had his own reasons to do so, domestic and foreign. His intervention in Lebanon was not popular with the Syrian military, and the inevitable casualties that an attack on the Christian enclave would have entailed would have made matters worse for him. Given the anti-Syrian feeling among most Christians, controlling their enclave would have been problematic. A full-scale invasion of the Christian sector would have elicited condemnation in the West as well as from leading Arab capitals.

The zenith of the Arab League Troika's efforts came in mid-September with the publication of a seven-point peace plan which included the convening of the Lebanese MPs in the Saudi city of Taif to discuss a draft National Reconciliation Charter. After his instant rejection of the Arab Troika's plan, Aoun reversed his position, aware that he was militarily inferior to his adversaries and that under the pressure of deadly shells and mortars the civilian morale in the Christian enclave had virtually collapsed.

The document that almost all the Lebanese parliamentarians present in Taif signed on 22 October 1989 was a compromise. The political reform conciliated the Muslim and Christian demands. While the powers of the president were curtailed, the practice of having a Maronite as the president was retained, and so too was the provision about having a Sunni prime minister, even though Sunnis were now less numerous than Shias. Despite their numerical superiority, the Muslims agreed to share parliamentary seats equally with the Christians. By accepting the Syrian military presence for two years after a national unity government had introduced reform, the Lebanese MPs conferred legitimacy on the Syrian presence, something that had been absent for seven years.

This was precisely what Aoun found objectionable about the Taif Accord. He had instructed the Christian MPs before their departure for Taif not to discuss constitutional reform until and unless they had secured written guarantees about a Syrian evacuation. His rejection of the Taif Accord was therefore predictable. But the national reconciliation process – blessed by Syria, Saudi Arabia, America, France and the Vatican – was too firmly in train to be derailed by Aoun, especially when he failed to secure the backing of other important Christian leaders for his policy.

By assembling inside Lebanon and endorsing the Taif Accord in early November, the Lebanese MPs turned it into a legal document. And by electing René Muawad, a member of the Suleiman Franjieh camp, they served notice on Aoun that his time was up. The assassination of Muawad a few weeks later made little difference to the way history was unfolding. Within days the Lebanese parliamentarians elevated Elias Hrawi, a fellow-MP from Zahle, to the presidency.

As the constitutionally elected president, Hrawi was within his rights to dismiss Aoun. He did. But Aoun was not a man to back down. He resorted to his populist tactics, which brought tens of thousands of his supporters to the presidential palace in Baabda to form a permanent human shield and thwart any plans of West Beirut and Damascus to overrun the palace militarily. The strategy worked, enabling Aoun to interpret the failure of his enemies to attack the Christian enclave as a victory for him. His prestige rose, but not sufficiently to overawe his leading Maronite rival, Geagea, the LF's commander, who advocated acceptance of the Taif Accord. On the other hand, freshly buoyed by the rising and vocal support for him, Aoun thought the time opportune to attack the LF and monopolize power in the Christian enclave. This turned out to be a miscalculation.

As the two Christian forces conducted 'the war of brothers', both West Beirut and Damascus kept away from the fray. Going by the past pattern, the Syrian intelligence agents most probably played a crucial clandestine role in bringing the simmering inter-Christian conflict to the boil. Assad's best bet was therefore to refrain from entering the combat overtly, especially when he knew that, as before, any such move would lead to the two Christian forces closing ranks to fight the non-Christians. Moreover, the longer the internecine violence continued, making civilian life increasingly unbearable, the greater was the chance of Aoun losing his popularity, an important element in his political armoury. In any case, while Assad wanted Aoun's downfall, he did not relish the idea of Geagea emerging as the clear victor, an outcome which would give the latter an unacceptable degree of power and independence. No wonder that, to prolong the inter-Christian combat, Assad permitted food and fuel supplies to the Aoun forces through the Syrian checkpoints, while allowing the LF fighters to retreat into West Beirut's southern suburbs and then move northwards to rejoin their colleagues in the LF-controlled part of East Beirut.

With the LF controlling two-thirds of the Christian enclave in early March, 1990, General Aoun lacking any worthwhile port and most Christian leaders openly calling for recognition of the Hrawi government, the general was in poor shape. Yet he hung on to power. While he had stopped talking about liberation from Syria, he bargained strenuously in his protracted talks with the West Beirut government through Vatican and Arab League mediators during June and July, demanding that an expanded national reconciliation cabinet should re-examine the Taif Accord. Such an idea was anathema to West Beirut and Damascus, but they were in no hurry to bring about Aoun's fall, which they perceived as benefiting Geagea's militia. In any case, President Hrawi needed Aoun's army virtually intact if he was to have a fighting chance of controlling the LF rather than becoming its hostage.

By early August, when Iraq attacked and occupied Kuwait, Aoun had lost any vestige of support abroad. Indeed, both Washington and Paris had grown weary of Aoun's stalling tactics. Assad's enrolment of Syria into the Washington-led coalition against Iraq ruled by Saddam Hussein, his long-time rival, prepared the ground for a deal between Damascus and Washington in mid-September to tackle the Aoun problem. There was, as always, Israel to be taken into account. But given the US complicity, reassuring Israel on the limited Syrian intentions proved to be a fairly routine business.

It was thus that the forces of Presidents Hrawi and Assad overpowered Aoun's men on 13 October 1990, forced the general to seek refuge at the French embassy, and ended the ordeal of the Lebanese people, which had lasted fifteen and a half years and left half a million casualties, including over 150,000 dead.

With this, the scene was set first to introduce constitutional reform, including parliamentary parity for Muslims and Christians, and then to formalize special relations between Lebanon and Syria. The result was the appointment of forty new MPs to replace those who had died and to raise the chamber's strength to 108, and the signing of the Treaty of Brotherhood, Co-operation and Co-ordination between Lebanon and Syria in May 1991.

Predictably, this upset Israel. Nine years after it had invaded Lebanon with a view to bringing it under its wing, it found Syria, its leading Arab rival, achieving that aim. The validity of the Syrian claim of special historical and geographical ties between the two Arab neighbours made little difference to the Israeli position. Reversing its previous policy, that it would pull out of south Lebanon when a strong government ruled in Beirut, it now declared that its troops would withdraw only after all other foreign forces had done so, *and* after an Israeli–Lebanese peace treaty had been signed.

To pacify Israel, the USA refrained from accepting the Lebanese argument that the Israeli withdrawal from south Lebanon should not be tied to the Middle East peace process because it was demanded, independently, by UN Security Council Resolution 425 of March 1978. In other words, whereas the Syrian–US deal, struck in the wake of the Kuwait crisis of August 1990, to use military force against Michel Aoun had resolved the internal aspect of the Lebanese civil war, only an American–Israeli agreement to tie in an Israeli evacuation of southern Lebanon with the concluding of a Lebanese–Israeli peace treaty contained the seed of settling the external aspect of the conflict concerning its territorial integrity.

Complete normalization in Lebanon therefore had to await a successful conclusion of the negotiations between Israel and its Arab neighbours which started in Madrid in October 1991. Meanwhile, the Lebanese and Syrian governments, pursuing a common policy, have stayed away from disarming the Hizbollah militia, and have allowed it to operate in south Lebanon – as a counterpoint to the Israeli-controlled South Lebanon Army in the self-declared security zone of Israel inside Lebanon. This is unlikely to change.

In a wider sense, though, noting that there were four fairly long periods of uneasy peace during the 1975–90 civil war, a question arises: will the current stretch of peace prove just another long lull before a recurring storm? The answer is no. The fatigue of the nation emerging slowly from sixteen years of nightmare and violent chaos is so deep that no domestic group, whether backed by a foreign power or not, has the motivation or will to ignite the smouldering cinders again. Moreover, the political imbalance, which condemned the Muslim majority to a minority status in parliament and provided it with a figurehead prime minister chosen from its ranks, has been addressed.

Yet one can only wonder how long the Muslim community, which forms 60 per cent of the total population, in a country with a multi-party democracy, can be content with a 50 per cent share of the political pie, and deny itself the office of the president; and how long the Shias, constituting the largest single sect, will tag along as junior partners in the Muslim camp. At present these remain open-ended questions.

APPENDIX 1
Chronology

1861
The Emirate of Mount Lebanon becomes an autonomous province of the Ottoman empire.

1920
September: As mandate power, France enlarges the Emirate of Mount Lebanon by adding areas to its north, west and south (hitherto belonging to Syria), and calling the new entity Greater Lebanon.

1926
France promulgates a republican constitution with parliament and an executive president elected by parliament.

1932
France suspends the constitution. Census produces figures for the sixteen recognized religious sects.

1936
France reinstates the constitution. Emile Edde is elected president.

1939
September: Second World War starts.

1940
Pro-German government formed in Vichy, central France, takes over French overseas territories, including Lebanon.

1941
June: Vichy government is defeated in Lebanon by the British and Free French troops.

1943
March: British envoy in Beirut offers a formula of six Christian MPs to five Muslim MPs, which forms the core of the National Pact.
July: France gives official sanction to the National Pact.
September: Bishara Khuri is elected president.

1945
Lebanon is one of the six founder-members of the Arab League.

1946
December: The French finally leave Lebanon.

1947
May: Parliamentary elections are held under an amended constitution.

1948
May: Israel is founded. Lebanon participates in the war against Israel declared by the Arab League.

1949
23 March: Lebanon and Israel sign a truce agreement.
September: Bishara Khuri is re-elected president.

1952
July: King Farouk of Egypt is overthrown by military officers.

1953
September: Khuri resigns. Camille Chamoun is elected president.

1956
October–November: British–French–Israeli invasion of Egypt.

1957
May: US president Dwight Eisenhower promises aid to any Middle East nation wishing protection against aggression from any regional country 'controlled by international Communism'. Chamoun subscribes to the Eisenhower doctrine.
June: Parliamentary elections are rigged.

1958
February: Formation of Egypt and Syria as the United Arab Republic.
8 May: Nasib Metni, an opposition Christian journalist, is assassinated.
12 May: Civil war erupts between pro-Western followers of President Chamoun and Arab nationalist supporters of Kamal Jumblatt.

14 July : Pro-Western King Faisal II of Iraq is overthrown.
18 July : 10,000 US marines and airborne ground troops begin arriving in Lebanon.
31 July : Parliament elects General Fuad Chehab president. Civil war ends.
23 September : Chehab becomes president.

1960
June : Elections to parliament, expanded from 77 seats to 99, are held.

1964
June : Parliamentary elections are conducted.
September : Charles Helou becomes president.

1967
5–11 June : Six Day Arab–Israeli War. Lebanon does not participate.

1968
May : Parliamentary elections are held.
28 December : Israeli commandos blow up thirteen civilian aircraft at Beirut airport.

1969
The National Progressive Front formed under the leadership of Kamal Jumblatt.
3 November : The Lebanese government signs an agreement with the PLO in Cairo, giving it certain rights inside Lebanon.

1970
23 September : Suleiman Franjieh becomes president.
15 November : Hafiz Assad comes to power in Syria in a bloodless coup.

1972
The PLO sets up its headquarters in Beirut.

1973
6–25 October : Arab–Israeli War. Lebanon does not participate.

1974
December : Israel bombs Palestinian camps in Beirut.

1975
26 February–1 March : A demonstration by Muslim fisherman in Sidon is put down by the army.

13 April: A retaliatory attack by the Phalange militia on a bus, killing twenty-seven Palestinians and Lebanese, heralds the start of a civil war. The Lebanese National Movement is formed under the leadership of Kamal Jumblatt.

1976

January: Unified military command of the Maronite militias, jointly called the Lebanese Forces, is formed under Bashir Gemayel. Lebanese army breaks up into Muslim and Christian segments.

14 February: President Franjieh issues a Constitutional Reform Document which specifies Muslim–Christian parity in parliament and transfer to parliament of the president's power to appoint the prime minister.

April: The LNM–PLO alliance controls two-thirds of Lebanon.

1 June: Syria intervenes in the war militarily and attacks LNM–PLO positions.

22 July: Ceasefire after Syria gains the upper hand.

23 September: Elias Sarkis becomes president.

26 October: Arab summit decides to form the Arab Deterrent Force of 30,000 troops drawn mainly from Syria and complemented by five other Arab nations.

November: Ceasefire in the civil war takes effect.

1977

16 March: Kamal Jumblatt is assassinated. His son, Walid, succeeds him as the clan leader. Grieving Druzes attack Christians in the Shouf region.

May: Likud-led government, headed by Menachem Begin, takes office in Israel.

19 November: President Anwar Sadat of Egypt visits Jerusalem in search of peace.

1978

11 March: A Palestinian group attacks a bus inside Israel, killing thirty-five passengers.

14–20 March: Israeli invasion of south Lebanon.

May: Maronite leaders Pierre Gemayel and Camille Chamoun visit Israel for arms supplies.

13 June: In a dawn raid a Phalange hit squad murders Tony Franjieh and his family.

1979

March: Egypt and Israel sign a peace treaty.

Mid-May: First clashes between the Phalange and the National Liberal Party militias.

22 November: Arab summit adopts a resolution calling for pressures on Israel to cease attacks on south Lebanon.

1980
3–4 and 7 July: The Phalange militia defeats NLP fighters.
27 October: The Phalange attacks the NLP in Zahle.
Early December: General Raphael Eitan of Israel visits Jounieh to promise Israeli back-up in case of a confrontation between the Christian forces and Syria.

1981
Late April: In the fighting between the Phalange and its opponents, Israel intervenes and shoots down two Syrian helicopters. Syria deploys surface-to-air missiles in the Beqaa valley.
23 May: Arab League members promise aid to Syria in its confrontation with Israel.
Late June: The Maronite Lebanese Forces leave Zahle.
9 July: Likud-led government is returned to power in Israel.
17 July: Israel bombs downtown Beirut.
25 July: Three-way understandings between Israel, Syria and the PLO are brokered by the USA on the eve of a ceasefire in south Lebanon.

1982
January: Israel's defence minister, Ariel Sharon, confers with LF commanders to plan an Israeli invasion of Lebanon.
Mid-February: Israeli arms shipments to the Maronite militias are resumed.
March: Four Iranian diplomats are kidnapped by a Christian militia.
April: Israel redeploys the troops withdrawn from the Sinai peninsula near its border with Lebanon.
3 June: An assassination attempt in London on the Israeli ambassador to Britain, Shlomo Argov, fails.
6 June: Israel invades Lebanon, deploying 76,000 troops backed by naval and air support. UN Security Council Resolution 409 calls on Israel to withdraw immediately to its borders with Lebanon.
11 June: Ceasefire between Israel and Syria in Lebanon.
12 June: Ceasefire between Israel and the PLO in Lebanon.
13 June: Israel besieges West Beirut.
19 July: David Dodge, an American citizen, is kidnapped by militant Shias.
25 July: Bashir Gemayel announces his presidential candidacy.
1–4 August: Saturation bombing of West Beirut by Israel.
12 August: Eleven and a half hours of saturation bombing of West Beirut, using phosphorus shells and cluster bombs, while water supplies are cut off.

13 August: Israel lifts the siege of West Beirut.

22–31 August: Syrian troops and PLO fighters leave West Beirut for foreign destinations.

23 August: Bashir Gemayel is elected president.

31 August: Israel's invasion ends with a death toll of 17,000 to 19,000 Palestinians and Lebanese, and 375 Israeli troops.

1 September: US president Ronald Reagan offers a Middle East peace plan. It is rejected immediately by Israel.

14 September: Bashir Gemayel is assassinated.

16–18 September: 2,000 Palestinian refugees are murdered by the Phalange militia in the Sabra and Shatila camps of West Beirut.

21 September: Amin Gemayel is elected president.

25 September: 400,000 Israeli protesters demand an inquiry into the Sabra and Shatila massacres and a recall of Israeli troops from Lebanon.

29 September: Israeli troops leave Beirut.

28 December: Tripartite talks begin between Lebanon, Israel and the USA on a draft Lebanese–Israeli peace treaty.

1983

February: Sharon is forced to resign as defence minister following a critical report on the Sabra and Shatila massacres by an Israeli commission.

18 April: Truck-bombing of the US embassy in West Beirut leads to sixty-three deaths, including seventeen American.

17 May: Israel signs the Lebanese–Israeli peace treaty after the Lebanese parliament adopts it by sixty-four votes to two. President Amin Gemayel withholds his signature.

29 August: Israeli prime minister Begin resigns due to continued deaths of Israeli soldiers in Lebanon. Yitzhak Shamir, a Likud leader, succeeds Begin.

3–25 September: Following the Israeli withdrawal from the Shouf, fighting erupts between the Druze–PLO alliance and the Lebanese army. USA and France intervene with warplanes and warships on the side of the Lebanese army.

23 October: Truck-bombing of US and French military headquarters in West Beirut leaves 300 American and French troops dead.

31 October–8 November: The First National Reconcilition Conference is held in Geneva.

11 November: Truck-bombing of the Israeli military headquarters in Tyre kills sixty people, half of them Israeli.

1984

3–7 February: Following an attack on West Beirut's Shia suburbs by the Lebanese army and the Lebanese Forces, fighting erupts between the army and the LF on one side and the Amal–Druze alliance on the other. US warships intervene against the Muslim forces. Following the defection of Muslims from the Lebanese army, the Amal–Druze alliance expels the army from West Beirut.

7 February: The US withdraws its marines from Beirut. France, Britain and Italy, the other members of the Western Multi-National Force, follow suit.

29 February: President Gemayel decides to annul the Lebanese–Israeli peace treaty.

5 March: The Lebanese parliament abrogates the Lebanese–Israeli treaty.

12–18 March: The Second National Reconciliation Conference is held in Lausanne, Switzerland.

16 March: William Buckley, the CIA station chief in Beirut, is abducted.

29 August: Pierre Gemayel, the founder-leader of the Phalange Party, dies.

Mid-September: A national unity government, led by the Labour leader Shimon Peres, is formed in Israel.

1985

8 March: A car bomb triggered by CIA agents to assassinate Shaikh Muhammad Hussein Fadlallah, the spiritual leader of the Hizbollah, kills eighty. Fadlallah is unharmed.

12 March: Samir Geagea, a member of the LF Command Council, takes over the LF in a coup.

5 May: The LF Command Council elects Elie Hobeika chairman, who appoints Geagea as his chief of staff.

20 May: Amal mounts a campaign against the Palestinian refugee camps in West Beirut.

6 June: Israel's military completes its withdrawal from Lebanon by handing over its positions in the border zone in south Lebanon to a Christian militia, called the South Lebanon Army, and leaves behind 1,000 Israeli troops.

30 June: Syria stops Amal's campaign against the Palestinian camps in West Beirut.

28 December: Nabih Berri, Walid Jumblatt and Elie Hobeika, the respective commanders of the Amal militia, the Druze militia and the LF, sign the National Agreement to Solve the Lebanese Crisis, a detailed document describing political reform and relations between Lebanon and Syria.

1986

8–14 January: Internecine conflict in the LF leads to the fleeing of Hobeika to Syria, thus spelling the end of the National Agreement.

3 November: Beirut-based *Al Shira* magazine reveals that the USA had sold arms to Iran clandestinely and that former US National Security Adviser, Robert McFarlane, had travelled to Iran on a goodwill mission.

1987
Early February : Amal is challenged militarily in West Beirut by the Druze Progressive Socialist Party and other left-of-centre Lebanese groups.
22 February : Syria sends its 85th Brigade, withdrawn in August 1982, to West Beirut to restore order.
April : The death toll in the twelve-year civil war reaches 120,000, plus another 10,000 who were killed after being kidnapped.
1 June : Prime Minister Rashid Karami is assassinated.
7 August : Camille Chamoun, former president and the current leader of the Maronite Lebanese Front, dies.
9 December : Palestinian intifada erupts in the Occupied Territories.

1988
Early April : Clashes between Amal and the Hizbollah in south Lebanon.
Mid-April : President Assad and US secretary of state, George Shultz, agree to co-ordinate policy on political reform in Lebanon.
28 May : Ceasefire between Amal and the Hizbollah.
22 September : Outgoing president Amin Gemayel calls on his chief of staff, General Michel Aoun, to form a 'temporary' military government.
23 September : Aoun appoints five military officers as cabinet ministers, but all three Muslim officers refuse to join the government.
22 October : Amin Gemayel goes into exile.

1989
14 February : Aoun attacks and subdues the LF in the Christian enclave.
6 March : Aoun imposes a blockade of all West Beirut ports.
14 March : Aoun declares a 'war of liberation' against Syria.
21 March : Syria imposes land and sea blockades on the Christian enclave.
25 May : The Arab summit appoints a Tripartite Committee of the heads of state of Algeria, Morocco and Saudi Arabia to settle the Lebanese crisis with the help of Lebanon's MPs within six months.
30 May : Ceasefire in Aoun's 'war of liberation'.
14 September : The Arab League Troika offers a seven-point peace plan which envisages the Lebanese MPs meeting outside Lebanon to discuss a National Reconciliation Charter.
22 September : Aoun accepts the Troika plan.
30 September–22 October : Fifty-eight of the sixty-two Lebanese MPs assembled in Taif, Saudi Arabia, approve the National Reconciliation Charter, popularly known as the Taif Accord. Aoun rejects the Taif Accord. The Maronite Lebanese Front accepts it.
5 November : Fifty-eight Lebanese MPs, gathered at Qulayaat in northern Lebanon, endorse the Taif Accord. Fifty-two MPs elect René Muawad president.
22 November : President Muawad is assassinated.

24 November: Forty-seven of the fifty-two Lebanese MPs, assembled at Shtura, vote for Elias Hrawi as president.
26–8 November: President Hrawi dismisses the cabinet of General Aoun, and then Aoun as the military chief of staff.
13 December: The LF says that the Taif Accord must be accepted.

1990
29 January–17 February: Fighting between the LF and Aoun's troops.
19 March: Renewed clashes between the LF and Aoun's troops.
3 April: LF leader Geagea declares allegiance to President Hrawi.
2 August: Iraq invades and occupies Kuwait.
Mid-August: Syria joins the US-led coalition against Iraq.
21 August: Forty-nine of the fifty-one Lebanese MPs vote for overhauling the constitution as outlined in the Taif Accord.
14 September: US secretary of state, James Baker, meets Assad in Damascus.
21 September: President Hrawi imposes land blockade on Aoun's enclave, now about one-third of the Christian sector, and is backed by the LF.
13 October: In a joint campaign the Lebanese and Syrian troops defeat Aoun's soldiers, thus bringing the civil war to an end. Aoun takes refuge at the French embassy in East Beirut. The fatalities in the fifteen and a half years of war are put at more than 150,000.
24 December: Omar Karami forms an expanded national unity government of thirty ministers, including former commanders of various militias.

1991
17 January: US-led coalition starts war against Iraq.
28 February: The Gulf War ends after the Iraqis are expelled from Kuwait.
9 May: Parliament passes a law giving Muslims and Christians parity in the chamber, and raises its total strength to 108.
22 May: Presidents Hrawi and Assad sign the Treaty of Brotherhood, Co-operation and Co-ordination between Lebanon and Syria.
8 August: John McCarthy, a British hostage in Lebanon, is released.
Mid-August: Parliament passes a law on war crimes.
27–9 August: The Lebanese government gives conditional amnesty to Aoun. He leaves for France.
30 October: Lebanon attends the Middle East peace conference in Madrid.
18 November: Terry Waite, a British hostage, and Thomas Sutherland, an American hostage, are freed.
1 December: Israel releases twenty-five Lebanese detainees.
2–4 December: The last three American hostages are freed.

APPENDIX 2

Important United Nations Security Council Resolutions on Lebanon: 425, 426, 508 and 509

United Nations Security Council Resolution 425
19 March 1978

The Security Council,

Taking note of the letters of the Permanent Representative of Lebanon (S/12600 and S/12606) and the Permanent Representative of Israel,

Having heard the statements of the Permanent Representative of Lebanon and Israel,

Gravely concerned at the deterioration of the situation in the Middle East, and its consequences to the maintenance of international peace,

Convinced that the present situation impedes the achievement of a just peace in the Middle East:

1 Calls for strict respect for the territorial integrity, sovereignty and political independence of Lebanon within its internationally recognized boundaries;

2 Calls upon Israel immediately to cease its military action against Lebanese territorial integrity and withdraw forthwith its forces from all Lebanese territory;

3 Decides, in the light of the request of the Government of Lebanon, to establish immediately under its authority a United Nations interim force for Southern Lebanon for the purpose of confirming the withdrawal of the Israeli forces, restoring international peace and security, and assisting the Government of Lebanon in ensuring the return of its effective authority in the area, the force to be composed of personnel drawn from Member States;

4 Requests the Secretary-General to report to the Council within twenty-four hours on the implementation of the present resolution.

Adopted by twelve votes to none, with two abstentions
(Czechoslovakia and the Soviet Union)

United Nations Security Council Resolution 426
19 March 1978

The Security Council,

1 Approves the report of the Secretary-General on the implementation of Security Council Resolution 425 (1978), contained in document S/12611 of 19 March 1978;

2 Decides that the force shall be established in accordance with the above-mentioned report for an initial period of six months, and that it shall continue in operation thereafter, if required, provided the Security Council so decides.

> Adopted by twelve votes to none, with two abstentions
> (Czechoslovakia and the Soviet Union)

United Nations Security Council Resolution 508
5 June 1982

The Security Council,

Recalling its resolutions 425 (1978), 426 (1978), and its ensuing resolutions and, more particularly, resolution 501 (1982),

Taking note of the letters of the Permanent Representative of Lebanon dated 4 June 1982 (S/15161 and S/15162),

Deeply concerned at the deterioration of the present situation in Lebanon and in the Lebanese–Israeli border area, and its consequences for peace and security in the region.

Gravely concerned at the violation of the territorial integrity, independence and sovereignty of Lebanon.

Reaffirming and supporting the statement made by the President and the members of the Security Council on 4 June 1982 (S/15163), as well as the urgent appeal issued by the Secretary-General on 4 June 1982,

Taking note of the support of the Secretary-General.

1 Calls upon all the parties to the conflict to cease immediately and simultaneously all military activities within Lebanon and across the Lebanese–Israeli border not later than 0600 hours, local time, on Sunday 6 June 1982;

2 Requests all Member States which are in position to do so to bring their influence to bear upon those concerned so that the cessation of hostilities declared by Security Council Resolution 490 (1981) can be respected;

3 Requests the Secretary-General to undertake all possible efforts to ensure the implementation of and compliance with the present resolution and to report to the Security Council as early as possible and not later than forty-eight hours after the adoption of the present resolution.

> Adopted by unanimous vote

United Nations Security Council Resolution 509
6 June 1982

The Security Council,

Recalling its resolutions 425 (1978) and 508 (1982),

Gravely concerned at the situation as described by the Secretary-General in his report to the Council,

Reaffirming the need for strict respect for the territorial integrity, sovereignty and political independence of Lebanon within its internationally recognized boundaries;

1 Demands that Israel withdraw all its military forces forthwith and unconditionally to the internationally recognized boundaries of Lebanon;

2 Demands that all parties observe strictly the terms of paragraph 1 of resolution 508 (1982) which called on them to cease immediately and simultaneously all military activities within Lebanon and across the Lebanese–Israeli border;

3 Calls on all parties to communicate to the Secretary-General their acceptance of the present resolution within twenty-four hours;

4 Decides to remain seized of the question.

Adopted by unanimous vote

The National Reconciliation Charter approved by the Lebanese MPs in Taif, Saudi Arabia, on 22 October 1989

I. General Principles and Reforms

I. *General Principles*

1 Lebanon is a sovereign, free and independent country, and a homeland for all its citizens.
2 Lebanon is Arab in heritage and identity. It is an active and founding member of the Arab League, and is committed to the League's charters. It is an active and founding member of the United Nations, and is committed to its charters. Lebanon is a member of the Non-Aligned Movement. The Lebanese state shall embody these principles in all areas and spheres without exception.
3 Lebanon is a democratic, parliamentary republic founded on respect for public freedoms, especially the freedom of expression and belief, social justice, and equality in rights and duties for all citizens without discrimination or preference.
4 The people are the source of authority. They are sovereign, and they shall exercise their sovereignty through constitutional institutions.
5 The economic system is a free system that guarantees individual initiative and private ownership, Culturally, socially and economically balanced development is a mainstay of the state's unity and of the system's stability.
6 Efforts shall be made to achieve comprehensive social justice through fiscal, economic and social reform.
7 Lebanon's territory is unified, and it belongs to all Lebanese. Every Lebanese is entitled to live in and enjoy any part of the country under the supremacy of the law. The people may not be categorized on the basis of any affiliation whatsoever, and there shall be no fragmentation or partition [of Lebanon], and no repatriation [of the Palestinians in Lebanon].
8 No authority violating the common co-existence charter shall be legitimate.

II. *Political Reforms*

(A) Chamber of Deputies

The Chamber of Deputies is the legislative authority which exercises full control over government policy and activities.

1 The Chamber's Speaker and Deputy Speaker shall be elected for the duration of the Chamber's term.
2 Two years after the Chamber elects its Speaker and Deputy Speaker, it may at the first session vote only once to withdraw confidence from the Speaker or Deputy Speaker with a two-thirds majority of its members following a motion [of no confidence] submitted by at least ten deputies. If confidence is withdrawn [from the Speaker or the Deputy Speaker], the Chamber shall convene immediately to fill the vacant post.
3 No urgent bill presented by the cabinet to the Chamber of Deputies may be passed unless it is included in the agenda of a public session and read in such a session, and unless the constitutionally stipulated grace period has passed without a resolution on such a bill, with the cabinet's approval.
4 A governorate shall be the basis of an electoral district.
5 Until the Chamber of Deputies passes an election law free of sectarian restrictions, parliamentary seats shall be divided on the following basis :
   (a) Equally between Christians and Muslims ;
   (b) Proportionately between the denominations of each sect ;
   (c) Proportionately between the districts ;
6 The size of the Chamber of Deputies shall be increased to 108 members, shared equally by Christians and Muslims. As for the [electoral] districts created on the basis of this document, and the districts where seats became vacant prior to the proclamation of this document, their seats shall be filled only once on an emergency basis through appointment by the National Reconciliation government that is planned.
7 With the election of the first Chamber of Deputies on a national, non-sectarian basis, a Senate shall be formed, and all the spiritual families shall be represented therein. Senate powers shall apply only to crucial issues.

(B) President of the Republic

The President of the Republic is the head of state and the symbol of the country's unity. He shall contribute to advancing the constitution, and preserving Lebanon's independence, unity and territorial integrity according to the provisions of the constitution. He is the supreme commander of the armed forces which are subject to the authority of the cabinet. The President shall exercise the following powers :
1 Chair cabinet meetings whenever he wishes, but without voting ;

2 Head the Supreme Defence Council;
3 Issue decrees and demand their publication. He shall also be entitled to ask the cabinet to reconsider any resolution it adopts within 15 days of the date of deposition of the resolution with the presidential office. Should the cabinet insist on sticking to the adopted resolution, or should the grace period pass without [the President] signing and returning the decree, the resolution or decree shall be valid and must be published;
4 Promulgate laws in accordance with the grace period stipulated in the constitution, and demand their publication on ratification by the Chamber of Deputies. After notifying the cabinet, the President may also request re-examination of laws within the grace periods provided by the constitution and in accordance with the articles of the constitution. If the laws are not signed or returned [by the President] before the end of the grace periods, they shall be valid and must be published;
5 Refer the bills presented to him by the cabinet to the Chamber of Deputies;
6 Name the Prime Minister-Designate after consulting the Chamber of Deputies' Speaker on the basis of mandatory parliamentary consultation, and officially informing the Speaker of his decision;
7 Issue the decree appointing the Prime Minister;
8 Following an agreement with the Prime Minister, issue the decree appointing the cabinet;
9 Issue decrees accepting the resignation of the cabinet or [individual] ministers, and decrees relieving ministers of their duties;
10 Appoint ambassadors, accept the accreditation of [foreign] ambassadors, and award state medals by decree;
11 Following an agreement with the Prime Minister, negotiate the conclusion and signing of international treaties which shall become valid on approval by the cabinet. The cabinet shall inform the Chamber of Deputies of these treaties without violating the country's interest or security. As for the treaties containing conditions concerning state finances and trade agreements, and other treaties which may require annual renewal, these may not be concluded without the Chamber of Deputies' approval;
12 When the need arises, address messages to the Chamber of Deputies;
13 Following an agreement with the Prime Minister, summon by decree the Chamber of Deputies to special sessions;
14 The President is entitled to present to a cabinet meeting any urgent issue not mentioned in its agenda;
15 Following an agreement with the Prime Minister, instruct the cabinet to hold a special session whenever he deems it necessary;
16 Grant special pardon by decree;
17 In the performance of his duties, the President shall not be liable unless he violates the constitution or commits high treason.

(C) Prime Minister

The Prime Minister is the head of the government. He represents it and speaks in its name. He is responsible for implementing the general policy drafted by the cabinet. The Prime Minister shall exercise the following powers:
1 Head the cabinet;
2 Hold parliamentary consultations to form the cabinet, and co-sign with the President the decree appointing it. The cabinet shall submit its common statement to the Chamber of Deputies for a vote of confidence within 30 days [of its formation]. The cabinet may not exercise its powers before gaining the [Chamber's] confidence or after its resignation or when it is considered to have retired – except within the narrow margin of disposing of [routine] matters.
3 Present the government's general policy to the Chamber of Deputies;
4 Sign all decrees, except the ones naming the Prime Minister, accepting the cabinet's resignation and declaring the cabinet to have retired;
5 Sign the decree calling for a special session [of the Chamber of Deputies] as well as the decrees proclaiming laws and requesting re-examination of laws;
6 Summon the cabinet to meet, draft its agenda, inform the President in advance of the issues included in the agenda and the urgent issues to be discussed, and sign the minutes of the meetings;
7 Oversee the activities of the public departments and institutions, co-ordinate the activities of the ministers, and issue general instructions to ensure smooth administration;
8 Hold working sessions with the appropriate state agencies in the presence of the concerned minister;
9 Act as the Deputy Chairman of the Supreme Defence Council.

(D) Cabinet

The cabinet shall exercise the following powers:
1 Supervise the implementation of laws and regulations, and the activities of all state agencies including the civilian, military and security departments and institutions;
2 The cabinet is the authority which controls the armed forces;
3 Appoint, dismiss and accept the resignations of state employees in accordance with the law;
4 The cabinet has the right to dissolve the Chamber of Deputies at the request of the President if the Chamber refuses to meet throughout an ordinary or special session lasting no less than one month, even when it is summoned twice consecutively, or if the Chamber sends back the budget in its entirety with the objective of paralyzing the government.

This right may not be exercised again for the same reason which called for the dissolving of the Chamber in the first instance;

5 When the President is present, he heads cabinet meetings. The cabinet shall meet periodically at special headquarters. The quorum is two-thirds of the ministers. The cabinet shall adopt its resolutions by consensus. If that proves impossible, then the resolutions shall be adopted by a majority of the ministers present. On major issues the approval of two-thirds of the cabinet ministers is required. The following shall be considered major issues: the state of emergency and its abolition, war and peace, general mobilization, international agreements and treaties, the general budget, comprehensive and long-term development plans, the appointment of top level civil servants or their equivalents, re-examination of the administrative division [of the country], dissolving the Chamber of Deputies, the electoral law, the citizenship law, the personal status laws, and the dismissal of cabinet ministers.

(E) Cabinet Minister

Cabinet minister's powers shall be reinforced in a manner compatible with the government's general policy and the principle of collective responsibility. A minister shall not be relieved of his position except by cabinet decree or withdrawal of confidence in him by the Chamber of Deputies.

(F) Cabinet Resignation, Considering Cabinet Retired, and Dismissal of Ministers

1 A cabinet shall be considered retired in the following cases:
(a) If its head resigns;
(b) If it loses more than a third of its members as listed in the decree appointing it;
(c) If its head dies;
(d) At the start of the President's term;
(e) At the start of the Chamber of Deputies' term;
(f) When the Chamber of Deputies withdraws its confidence from it following an initiative by the Chamber and on the basis of a vote.
2 A cabinet minister shall be relieved of his job by a decree signed by the President and the Prime Minister with the approval of the cabinet.
3 When the cabinet resigns or is considered retired, the Chamber of Deputies shall, by law, be considered to be convened in a special session until a new cabinet is formed. A vote of confidence session shall follow.

(G) Abolition of Political Sectarianism

Abolishing political sectarianism is a fundamental national objective. To achieve it, efforts must be made according to a phased plan. The Chamber of Deputies elected on the basis of parity between Christians and Muslims shall adopt proper measures to achieve this objective and to form a National Council headed by the President which shall include – besides the Prime Minister and the Chamber of Deputies' Speaker – political, intellectual and social leaders. The Council's task will be to examine and propose the means to abolish sectarianism, present them to the Chamber of Deputies and the cabinet, and to oversee the implementation of the phased plan. The following shall be done in the interim period:

(a) Abolish the sectarian representation base and rely on merit and specialized skills in public jobs – the judiciary and the military, security and public institutions – and in the independent [public] agencies according to the terms of the National Reconciliation Charter, excluding the top level jobs and their equivalents, which shall be shared equally by Christians and Muslims without allocating a particular job to a particular sect.

(b) Abolish the mention of sect and denomination on identity cards.

III. *Other Reforms*

(A) Administrative Decentralization

1 The Lebanese state shall be a single and united state with a strong central authority.
2 The powers of the governors and district administrative officers shall be expanded, and all public services shall be available at the highest possible level in the administrative governorates in order to facilitate serving citizens and meeting their needs locally.
3 The administrative division [of the country] shall be reconsidered in a manner that emphasizes national integration within the framework of preserving common co-existence and unity of the land, people and institutions.
4 Administrative decentralization shall be adopted at the level of smaller administrative units (districts and smaller units) through the election of a [local] council, headed by the district officer, in every district to ensure local participation.
5 A comprehensive and unified development plan capable of developing the governorates economically and socially shall be adopted, and the resources of the municipalities and municipal unions shall be reinforced with necessary financial resources.

(B) Courts

I. To guarantee that all officials and citizens are subject to the supremacy of the law and to ensure harmony between the actions of the legislative and executive authorities on one hand, and the principles of common co-existence and basic rights of Lebanese citizens as stipulated in the constitution on the other hand :

1 The Higher Judicial Council stipulated by the constitution, with powers to try presidents and ministers, shall be formed.

2 A Constitutional Council shall be created to interpret the constitution, to examine constitutionality of laws, and to settle disputes concerning presidential and parliamentary elections.

3 The following authorities shall be entitled to revise the Constitutional Council's decisions in the matters pertaining to interpreting the constitution and examining constitutionality of laws :

(a) The President of the Republic ;

(b) The Chamber of Deputies' Speaker ;

(c) The Prime Minister ;

(d) A certain proportion of the members of the Chamber of Deputies.

II. To ensure harmony between religion and state, the heads of the Lebanese sects may revise the Constitutional Council's decisions in the matters pertaining to :

(a) Personal status affairs ;

(b) Freedom of religion and the performance of religious rites ;

(c) Freedom of religious education.

III. To ensure the judiciary's independence, a certain proportion of Higher Judicial Council members shall be elected by judges.

(C) Parliamentary Election Law

Parliamentary elections shall be held according to a new electoral law based on the governorates [as electoral districts], and in the light of rules which guarantee common co-existence between Lebanese, and which ensure sound and efficient political representation of all factions and generations of citizens. This shall be done after reviewing the administrative division within the framework of the unity of the people, land and institutions.

(D) Socio-economic Council for Development

A Socio-economic Council for Development shall be created to ensure that representatives of various sectors participate in drafting the state's socio-economic policy and are provided with advice and proposals.

(E) Education

1 Education shall be provided to all and shall be compulsory up to the elementary stage at least.

2 Freedom of education shall be emphasized according to general laws and regulations.

3 Private education shall be protected, and state control over private schools and text books shall be strengthened.

4 Administrative, vocational and technological education shall be reformed, strengthened and developed in a manner that meets the country's development and reconstruction needs. The Lebanese University shall be reformed, and aid provided to it, especially to its technical colleges.

5 The curricula shall be reviewed and developed in a way which strengthens national integration as well as spiritual and cultural openness, and which harmonizes text books on history and national education.

(F) Information

All information media shall be reorganized under the canopy of the law and within the framework of responsible behaviour which fosters cautious tendencies [in reporting] and furthers the objective of ending the state of war.

II. Extending the Sovereignty of the Lebanese State over all Lebanese Territory

Considering that all Lebanese factions have agreed to the establishment of a strong state founded on the basis of the National Reconciliation Charter, the National Reconciliation government shall draft a detailed one-year plan with the objective of extending the sovereignty of the Lebanese state over all Lebanese soil, using its own forces. The broad lines of the plan shall be as follows:

1 Disbanding of all Lebanese and non-Lebanese militias shall be announced, the militias' weapons shall be surrendered to the Lebanese state within a period of six months, beginning with the approval of the National Reconciliation Charter; the President shall be elected; a National Reconciliation cabinet shall be formed; and political reforms shall be approved constitutionally.

2 The internal security forces shall be strengthened by:
(a) Opening the door of voluntary enrolment to all Lebanese without exception, initiating central training for volunteers, distributing them among the units in the governorates, and providing them with periodic [refresher] training courses;
(b) Strengthening the security apparatus to ensure control over the arrival and departure of individuals across the borders by land, sea and air.

3 Strengthing the armed forces:
(a) The fundamental task of the armed forces is to defend the homeland

and, if necessary, protect public order when the threat to it is greater than what the internal security forces can handle on their own;

(b) The armed forces shall be used to support the internal security forces in preserving security under conditions determined by the cabinet;

(c) The armed forces shall be unified, prepared and trained to enable them to shoulder their responsibilities in confronting Israeli aggression;

(d) When the internal security forces are ready to undertake their security duties, the armed forces shall return to their barracks;

(e) The armed forces' intelligence shall be reorganized to serve military purposes to the exclusion of all others.

4 The problem of the displaced Lebanese shall be solved, and the right of every Lebanese displaced since 1975 to return to the place from where he was displaced shall be established. Legislation to guarantee this right and to ensure the means of reconstruction [to the displaced person] shall be passed. Considering that the objective of the Lebanese state is to extend its authority over all Lebanese soil by using its own forces, represented primarily by its internal security forces – and in view of the fraternal relations binding Syria to Lebanon – the Syrian forces shall assist the forces of the legitimate Lebanese government to extend the authority of the Lebanese state within a period not exceeding two years, beginning with the ratification of the National Reconciliation Charter, the election of the President of the Republic, the formation of the National Reconcil-iation cabinet, and the approval of political reforms constitutionally. At the end of this period, the two governments – the Syrian government and the Lebanese National Reconciliation government – shall decide on the redeployment of the Syrian forces in the Beqaa region from Dahr al Baidar to the Hammana–Mudairij–Ain-Dara line, and if necessary at other positions to be determined by a joint Lebanese–Syrian military committee. An agreement shall also be concluded by the two governments to determine the strength and duration of the presence of the Syrian forces in the above-mentioned areas, and to define their relationship with the Lebanese state authorities where they are deployed. The Arab Tripartite Committee is prepared to assist the two states, if they so wish, to develop this agreement.

III. Liberating Lebanon from the Israeli Occupation

Regaining state authority over the area extending to the internationally recognized Lebanese borders requires the following:

(a) Efforts to implement Resolution 425 and all other UN Security Council resolutions calling for the total elimination of the Israeli occupation.

(b) Adherence to the armistice agreement [between Lebanon and Israel] signed on 23 March 1949.

(c) Taking all necessary steps to liberate all Lebanese territory from the

Israeli occupation, to extend state sovereignty to all Lebanese soil, and to deploy the Lebanese army in the border area adjacent to Israel; and endeavouring to reinforce the presence of the UN forces in South Lebanon to ensure the Israeli withdrawal and to allow the return of security and stability to the border area.

IV. Lebanese–Syrian Relations

Lebanon, with its Arab identity, is tied to all Arab countries by true fraternal relations. Between Lebanon and Syria there is a special relationship which derives its strength from the roots of kinship, history and joint fraternal interests. This is the concept on which co-ordination and co-operation between the two countries is founded, and which will be embodied into the agreements between them in all fields to the mutual benefit of both fraternal countries and within the framework of the sovereignty and independence of each of them. In view of this, and because strengthening the bases of security creates the climate needed to develop these special bonds, Lebanon should not be allowed to become a source of threat to Syria's security, and Syria should not be allowed to become a source of threat to Lebanon's security under any circumstances. Consequently, Lebanon should not allow itself to become a passage or base for any force, state or organization seeking to undermine its security or Syria's security. Syria, which desires Lebanon's security, independence and unity, and harmony among its citizens, shall not permit any act that poses a threat to Lebanon's security, independence and sovereignty.

The Treaty of Brotherhood, Co-operation and Co-ordination between Lebanon and Syria (1991)

The Lebanese Republic and the Syrian Arab Republic:
By virtue of the distinctive brotherly ties that bind them and that derive their strength from the roots of kinship, history, common destiny and fraternal interests;
Convinced that achievement of the widest scope of co-operation and co-ordination would serve their interests; furnish the means to guarantee their development, progress and safeguarding of their national security; provide prosperity and stability; and enable them to confront all regional and international developments, and meet the aspirations of the peoples of the two states in keeping with the Lebanese National Reconciliation Charter approved by the [Lebanese] Chamber of Deputies on 5 November 1989, Agree on the following:

Article 1
The two states will strive to realize the highest degree of co-operation and co-ordination between them in all political, security, cultural, scientific and other fields in pursuit of the interests of the two brotherly countries within the framework of the sovereignty and independence of each of them, so as to enable the two countries to utilize their political, economic and security resources to provide prosperity and stability, guarantee their national security, and expand and strengthen their common interests in affirmation of [their] brotherly relations and for the preservation of their common destiny.

Article 2
The two states will strive to achieve co-operation and co-ordination between the two countries in the fields of economics, agriculture, industry, commerce, transportation, communications, customs, initiation of joint projects, and co-ordination of development plans.

Article 3
The intertwining of the two countries' security requires that Lebanon not be made a source of threat to Syria's security, or Syria to Lebanon's

security, in any circumstances whatsoever. Lebanon shall therefore not allow itself to become a passage or base for any force, state or organization seeking to undermine the security of Lebanon or Syria. And Syria, which desires Lebanon's security, independence and unity, and harmony among its citizens, shall not permit any act that poses a threat to Lebanon's security, independence and sovereignty.

Article 4
After the approval of political reform constitutionally, as the Lebanese National Reconciliation Charter provides, and when the periods specified in the Charter expire, the Syrian and Lebanese governments shall decide on the redeployment of the Syrian forces in the Beqaa region from Dahr al Baidar to the Hammana–Mudairij–Ain-Dara line, and if necessary at other positions to be determined by a joint Lebanese–Syrian military committee. An agreement shall also be concluded by the two governments to determine the strength and duration of the presence of the Syrian forces in the above-mentioned areas, and to define their relationship with the Lebanese state authorities where they are deployed.

Article 5
The two countries' foreign policy, Arab and international, shall be based on the following principles :
1. Lebanon and Syria are two Arab countries committed to the Charter of the League of Arab States and the Arab joint defence and economic co-operation treaty and all other agreements concluded within the framework of the League. They are also members of the United Nations and committed to its charter, and members of the Non-Aligned Movement.
2. The common destiny and fraternal interests of the two countries.
3. Each will support the other in matters relating to its security and its national interests in keeping with the provisions of this treaty. The governments of the two countries shall therefore strive to co-ordinate their Arab and international policies, realize the greatest possible co-operation in Arab and international institutions and organizations, and co-ordinate their positions on various regional and international issues.

Article 6
The following agencies shall be instituted to achieve the objectives of this treaty, and other agencies can be established by a decision by the Higher Council mentioned below :

1. *The Higher Council*
(a) The Higher Council shall be composed of the President of the Republic of each of the two contracting states – and the Speaker of the People's Council [Parliament], the Prime Minister and the Deputy Prime Minister

of the Syrian Arab Republic, and the Speaker of the Chamber of Deputies, the Prime Minister and the Deputy Prime Minister of the Lebanese Republic.

(b) The Higher Council shall meet once a year and when the need arises, the venue to be agreed upon.

(c) The Higher Council shall define the general policy for co-ordination and co-operation between the two states in the political, economic, security, military and other fields, and shall oversee its implementation. It shall also approve the plans and decisions of the Follow-Up and Co-ordination Commission, the Foreign Affairs Committee, the Economic and Social Affairs Committee, the Defence and Security Affairs Committee, and any other committee that may be created later.

(d) The decisions of the Higher Council are binding and applicable within the framework of each of the two countries' constitutional rules.

(e) The Higher Council shall determine the subjects on which the specialized committees are authorized to make decisions which are automatically accomplishable either because they are in accord with the constitutional rules and principles in each of the two countries, or because they do not conflict with those rules and principles.

2. *The Follow-Up and Co-ordination Commission*
The Follow-Up and Co-ordination Commission shall be composed of the Prime Ministers of the two countries and a number of ministers involved with relations between the two states, and it shall have the following tasks:

(a) Following up the implementation of the decisions of the Higher Council and reporting to the Council on the stages of implementation;

(b) Co-ordinating the recommendations and decisions of the specialized committees, and referring their suggestions to the Higher Council;

(c) Holding meetings with the specialized committees when necessary;

(d) The Commission shall meet once every six months and whenever the need arises, the venue to be agreed upon.

3. *The Foreign Affairs Committee*
(a) The Foreign Affairs Committee shall be composed of the foreign ministers of the two countries;

(b) The Foreign Affairs Committee shall meet once every two months and whenever the need arises in one of the two countries in rotation;

(c) The Foreign Affairs Committee shall strive to co-ordinate the foreign policies of the two states in their relations with all states, and shall also strive to co-ordinate their activities and positions in the Arab and international organizations and shall, for that purpose, prepare plans for approval by the Higher Council.

4. *The Economic and Social Affairs Committee*

(a) The Economic and Social Affairs Committee shall be composed of the ministers concerned with the economic and social affairs in the two countries;

(b) The Economic and Social Affairs Committee shall meet in one of the two countries in rotation once every two months and whenever the need arises;

(c) The task of the Economic and Social Affairs Committee shall be to strive for economic and social co-ordination between the two states and prepare recommendations to that end;

(d) The recommendations of the Economic and Social Affairs Committee shall be implemented, in accordance with the constitutional principles of each of the two countries, when they are approved by the Higher Council.

5. *The Defence and Security Affairs Committee*

(a) The Defence and Security Affairs Committee shall be composed of the ministers of defence and interior in each of the two countries;

(b) The task of the Defence and Security Affairs Committee shall be to study the means by which the security of the two states can be preserved and to propose joint measures to confront any aggression or threat to their national security or any disturbances that jeopardize the internal security of either state;

(c) All plans and recommendations by the Defence and Security Affairs Committee shall be referred to the Higher Council for approval in accordance with the constitutional principles of each of the two countries.

6. *The Secretariat General*

(a) A Secretariat General shall be established to follow up the implementation of the provisions of this treaty;

(b) The Secretariat General shall be headed by a Secretary-General appointed by a Higher Council decision;

(c) The headquarters, jurisdiction, staff and budget of the Secretariat General shall be determined by a Higher Council decision.

Final Rules

1. Special arrangements shall be signed by the two countries in the fields covered by this treaty, such as the economic, security, defence and other fields in accordance with the constitutional principles of the two countries; and these shall be considered complementary to this treaty;

2. This treaty shall go into effect when it is promulgated by the authorities concerned in accordance with the constitutional principles of the two contracting states;

3. Each of the two states shall take action to annul the laws and regulations that are not in conformity with this treaty without violating the rules of the constitution of each of the two countries.

Signed: Signed:
Elias Hrawi   Hafiz Assad
President of the Lebanese Republic   President of the Syrian Arab Republic

Damascus, 22 May 1991

APPENDIX 5 : Armed forces of Lebanon, Syria and Israel, 1975

	Lebanon	Syria	Israel
Total regular armed forces			
Active	15,300	177,500	156,000
Reserves	–	102,500	244,000
Ground forces			
(A) Regular army			
Active	14,000	150,000	135,000
Reserves	–	100,000	240,000
(B) Paramilitary			
Active	5,000	1,500	9,000
Reserves	–	–	–
In-service equipment			
Battle tanks	103	2,100	2,700
Armoured combat vehicles	196	1,100	6,900
Major artillery	50	775	660
Air forces			
Regular air force	1000	25,000	15,000
In-service equipment			
Combat aircraft	19	400	461
Combat helicopters	16	60	72
Naval forces			
Regular navy	300	2,500	4,000
In-service equipment			
Patrol and coastal combatants	5	12	24
Submarines	–	–	2

Source: *Adapted from The Military Balance 1975–1976*, International Institute of Strategic Studies, London, 1975

APPENDIX 6: *Armed forces of Lebanon, Syria and Israel, 1990*

	Lebanon	Syria	Israel
Total regular armed forces			
Active	21,900	404,000	141,000
Reserves	–	400,000	504,000
Ground forces			
(A) Regular army			
Active	21,000	250,000	104,000
(Lahoud)	10,000		
(Aoun)	11,000		
Reserves	–	50,000	494,000
(B) Paramilitary			
Active	8,000	11,800[1]	6,000
Reserves	–	–	–
In-service equipment			
Battle tanks	232	4,000	4,288
Armoured combat vehicles	300	3,750	5,900
Major artillery	110	2,252	1,395
Air forces			
Regular air force	800	40,000	28,000
In-service equipment			
Combat aircraft	3	558	393
Combat helicopters	1	100	75
Naval forces			
Regular navy	100	6,000	9,000
In-service equipment			
Frigates	–	2	–
Patrol and coastal combatants	–	20	63
Submarines	–	3	3
Militias			
Christian			
Lebanese Forces			
Active	10,000	–	–
Reserves	25,000	–	–
South Lebanon Army[2]	2,500		
Muslim			
Amal			
Active	5,000	–	–
Reserves	10,000	–	–
Hizbollah			
Active	3,500	–	–
Reserves	11,500	–	–
Progressive Socialist Party (Druze)			
Active	5,000	–	–
Reserves	10,000	–	–

[1] Excludes 4,500-strong Palestine Liberation Army controlled by Syria.
[2] Controlled by Israel.

Source: Adapted from *The Military Balance 1990–1991*, International Institute of Strategic Studies, London, 1990.

—————— NOTES ——————

Introduction: the background

1 Ismailis or Seveners form one of the three branches within the Shia school of Islam, the others being Zaidis or Fivers, and Imamis or Twelvers. Of the twelve Shia Imams (religious leaders), Ismailis share the first six Imams with Twelvers and then follow a different line, beginning with Ismail, the older, militant son of Jaafar al Sadiq.

2 Itamar Rabinovich, *The War for Lebanon: 1970–85*, Cornell University Press, Ithaca and London, 1985, p. 21.

3 Later the 6:5 ratio was to be applied to posts in the civil service, judiciary and military.

4 Some of the sixteen recognized religious sects were too small to merit a parliamentary seat. According to the 1932 census, the size of the (all-male) electorate affiliated to each of the recognized Christian sects, was: Armenian Catholic, 5,694; Assyrian and Chaldean Catholic, 528; Greek Catholic, 45,999; Maronite Catholic, 226,378; Roman Catholic, 232; Syrian Catholic, 2,675; Armenian Orthodox, 25,462; Greek Orthodox, 76,522; Syrian Orthodox, 2,574; and Protestant, 6,712. The small, recognized non-Muslim minorities of Bahais and Jews were combined with Protestants and together given one seat. The figures for the voters from the Muslim sects were: Alawi, 353; Druze, 53,047; Shia, 154,208; and Sunni, 175,925. In 1960 the parliamentary seats were increased to 99. Of these, 54 were allocated to Christians – with Maronite Catholics receiving 30, Greek Orthodox 11, Greek Catholics 6, Armenian Catholics and Armenian Orthodox 5, and Protestants and non-Muslim minorities (Jews and Bahais) two. The 45 Muslim seats were divided among 20 Sunnis, 19 Shias and 6 Druzes.

5 Between 1922 and 1972 the number of parliamentary deputies from the eminent Lebanese families remained basically unaltered. Marius Deeb, *The Lebanese Civil War*, Praeger Publishers, New York, 1980, p. 75.

6 See Wilbur Crane Eveland, *Ropes of Sand: America's Failure in the Middle East*, W. W. Norton, New York and London, 1980, pp. 251–2.

7 Ibid., p. 275; and Jonathan Randal, *The Tragedy of Lebanon:*

249

Christian Warlords, Israeli Adventures and American Bunglers, Chatto and Windus, London, p. 73.

8 Dilip Hiro, *Inside the Middle East*, Routledge and Kegan Paul, London, and McGraw-Hill, New York, 1982, p. 47.

9 Phalange is a derivative of phalanx (or battalion), the literal translation of the Arabic word *Kataeb*, the full name of the organization being the Lebanese Kataeb Social Democratic Party.

10 Tabitha Petran, *The Struggle Over Lebanon*, Monthly Review Press, New York, p. 123.

11 Sandra Mackey, *Lebanon: Death of a Nation*, Congdon and Weed, New York, 1989, p. 154.

12 Like Ismailis, Alawis believe in the first seven Imams of the Shia sect. They hold Imam Ali, a son-in-law of Prophet Muhammad, in higher esteem than any of the earlier prophets mentioned in the Quran.

13 Between mid-1968 and mid-1974 Israel mounted forty-four major attacks on Lebanon, killing 880 Lebanese and Palestinians. Frederick C. Hof, *Galilee Divided: The Israel–Lebanon Frontier, 1916–1984*, Westview Press, Boulder, Co., p. 74.

14 Winslow Peck in *Anti*, an Athens-based magazine, 17 April 1976, cited in *Arab Report and Record, 1976*, p. 256. See also Bob Woodward, *Veil: The Secret Wars of the CIA 1981–1987*, Simon and Schuster, New York and London, 1987, p. 204.

15 *Arab World File*, 12 May 1976.

16 Peter Mansfield (ed.), *The Middle East: A Political and Economic Survey* (4th edn), Oxford University Press, London and New York, 1973, p. 72.

17 Kamal S. Salibi, *Crossroads to Civil War: Lebanon, 1958–1976*, Ithaca Press, London, and Caravan Books, Delmar, NY, 1976, p. 119. Amal recruits were initially trained by the officers of Fatah, the leading constituent of the PLO.

1. *Ascendancy of the reformist alliance*

1 Woodward, *Veil* op. cit., p. 204.
2 *Guardian*, 20 April 1976.
3 To reassure France of his peaceful intentions, Assad despatched his foreign minister to Paris to make the point.
4 *Middle East Contemporary Survey, 1980–81*, p. 172.

2. *Syrian intervention and hegemony*

1 These were two of the sixteen Palestinian camps in Lebanon – situated in and around Tripoli (Nahir al Barid and Badawi), Baalbek (Wavel), Beirut (Dubaya, Mar Elias, Shatila, Sabra and Burj al Barajina), Sidon

(Miya Miya and Ain al Hilwa), Nabatiya (Nabatiya), and Tyre (Bass, Burj al Shimali and Rashidiya).

2 By October 1976, the Phalange and NLP militias had received from Israel 110 tanks, 5,000 machine-guns and 12,000 rifles. See Hiro, *Inside the Middle East*, op. cit., p. 116.

3 Rabinovich, *The War for Lebanon* op. cit., p. 57.

4 The 12,000 armed Palestinians were made up of the troops of the PLO-controlled Palestine Liberation Army and the fighters belonging to each of the seven constituents of the PLO, including the small pro-Syrian Saiqa Organization. The 5,000 predominantly Muslim Lebanese militiamen belonged to the PSP, Communists, Murabitoun, pro-Libyan Nasserites, pro-Iraqi Baath Party and pro-Syrian SSNP.

5 In the event, the final phase was not implemented because of the absence of a reconstituted Lebanese army.

6 By now South Yemen had withdrawn its 1,000 troops.

3. *The first Israeli invasion and aftermath*

1 *International Herald Tribune*, 21 March 1978; *The Middle East*, June 1978, p. 28.

2 Mackey, *Lebanon: Death of a Nation*, op. cit., p. 171.

3 *The Middle East*, September 1978, pp. 14 and 23.

4 Cited in *Middle East Contemporary Survey, 1977–78*, p. 609.

5 Randal, *The Tragedy of Lebanon*, op. cit., p. 132.

6 A few days later the Lebanese Front leaders rejected 'any political solution' before 'the foreign forces, Syrian or other' had left Lebanon. Middle East News Agency, 7 September 1978.

7 Bashir Gemayel, an 'asset' of the CIA, was introduced to the Israeli intelligence service, Mossad, and had become a 'shared CIA–Mossad intelligence asset'. Woodward, *Veil*, op. cit., p. 217.

8 *The Middle East*, June 1981, p. 7.

9 *The Middle East*, December 1978, p. 11. Interestingly, first France and then America blamed the right-wing Christians for the latest flare-up.

10 *Sunday Times*, 15 October 1979.

4. *Consolidation of the Christian mini-state*

1 *Foreign Broadcast Information Service*, 9 August 1979.

2 Following the withdrawal of the Saudi troops from the ADF in March 1979, the role of policing the Green Line in Beirut on the Christian side had been taken up by the Lebanese army.

3 Earlier too the Armenian militia had fought back when, faced with a Syrian onslaught in October 1978, the Maronite militias had tried to compel it to end its neutrality and join them in their anti-Syrian struggle.

4 *Al Anwar*, 21 November 1979.

5 *Middle East Contemporary Survey, 1977–78*, p. 623. By June 1980 the actual payments to Lebanon by the Gulf monarchies and Iraq amounted to $142 million, *Middle East Contemporary Survey, 1979–80*, p. 596

6 The ADF's tenure was extended from 26 July 1980 to 26 January 1981.

7 *The Middle East*, August 1980, pp. 135–6; and Randal, *The Tragedy of Lebanon*, pp. 135–6. In all there were fifteen illegal sea and airports, and they handled 75 per cent of the country's imports and exports. *Middle East Contemporary Survey, 1980–81*, p. 665.

8 The vote was forty-one to six, with two abstentions, the rest of the ninety-three surviving deputies being absent. *Arab World File*, 11 February 1981.

9 There was a precedent here. In October 1978 Israel had promised air support for the Maronites if the Syrians used airpower in their offensive against the Maronites. Yair Evron, *War and Intervention in Lebanon: The Israeli-Syrian Deterrence Dialogue*, Croom Helm, London, 1987, p. 92.

10 *Guardian*, 25 May 1981.

11 Evron, *War and Intervention in Lebanon*, op. cit. pp. 93–4 and 100–1.

12 *Middle East Contemporary Survey, 1980–81*, p. 674.

13 Of the 200 corpses recovered, 175 were civilian; and so were 700 of the injured, including 197 children. *The Economist*, 25 July 1981, p. 44.

14 Patrick Seale, *Asad*, p. 371.

15 Damascus was suspicious of Bashir Gemayel, who was then aiding the chief Syrian opposition party, the Muslim Brotherhood, engaged in an armed struggle against the government, with the Phalange radio broadcasting the Brotherhood's successes in Syria. *The Middle East*, October 1981, pp. 30 and 33.

16 Later, at its meeting on 24 March 1982, Lebanon put before the Follow-Up Committee the idea of a Unified Arab Command for south Lebanon. The Committee in turn passed on the plan to the chiefs of staff of the member countries, but nothing came of it.

17 Randal, *The Tragedy of Lebanon*, op. cit., p. 245.

18 *Al Nahar*, 19 March 1982.

19 However, random acts of violence continued, with the US embassy being severely damaged by a rocket on 12 April 1982. A fortnight later, Shaikh Ahmad Assaf, president of the Islamic Centre and chairman of the (Sunni) Islamic Alignment, was assassinated.

20 The death toll during the first five years amounted to about 35,000. *The Middle East*, March 1980, p. 28.

21 *Middle East Report*, January–February 1990, pp. 5–6.

22 *The Middle East*, December 1984, p. 7.

5. *The second Israeli invasion and aftermath*

1 Trevor N. Dupuy and Paul Martell, *Flawed Victory: The Arab–Israeli Conflict and the 1982 War in Lebanon*, Brassey's Defence Publishers, Fairfax, Va, 1986, pp. 86–90.

2 *The Times*, 26 July 1982; and *The Middle East Military Balance 1983*, Jaffee Centre for Strategic Studies, Tel Aviv, 1983, p. 260.

3 Sean MacBride *et al.*, *Israel In Lebanon: The Report of the International Commission*, London, 1983, p. 226. The use of cluster bombs had been confirmed earlier by the surgeons who operated on the victims whose limbs had been shattered by these bombs supplied to Israel by the USA. Unsurprisingly, the Palestinians and most Lebanese Muslims regarded America as a 'silent partner' of Israel in the death and destruction rained upon them.

4 Richard A. Gabriel, *Operation Peace for Galilee: The Israeli–PLO War in Lebanon*, Hill and Wang, New York, 1984, p. 144.

5 Mackey, *Lebanon: Death of a Nation*, op. cit., p. 178.

6 *Washington Post*, 3 September 1982; *L'Orient le Jour*, 30 November 1982; Seale, *Asad*, op. cit., p. 395; Mackey, *Lebanon: Death of a Nation*, op. cit., p. 190. See also Chapter 4, p. 77.

7 Shartuni was recruited by the SSNP in 1979 when he was a student in Paris. His arrest stemmed from a hysterical outburst of his sister when she blurted out that Shartuni had telephoned her to leave the building minutes before the explosion. Another suspect, Nabil Alam, escaped to Syria. *Le Monde*, 11 September 1985; and Randal, *The Tragedy of Lebanon*, p. 150.

8 Interview on 27 September 1986. Seale, *Asad*, op. cit. p. 392.

9 *Al Sayyad*, 22 October 1982.

10 Simultaneously, Assad allowed the Iranian revolutionary guards to set up their headquarters in the Syrian border town of Zabadani. Augustus Richard Norton, *Amal and the Shia: Struggle for the Soul of Lebanon*, University of Texas Press, Austin, Tex., 1987, p. 88.

11 Woodward, *Veil*, op. cit., p. 347.

12 *BBC Summary of World Broadcasts*, 21 March 1983.

13 *Davar*, 17 May 1983. For a full text of the draft treaty between Lebanon and Israel, see *Middle East Contemporary Survey, 1982–83*, pp. 690–7.

14 The number of MPs accepting the treaty was about the same as those who had voted for Bashir Gemayel as president, but thirteen fewer than had elected Amin Gemayel president. This time the pro-Syrian deputies from the north and Beqaa stayed away, voted against the treaty or abstained.

15 *Observer*, 30 October 1983.

16 The full text of the National Salvation Front charter was broadcast on 23 July 1983. *BBC Summary of World Broadcasts*, 26 July 1983.

17 Since Amin Gemayel's niece was married to Fadi Afram, the chairman of the Lebanese Forces Command Council, it was hard for the president to distance himself sufficiently from the LF.

18 *Guardian*, 12 August 1983.

19 According to one source, published in December 1982 in *Ha'Aretz*, an Israeli newspaper, before the assassination of Kamal Jumblatt in 1977 the Aley area had 52,000 Christians and 46,000 Druzes.

20 The US military assistance of $150 million included the supply of 124 armoured personnel carriers. *Middle East Contemporary Survey, 1982–83*, p. 663.

21 Of the 33,000 men in the Lebanese army, whose ranks were 60 per cent Christian and 40 per cent Muslim, only 14,000 were combat forces equipped with 114 tanks.

22 See above, p. 3.

23 Cited in Robin Wright, *Sacred Rage: The Wrath of Militant Islam*, Simon and Schuster, New York, 1985, p. 83.

24 Arthur J. Arberry (trans.), *The Koran Interpreted*, Oxford University Press, London and New York, 1964, 3 :164.

25 Cited in *The Economist*, 25 October 1983, p. 25, and *Time*, 31 October 1983, p. 18.

26 David Gilmour, *Lebanon: The Fractured Country*, Sphere Books, London, 1987, pp. 196–7.

27 *Middle East Report*, 23 February 1985.

28 Cited in *Middle East Contemporary Survey, 1983–84*, p. 545.

29 *BBC Summary of World Broadcasts*, 6 March 1984.

6. *Return of Syrian hegemony*

1 Outside the Christian enclave north of Beirut, this was the only area where Christians were in the majority.

2 *Daily Star*, 21 May 1984.

3 Elie Hobeika was also involved in the Tal Zaatar massacre, according to Raymond Edde. Cited in Petran, *The Struggle for Lebanon*, op. cit., p. 361.

4 In contrast, according to a broadcast by the Voice of Free Lebanon, a Christian radio station, on 23 September 1985, the strengths of the other militias were: Hizbollah, 1,500; Organization of Communist Action, 1,000; Murabitoun, 900; Baath Party's Assad Brigade, 600; SSNP, 550; Lebanese Communist Party, 300.

5 At the end of June 1985, of the 650 killed, 500 were Amal militiamen. Petran, *The Struggle for Lebanon*, op. cit., p. 363.

6 Beirut Radio, 8 and 11 July 1985.

7 *Middle East Contemporary Survey, 1984–85*, pp. 535–6.

7. *Limits of Syrian power*

1 According to official sources, in March 1984 there were 255,015 registered Palestinian refugees in Lebanon. *Al Safir*, 6 June 1984.
2 See Dilip Hiro, *The Longest War: The Iran–Iraq Military Conflict*, Grafton, London, 1989, and Routledge, New York, 1991, pp. 215–19.
3 *Al Watan*, 28 January 1987.
4 In early February 1987 Jumblatt allowed the Communist Party to hold its fifth congress in the Druze town of Baaqlin, and addressed it. In September Jumblatt despatched 900 Druze and Sunni fighters to Libya in return for financial and military aid from Libya. They included Communist Party members.
5 *Middle East Contemporary Survey, 1987*, p. 520.
6 See Woodward, *Veil*, op. cit., pp. 395–7.
7 *Al Rai al Aam*, 15 June 1987; and *Jerusalem Post*, 2 August 1987. By the end of 1987 Salibi had not been extradited to Lebanon.
8 *Foreign Broadcast Information Service*, 30 October and 3 November 1987; and *Middle East International*, 19 December 1987.
9 *Al Safir*, 4 March 1988.
10 *Al Safir*, 16 May 1988.
11 Direct talks between Amin Gemayel and Hafiz Assad at the Arab summit in Algiers in June 1988 (called to discuss the Palestinian intifada) foundered on the question of political reform.
12 *Al Safir*, 27 May 1988.
13 On his return to West Beirut, the Hizbollah spokesman cited President Assad telling the Hizbollah delegation: 'You represent the true Islam in Lebanon as against the Islam deputed by imperialism to hit [true] Islam. You are the Islamic struggle in Lebanon which I have referred to in my speeches'. *Al Safir*, 28 May 1988.
14 In the Hoss cabinet, two of the three remaining Christian ministers refused to serve.
15 The average Lebanese family of four needed $56 a month to survive. *Al Nahar*, 18 October 1987.
16 By 1987 the total public debt was L£147 billion. *The Economist*, 12 September 1987. Inflation fell to 155 per cent in 1988.
17 *Middle East Report*, January–February 1990, pp. 7–8.

8. *War of liberation, Aoun style*

1 Aoun's inner circle consisted of Amir Shihab, chief of intelligence; Amir Shahin, commander of the commandos; Adil Sassim, head of military police; Salim Kalas, commander of the 8th Brigade; and officers Fawzi Abu Farhat, Fuad Aoun and Izzat Haddad.
2 During the Israeli invasion of Lebanon, President Sarkis personally had to restrain General Aoun from firing at the Israelis (whom he described

as enemies) as they approached the presidential palace. Later Aoun refused to hand over the Sabra and Shatila camps to the IDF, and that was why the IDF let loose the Lebanese Forces into these camps. *The Middle East*, June 1989, p. 20. However, in early 1989 while he personally undertook the task of expelling the Syrians from Lebanon, he called on the United Nations to remove the Israelis from the south.

3 *Middle East Contemporary Survey, 1989*, p. 507.
4 These were 5th, 8th, 9th and 10th Brigades, with up to a fifth of their troops being Muslim. The remaining six brigades – with their strength, sectarian make-up and deployment area – were: 1st Brigade (3,000, Shia), Beqaa; 2nd Brigade (3,000, Sunni–Christian), Tripoli; 6th Brigade (4,500, Shia), West Beirut; 7th Brigade (1,000, Christian), Batroun, and (750, Sunni–Shia), commando units; 11th Brigade (1,100, Druze), Hammana; and 12th Brigade, (2,500, Sunni), Sidon. *Middle East Contemporary Survey, 1989*, p. 530.
5 Later, in his interviews with the Western press, he justified banning the Muslim ports thus: 'I moved to stop the smuggling of narcotics in and out of Lebanon through control of such harbours'. *Washington Post*, 12 April 1989.
6 *Al Nahar*, 15 March 1989; and *Daily Telegraph*, 15 March 1989.
7 *The Economist*, 1 April 1989, p. 33.
8 *Observer*, 2 April 1989.
9 *New York Times*, 14 April 1989. By now the supplies from Iraq amounted to about a third of the Christian side's heavy military equipment. *Middle East Contemporary Survey, 1989*, p. 514.
10 Cited in *The Middle East*, June 1989, p. 20.
11 *Foreign Broadcast Information Service*, 18 April 1989; and *Guardian*, 19 April 1989.
12 *Al Safir*, 26 May 1989. Earlier, Syria's information minister, Muhammad Salman, had spelled out the preconditions of the Syrian withdrawal thus: implementation of political reform, election of the president, and Israeli evacuation of all Lebanese territory. *The Middle East*, June 1989, p. 20.
13 *The Middle East*, June 1989, p. 20.
14 *Al Nahar*, 27 September 1989.
15 *Independent*, 7 July 1989.
16 *Al Nahar*, 27 September 1989.
17 In Prime Minister Hoss's office in West Beirut, a correspondent of the *Guardian* noticed 155 mm phosphorus bomb shells marked in Hebrew and 240 mm mortars 'as thick as a man's thigh': these had fallen on the central sector of West Beirut, populated mainly by Sunnis. *Guardian*, 28 July 1989.
18 In a letter to his wife, David Dodge had said that his freedom depended on the release of the Iranians kidnapped earlier by Maronite militiamen.

Guardian, 1 August 1989. Later, Samir Geagea confirmed that the Iranian diplomats, picked up at an LF checkpoint, had been killed soon after they were captured. *New York Times*, 19 November 1991.

19 Each of these hostages was bought from the kidnappers by Libyan agents in Beirut. So too were two British teachers, Leigh Douglas and Philip Padfield, who were then killed. Robert Fisk, *Pity the Nation: Lebanon at War*, André Deutsch, London, 1990, p. 616.

20 Interestingly, only 28 per cent of those polled in the USA wanted President Bush to use force against the hostage-takers, while 42 per cent favoured negotiations with the kidnappers for hostage release. 60 per cent backed his erstwhile policy of doing nothing. *The Times*, 4 August 1989.

21 Artesian wells became the main source of water supply. In East Beirut the petrol ration was 20 litres a week per car. *Guardian*, 26 July 1989.

22 *Al Nahar*, 17 August 1989.

23 *Independent*, 14 August 1989.

24 *Independent*, 15 August 1989. General Aoun was the chief guest of honour at the Iraqi embassy in East Beirut (the only Arab mission to be based there) to celebrate the Baathist seizure of power in Iraq in 1968. *Guardian*, 26 July 1989.

25 *Financial Times*, 16 August 1989; and *Guardian*, 16 August 1989.

26 *Independent*, 16 August 1989.

27 *The Times*, 17 August 1989.

28 *Guardian*, 21 August 1989.

29 *Independent*, 21 August 1989.

30 *The Times*, 17 August 1989.

31 *Lebanon Information Processing Service*, 24 October 1989, p. 1.

9. *The Taif Accord, a trigger for inter-Christian conflict*

1 Following the Lebanese administration's demand, during the Israeli siege in 1982, for the withdrawal of the Syrian troops, the Arab League called on the Beirut government to negotiate the evacuation with Damascus. But according to Prime Minister Hoss, President Amin Gemayel never raised the subject in any of his twelve meetings with President Assad during his six-year tenure. *The Times*, 30 August 1989.

2 *Middle East International*, 3 November 1989, p. 4.

3 *Guardian*, 26 October 1989.

4 *Independent*, 26 October 1989.

5 *Guardian*, 26 and 30 October 1989.

6 *New York Times*, 5 November 1989.

7 *Independent*, 17 May 1989. In 1932, when the total population was 775,624, the figures for the three leading sects were: Maronites, 226,378; Sunnis, 175,925; and Shias, 154,205. As the poorest segment

of society, Shias had the highest birth rate. The natural increase in Maronite population was reduced by a comparatively high rate of emigration among Christians, who joined the large Lebanese Christian communities settled in North America, Argentina and Australia.

8 *Al Safir*, 8 November 1989.

9 The US ambassador, Ryan Crocker, formally presented his credentials to President Muawad on 19 November 1989.

10 Interestingly, the Aoun camp, the prime suspect, put it about that Israel, perhaps working with the Iranian-backed Hizbollah, was behind Muawad's assassination. Its analysis was that the Arab and American-backed peace plan, of which Muawad's election was the first practical step, tilted the balance of influence in Lebanon too strongly in favour of the Arabs and Americans, something disliked by Israel and Iran, albeit for different reasons. *Sunday Times*, 26 November 1989.

11 *Guardian*, 1 December 1989. The other assassinations for which Shaikh Najar held Syria responsible were: Kamal Jumblatt, Bashir Gemayel and Shaikh Hassan Khalid.

12 *Guardian*, 30 November 1989.

13 *Foreign Broadcast Information Service*, 30 November 1989.

14 *Guardian*, 4 December 1989.

15 *Middle East Contemporary Survey, 1989*, p. 524.

16 *Observer*, 10 December 1989.

17 The figure of 2,250 injured was nearly half of such casualties in the war of liberation. *Lebanon Information Processing Service*, February 1990, p. 5.

18 Significantly, the next day, 19 June 1990, the LF and Aoun loyalists clashed north of East Beirut.

19 West Beirut leaders claimed that the assassination attempt on Michel Aoun was stage-managed. But the fact that Habib Hilal was released on 16 October, a few days after Aoun's overthrow, showed that he had acted on behalf of the anti-Aoun camp.

20 The other 'red lines' were: (a) Syria was not to move its military units towards Israel or station surface-to-air missiles inside Lebanon; and (b) Syria was to refrain from attempting to change the status of the Israeli-occupied 'security zone' inside Lebanon. These 'red lines', spelled out by the Israeli defence minister Yitzhak Rabin and conveyed to Damascus via Washington, were revealed by Rabin five years later. *Middle East International*, 31 May 1991, p. 5.

21 However, to avoid any misunderstanding, America had cleared the precise flight path of the Syrian warplanes with Israel through its embassy in Nicosia, Cyprus. *Middle East International*, 26 October 1990, p. 8. Unlike America, France opposed the Syrian–Lebanese military action against General Aoun. This, and giving asylum to Aoun, created ill-will between Beirut and Paris.

22 Bashir Gemayel's brother, Amin, living in Paris, protested at Shartuni's release, but in vain.

23 About half of this sum was finally recovered from Aoun and his two aides. *Lebanon Information Processing Service*, December 1990, p. 2.

24 By the end of 1989, the estimate of the dead was 150,000. *Middle East Report*, January–February 1990, p. 10. To this must be added the 1990 death toll of 2,530, arising from the LF–Aoun clashes, the Syrian–Lebanese attack on Aoun's forces and the Amal–Hizbollah fighting.

25 At the average (natural) annual growth of 3 per cent, the Lebanese population of 2.59 million in 1976 should have risen to about 4 million in 1987. Since the estimated figure in 1987 was actually about 3.4 million, the loss due to emigration was 600,000. To this must be added another 150,000 emigrants during the next two and a half years. The Lebanese figures exclude some 350,000 Palestinian civilians living in Lebanon in 1990. See *Middle East Report*, January–February 1990, pp. 10 and 23.

26 *Lebanon Information Processing Service*, September 1990, p. 8. Lebanon's parallel economy too had suffered. Between 1987 and 1989 its farmers had produced 700 to 900 tons of hashish mainly in the Beqaa valley, most of it for export; but in 1990 hashish production declined to about 100 tons due to bad weather. *Lebanon Information Processing Service*, April 1991, p. 5.

10. *Peace at last, Syria ascendant*

1 Checkpoints were a major source of revenue for the militias. The Druze militia, for example, stood to lose L£10 million daily in revenue from the trucks on the back-roads to Damascus through the Shouf mountains.

2 Following the defeat of General Aoun's men on 13 October, the Syrian troops had remained mainly on the southern and eastern edge of the Metn, away from the densely populated Christian settlements.

3 *Middle East International*, 31 May 1991, p. 5.

4 According to a private poll conducted for a Christian organization, Christians were 39 per cent of the total Lebanese population. *Observer*, 13 August 1990.

5 *Middle East International*, 31 May 1991, p. 4.

6 However, on the whole, the various militias retained their small arms.

7 Syria's foreign minister, Farouk al Shaara, pointed out, rightly, that it was the first time Syria had formally acknowledged Lebanon's independence. Cited in *Middle East International*, 31 May 1991, p. 3. The fact that Syria and Lebanon had always lacked embassies in each other's capital was illustrative.

8 *International Herald Tribune*, 23 May 1991.

9 Ibid.

10 Cited in *Middle East International*, 31 May 1991, p. 6.

11 *International Herald Tribune*, 23 May 1991.

12 *Guardian*, 24 May 1991. Earlier, on 19 April, in a drive to establish its authority in the south, the Lebanese army arrested six guerrillas of the Popular Front for the Liberation of Palestine while trying to infiltrate into the Israeli-occupied security zone. It was the first action of its kind. *Lebanese Information Processing Service*, September 1991, p. 4.

13 To Geagea's chagrin, Elie Hobeika was appointed a Maronite MP for East Beirut, a stronghold of the Phalange Party.

14 *Lebanese Information Processing Service*, September 1991, p. 4.

15 *The Middle East*, September 1991, p. 5; *The Military Balance 1991–1992*, International Institute of Strategic Studies, London, 1991, p. 112.

16 However, on his arrival in France on 29 August, Aoun made several accusations, and this annoyed the host government. *Lebanese Information Processing Service*, September 1991, p. 5.

17 *Middle East International*, 30 August 1991, p. 13.

18 James Baker responded to the Lebanese demands with a written response which was passed on to the Lebanese foreign minister by the US ambassador Ryan Crocker, on 19 October. Its contents were not divulged. *Middle East International*, 25 October 1991, p. 7.

- SELECT BIBLIOGRAPHY -

Azar, Edward E. (ed.), *The Emergence of a New Lebanon: Fantasy or Reality?* Praeger Publishers, New York, 1984.

Dawisha, Adeed I., *Syria and the Lebanese Crisis*, Macmillan, London, 1980.

Deeb, Marius, *The Lebanese Civil War*, Praeger Publishers, New York, 1980.

Eveland, Wilbur Crane, *Ropes of Sand: America's Failure in the Middle East*, W. W. Norton, New York and London, 1980.

Evron, Yair, *War and Intervention in Lebanon: The Israeli-Syrian Deterrence Dialogue*, Croom Helm, London, 1987.

Fisk, Robert, *Pity the Nation: Lebanon at War*, Andre Deutsch, London, 1990.

Gabriel, Richard A., *Operation Peace for Galilee: The Israel–PLO War in Lebanon*, Hill & Wang, New York, 1984.

Gilmour, David, *Lebanon: The Fractured Country*, St Martin's Press, New York, 1984/Sphere Books, London, 1987.

Harik, Iliya, *Lebanon: Anatomy of Conflict*, American Universities Field Staff, Hanover, NH. 1981.

Hiro, Dilip, *Inside the Middle East*, Routledge & Kegan Paul, London, 1982/McGraw Hill, New York, 1982.

Jansen, Michael, *The Battle for Beirut: Why Israel Invaded Lebanon*, Zed Press, London, 1982.

Khalaf, Samir, *Lebanon's Predicament*, Columbia University Press, New York, 1987.

Khalidi, Walid, *Conflict and Violence in Lebanon*, Centre for International Affairs, Harvard University, Cambridge, Mass., 1979.

MacBride, Sean, et al., *Israel in Lebanon: The Report of the International Commission*, London, 1983.

Mackey, Sandra, *Lebanon: Death of a Nation*, Congdon & Weed, New York, 1989.

Meo, Leila, *Lebanon, Improbable Nation: A Study in Political Development*, Greenwood Press, Westport, CT, 1965; reprinted 1976.

Middle East Contemporary Survey, Vol. II, 1977–78; Vol. V, 1980–81;

Vol. VII, 1982–83; Vol. VIII, 1983–84; Volume IX, 1984–85; Vol. XI, 1987; and Vol. XIII, 1989; The Shiloah Institute, Tel Aviv University, Tel Aviv, Distributed by Westview Press, Boulder, Co., and Oxford.

Norton, Augustus Richard, *Amal and the Shia: Struggle for the Soul of Lebanon*, University of Texas Press, Austin, Texas, 1987.

Petran, Tabitha, *The Struggle Over Lebanon*, Monthly Review Press, New York, 1987.

Rabinovich, Itamar, *The War for Lebanon: 1970–85*, revised edition, Cornell University Press, Ithaca and London, 1985.

Randal, Jonathan, *The Tragedy of Lebanon: Christian Warlords, Israeli Adventurers and American Bunglers*, Chatto & Windus, London, 1983/ *Going All the Way: Christian Warlords, Israeli Adventurers and American Bunglers*, Viking Press, New York, 1983.

Salibi, Kamal, *Crossroads to Civil War: Lebanon, 1958–76*, Ithaca Press, London, 1976; and Caravan Books, Delmar, NY, 1976.

Schiff, Ze'ev and Ehud Ya'ari, *Israel's Lebanon War*, Simon and Schuster, New York, 1984.

Seale, Patrick, *Asad: The Struggle for the Middle East*, I. B. Tauris, London, 1988.

Woodward, Bob, *Veil: The Secret Wars of the CIA 1981–1987*, Simon and Schuster, New York and London, 1987.

Wright, Robin, *Sacred Rage: The Wrath of Militant Islam*, Simon and Schuster, New York, 1985/Andre Deutsch, London, 1986.

Newspapers and Periodicals

(For a name starting with Al, L' or The, see its second part.)

Al Anwar (Beirut)
Arab World File (Nicosia)
BBC Summary of World Broadcasts (Reading)
Daily Star (Beirut)
Daily Telegraph (London)
Economist (London)
Financial Times (London and New York)
Foreign Broadcast Information Service (Washington)
Guardian (London)
Independent (London)
International Herald Tribune (London)
Jerusalem Post (Jerusalem)
Lebanon Information Processing Service (London)
MERIP Middle East Report (Washington)
The Middle East (London)
Middle East International (London)
Middle East Report (Washington)

SELECT BIBLIOGRAPHY

Al Nahar (Beirut)
New York Times (New York)
Observer (London)
L'Orient le Jour (Beirut)
Al Safir (Beirut)
Al Sayyad (Beirut)
Sunday Times (London)
Time (New York)
The Times (London)
Washington Post (Washington)
Al Watan (Kuwait)

INDEX

For a name starting with Al, El, Le or The, see its second part.

Peres, Shimon, 115, 209
Perez de Cuellar, Javier, 156, 199
Petran, Tabitha, 12
Phalange Party and Phalangists, 10, 14, 19, 20,
  21–2, 26, 31, 32, 33, 34, 45, 46, 50, 53, 56, 58,
  63, 64, 66, 67–68, 70, 74, 75, 92, 96, 109, 113,
  115–16, 127, 141, 147, 164, 165, 166, 176, 182,
  185–86, 187, 189
Poindexter, John, 125
Polhill, Robert, 152
Popular Front (French), 4
Popular Front for the Liberation of Palestine
  (PFLP), 27, 194
Popular Front for the Liberation of Palestine-
  General Command (PFLP-GC), 155
Popular Nasserite Organization, 26, 129, 187
Popular Struggle Front, 194
Progressive Front, *see* Front of National and
  Progressive Parties and Forces
Progressive Socialist Party (PSP), 6, 16, 24, 25, 118,
  126, 129, 145, 155, 166, 191, 197
Protestants, 5
Puente, Pablo, 172, 176

Qadhafi, Muammar, 153
Qadri, Nazim, 168
Qansu, Asim, 25, 99
Qarantina, 172
Qassis, Sherbal, 23
Qatar, 60, 188
Qom, 16
Qulaya, 48, 50
Qulayaat, 165
Qulaylat, Ibrahim, 25
Quran, 105

Raad, Inaam, 26, 99
Rabat, 149, 151
Rabinovich, Itamar, 4
Rafii, abdul Majid, 25
Rafsanjani, Ali Akbar Hashemi, 124, 126, 153, 191
Rashaya, 83
Rashidiya, 188, 198
Reagan, Ronald, 83, 84, 86, 90, 103, 105, 106, 107,
  124, 126, 192, 210–11
'Red line' agreements (Syrian-Israeli), 39, 48, 189,
  206, 209
Le Réveille, 50, 141
Revolutionary Justice Organization (RJO), 109,
  131, 152, 156
Revolutionary Organization of Socialist Muslims,
  153
Roman Catholics, 25
Rome, 118, 174
Rosan, Nawal, 77
Rumaish, 48, 51
Runcie, Robert, 153

Saad, Adib, 58
Saad, Maruf, 18
Saad, Mustafa, 26, 187, 194
Saade, Antun, 25, 26
Saade, Georges, 147, 161, 168, 177, 187
al Sabah, Sabah, 143

Sabra, 14, 18, 88, 92–93 94, 97, 117, 207
Sadat, Anwar, 50, 204
Sadr, Musa, 16–17, 26–27, 32, 66, 76
Sadr, Sadr al Din, 76
al Said, Nuri, 7
Saida, *see* Sidon
Saiqa Organization, 27, 51
Salam, Saeb, 13, 16, 63, 89, 91, 92, 93, 109–10
Salibi, Elie Louis, 128
Salim, Elie, 95
Saqr, Etienne, 23
Sarkis, Elias, 12–13, 24, 38–39, 40, 43, 45, 47, 50,
  51, 53, 54, 57, 58, 60, 61, 62, 63, 64, 65, 66–67,
  68, 71, 74, 84, 85, 136, 176, 203, 205, 207
Sassine, Michel, 177, 187
Saudi Arabia, 36, 41, 43, 44, 45, 58, 60, 62, 72, 103,
  113, 128, 138, 158–59, 167, 179, 203, 213, 215
Scheer, François, 157
Security Commission, 185
Second Bureau (Lebanese), 8
Seale, Patrick, 93
Second World War (1939–45), 4
Sfier, Nasrallah Boutros, 128, 131, 136, 142,
  144–45, 147, 157, 164, 165, 170, 174, 175, 192
Shalhat, Nihad, 22
Shamali, Fuad, 23
Shamir, Yitzhak, 102, 106
Shams al Din, Muhammad Mahdi, 66, 76, 128
Sharon, Ariel, 75, 76, 81, 84, 85, 86, 88, 92, 93, 94,
  95, 97, 193, 207
Shartuni, Habib Tanios, 92, 182
Shatila, 14, 18, 88, 92–93, 97, 117, 126, 132, 207
Shawi, Niqula, 24
Shehabi clan, 2
Shehabi, Bashir II, 3
Shehabi, Bashir III, 3
Shehabi, Yusuf, 2–3
Shias: (Kuwait), 118, 124; (Lebanon), 2, 5, 9, 15,
  16–17, 19, 26–27, 32, 35, 62, 75–76, 89, 96, 99,
  100–1, 103, 104, 106–7, 108, 109, 113, 115,
  116, 118, 119, 130, 131, 132–33, 134, 149, 152,
  153, 166, 179, 187, 191, 199, 208, 209, 211,
  214, 218
Al Shiraa, 124
Shiyya, 53, 185
Shouf Mountains, 1, 8, 93, 101, 146, 184, 209
Shtura, 49, 118, 167
Shultz, George, 85, 90, 97, 106, 131, 132, 211
Sidon, 1, 3, 18, 26, 35, 41, 73, 81, 82, 109, 114, 115,
  116, 129, 170, 189, 193, 194, 195
Sinai Peninsula, 10, 15, 75
Six Day War, *see* Arab-Israeli Wars
Socialist National Front (SNF), 6, 7–8, 24
Sofar, 85
Solh, Rashid, 18, 19, 32
Solh, Riad, 5
Solh, Taqi al Din, 14, 15, 17, 68
Souq al Gharb, 102, 103, 104, 108, 145, 150, 154,
  181, 183
South Lebanese Army (SLA), 53, 115, 117, 128,
  130, 137, 138, 140, 188, 189, 194–95, 196, 199,
  211, 217
South Lebanon, *see* Lebanon, South
South Yemen, 11, 43, 45, 192, 203